D1559187

Limits to Autocracy

LIMITS TO AUTOCRACY

*From Sung Neo-Confucianism
to a Doctrine of Political Rights*

ALAN T. WOOD

UNIVERSITY OF HAWAI'I PRESS, HONOLULU

95 96 97 98 99 00   5 4 3 2 1

Library of Congress Cataloging-in-Publication Data
Wood, Alan Thomas.
Limits to autocracy : from Sung Neo-Confucianism to
a doctrine of political rights / Alan T. Wood.
p.   cm.
Includes bibliographical references and index.
ISBN 0–8248–1703–6
1. Political science—China—History.   2. China—Politics and
government.   3. Neo-Confucianism.   I. Title.
JA84.C6W66   1995
320'.0951—dc20   95–9836
CIP

University of Hawai'i Press books are printed on
acid-free paper and meet the guidelines for
permanence and durability of the Council on
Library Resources

Designed by Kenneth Miyamoto

To my parents,
Herb and Katherine Wood,
my wife, Wei-ping, and
Brian and Irene

Contents

Preface

THE main thesis of this study is that the leading neo-Confucian political thinkers of the Sung dynasty, who promoted a policy of "revering the emperor and expelling the barbarians" *(tsun-wang jang-i),* intended not to increase the power of the emperor, as they are often accused of doing, but instead to limit it. They believed that China's vulnerability to rebellion from within or invasion from without was due to a moral failure of China's society and could therefore be rectified only by a revival of fundamental Confucian values. Central to this revival was thought to be the institution of the emperor, who represented the indispensable link between the timeless values of cosmic harmony and the temporal reality of government policy. The priority that Sung thinkers placed on the crucial role of the emperor has caused many modern scholars to conclude that they advocated a form of blind obedience to the ruler and in so doing laid the ideological foundations for the growth of autocratic institutions in China.

During most of the twentieth century, the leading intellectuals in China have tended to blame Confucianism—especially neo-Confucianism—for China's failure to develop a modern democracy. In attempting to throw off the chains of Confucian authoritarianism, some of them embraced a Western ideology of Marxism-Leninism that condemned the Chinese past wholesale and promoted socialism as the agent of national salvation. Others rejected Marxism-Leninism, but were disillusioned by the wartime corruption and incompetence of the Kuomintang, and chose to settle in the United States. There, as scholars of Chinese history in American universities, they continued to search for the underlying source of China's weakness and often found it in Confucianism. If this is true—if Confucianism did advocate absolute loyalty to the emperor—then the Chinese intellectual tradition would indeed be hostile to modern notions of democracy and human rights. Those doctrines could then legitimately be regarded as little more than foreign imports from the West, exotic indoor plants unable to survive on their own in the Chinese climate. The current leaders in Beijing would be correct when they claim that the concept of human rights is of Western origin with no roots in Chinese soil.

This study takes a different view, arguing that in fact the neo-Confucian political thinkers of the Northern Sung—who defined the terms of orthodox Confucian political thought for the last thousand years—sought to reduce the power of the emperor, not enhance it. To be sure, the leading Sung political thinkers, who embedded their most important ideas in commentaries on the Confucian *Spring and Autumn Annals,* did advocate enhancing the authority of the emperor. Authority, however, is not power. Although many Sung literati may have advocated centralizing the authority of the emperor, at the same time they also hoped that he would delegate his actual power to them. In other words, the neo-Confucians hoped to appropriate for themselves the emperor's power through their dominance of the government bureaucracy. They believed that they deserved that dominance, of course, because they considered themselves to be the only group educated enough to understand fully the moral laws governing the natural and the human worlds. What they appeared to be granting him with their left hand, in effect, they were planning on taking away with their right. Since my case rests on making a plausible distinction between *power* and *authority,* I focus the first chapter on explaining how modern political theorists define those terms.

How could Sung scholar-officials ever hope to pull off such a political sleight of hand since they were only servants of the emperor and had no institutional base in an aristocracy? Part of the explanation lies in naïveté about the reality of court politics, but part of it also lies in their enormous self-confidence. To demonstrate why they might entertain such tremendous faith in their own powers, I outline the background of the neo-Confucian revival—the broader social and economic conditions of the Northern Sung that shaped the attitudes and concerns of the neo-Confucian movement as a whole. In the end, of course, they could not sustain such confidence. Emperors were not about to surrender their power, and the officials themselves were so divided by differences of policy and personality that they could not act together. By the Southern Sung, as Peter Bol and Robert Hymes have argued, their attention shifted from national to local affairs, still hoping for a moral renewal, but now from the bottom up, not the top down.

This study draws attention to the importance—often neglected in twentieth-century scholarship—of the *Spring and Autumn Annals* in Chinese political thought. One chapter is devoted to a review of the major commentaries prior to the Sung and another to the major commentaries in the Northern Sung. The final chapter notes that the *Annals* have been a source of counsel for modern-day reformers in Japan as well as China. In late Tokugawa Japan, the slogan *sonnō jōi* (revere the emperor and expel the barbarians), which originated in the Sung commentaries on the *Annals,* became a rallying cry for the radicals who overthrew the shogunate and founded the Meiji Restoration. In China, late nineteenth-century proponents of a limited, constitutional monarchy such as K'ang Yu-wei and Liang Ch'i-ch'ao drew on commentaries to the *Annals* to justify their proposals.

These modern thinkers were the heirs of a long tradition of belief in the efficacy of moral principle in practical policy. The crucial point of this study is that the principal Northern Sung political thinkers believed passionately in the existence of a moral universe governed by laws, known as *t'ien-li* (heavenly principle), that were accessible to human understanding and that transcended the ruler and therefore obliged him to obey them. This doctrine did not support blind obedience to a ruler. On the contrary, by offering a source of moral law higher than the ruler, it was intended to be used to set limits to his power rather than expand it. Since this view runs counter to the prevailing climate of opinion among much of contemporary scholarship on Chinese history in the United States, I demonstrate how a similar doctrine of universal moral law in late medieval Europe—natural law—also provided a basis in the European context for limiting the power of the ruler, ultimately laying the foundation for a doctrine of human rights that in turn became the rationale for later theories of democratic politics. By the time it got to Locke and the empiricists of the eighteenth and nineteenth centuries, that democratic theory had become fully secularized and morally defanged, its origins in natural law no longer acknowledged, but the pedigree is there for those who wish to find it.

I am prepared to concede that there are important differences between natural law as it was developed in Europe and the system of cosmic laws expressed by the neo-Confucian thinkers (I discuss those differences in greater detail in chapter 6). Nevertheless, for the limited purposes of my study, there are sufficient similarities between the two experiences for a comparison to be useful. In both cases, all levels of the cosmic order were understood to be animated by a moral force that tied the parts into a coherent and intelligible whole. Life and thought, heart and mind, subject and object, were integrated into a harmonious unity of meaning. The fact that European theories of natural rights grew out of an understanding of universal laws very similar to that of China offers promise for China as well. The doctrine of Confucianism in China can become the basis of a Chinese theory of human rights that would absorb elements from the Confucian heritage as well as the West. The most important task confronting Chinese political thinkers in the modern world is to reconcile the influences emanating from the West with the traditional ideas and institutions of China. How to be fully modern and fully Chinese has been the great challenge of the twentieth century and will no doubt continue to be for the twenty-first as well.

A syncretic, Confucian/Western doctrine of human rights could, I believe, flourish in China, even in the harsh climate of Beijing. In spite of the confusion about the meaning of the term *democracy* manifested by the students in Tiananmen Square in June 1989 (although they constantly invoked its ideals as the object of their actions), and in spite of the fact that those students did not always demonstrate in their own conduct a commitment to democratic methods of leadership, no one who witnessed the acts of courage by them and so many other people in Beijing can ever again doubt that the Chinese desire freedom with a passion that is perhaps greatest among those who have been denied its fruits for so long. The people of Beijing are an inspiration to us all, and while I recognize the dangers to truth of relating scholarship to life, I also believe that we who live by the pen bear some measure of obligation, however tenuous, to those who die by the sword.

Acknowledgments

I HAVE incurred many debts in writing this book. I wish first to acknowledge the assistance rendered by Professor Hok-lam Chan, who suggested that I concentrate on the Northern Sung commentaries on the *Ch'un-ch'iu* for my Ph.D. dissertation, and then skillfully guided that project through to conclusion. Jack Dull applied his superb critical skills to the manuscript at an early point and improved it immeasurably. My greatest intellectual debt is owed to Donald Treadgold, whose balance, wisdom, encyclopedic knowledge, and powers of synthesis have been a model of inspiration for me during the last twenty-five years. I had looked forward to giving him a copy of this book as a small token of my regard for him but his sudden death in December 1994 deprived me of that opportunity. I also want to thank David Keightley at the University of California, Berkeley, for his words of encouragement, which came at a crucial moment and gave me the courage to revise the dissertation for publication.

The example of Professor Hsiao Kung-ch'üan is always before me. Although he had retired from teaching at the University of Washington before I began graduate school there, he continued to attend colloquia on campus. His comments on papers by visiting scholars were invariably so full of wisdom, kindness, and erudition that he became, at least in my mind, a living example of the best of the Confucian tradition in the modern world. Professor Hsiao's son and daughter-in-law, David and Martha Hsiao, established a scholarship in Professor

Hsiao's honor that I received one year while working on the dissertation, for which I am grateful.

More recently, I received a summer research grant from the University of Washington graduate school that made it possible to complete the final revisions of this manuscript. Jane Decker, my department chair at the University of Washington, Bothell, helped in innumerable ways to bring this project to completion. Ying-wo Chan read through the whole manuscript and offered invaluable advice, particularly on the section on modern Japan in the concluding chapter.

I want to thank as well the anonymous readers of the manuscript whose comments I have largely followed. I have been most fortunate in having Patricia Crosby as editor at the University of Hawai'i Press. Her suggestions at several stages of the editorial process greatly improved the manuscript. The managing editor, Sally Serafim, kept the whole project moving forward with admirable efficiency and speed. No scholar could ask for a better copy editor than Joe Brown, whose ability to locate inconsistencies and errors is nothing short of amazing. I take full responsibility, of course, for whatever sins of commission and omission remain.

Last I would like to thank my family, to whom this whole project is dedicated. My parents, Herb and Katherine Wood, grew up in the Midwest but first met each other in Canton, China, in 1930, where my father was teaching at Lingnan University and my mother at True Light Middle School. They fell in love with China, as well as each other, during the years they lived there, from 1930 to 1933, and they passed that affection for things Chinese on to their youngest son.

My wife, Wei-ping, is the reason this book was written. Without her inspiration it would not have been started, and without her patience and encouragement it could not possibly have been finished. Our children, Brian and Irene, have also made many sacrifices through the years, in lost time with Daddy, for this project. Words cannot convey the gratitude I have for my family.

1

Introduction

> Thus can the demigod, Authority,
> Make us pay down for our offense by weight.
> The words of heaven;—on whom it will, it will;
> On whom it will not, so; yet still 'tis just.
> —*Measure for Measure*

P OLITICAL thought is the child of chaos and the father of
order. It is no coincidence that most of the great pioneer-
ing works of political thought in the West have followed closely
on times of political disorder. Plato's *Republic* was written after
the Athenian loss to the Spartans in the Peloponnesian War,
Augustine's *City of God* after the disintegration of the Roman
Empire, Machiavelli's *Prince* after the decline of the republican
city-states in Italy, and Hobbes' *Leviathan* after the Thirty Years'
War on the Continent and the Civil War in England. Our effort
to understand the forces of order and civilization, it seems, has
often come only after those forces have ceased to prevail.
Hegel's metaphor—that the owl of Minerva flies only at dusk—
continues to apply.

This is not to say that during every period of disorder there
will inevitably arise a fundamental reexamination of conventional political philosophy. This certainly did not happen, for
example, during the Six Dynasties period (220–589) in China,
when Buddhism established itself for the first time in the aftermath of the fall of the Han dynasty. Nevertheless, in the main,
the Chinese tradition is no different from that of the West, at
least with regard to the relation between disorder and intellectual creativity. Confucius, Mencius, and Hsün Tzu all wrote out
of a desire to restore order in times of chaos and unrest. Similarly, in the Sung dynasty (960–1279), a period that followed
more than a century of civil war, the Confucian tradition under-

1

went a revival of major proportions. This rebirth of Confucian thought in the Sung created a new frame of reference for Chinese political thought that lasted for the next thousand years until the twentieth century. As before, the thinkers responsible for this revival were motivated in large part by fear of disorder. The effect was, not unexpectedly, that they undertook to reexamine some of the most fundamental problems of the Confucian political heritage, centering on the question of obedience to the ruler.

The Nature of Obedience and Authority

This problem of whom to obey, and when, was not just one of a large number of political problems that commanded more or less equal attention among those who thought deeply about politics in both China and the West. In many ways it was, and is, the central problem of politics. One of the foremost political thinkers of the twentieth century, A. P. d'Entrèves, once remarked that political theory is "first and foremost the history of the attempts to solve the problem of political obligation."[1] Isaiah Berlin has written that the question, "Why should anyone obey anyone else?" is perhaps "the most fundamental of all political questions."[2]

In Western political theory, there have been two principal responses to the general problem of the nature of political obligation. The first rejects overarching moral or metaphysical dimensions and recognizes only the agency of the human will acting in conscious pursuit of self-interest, either narrowly or broadly conceived, as the motive force in compelling obedience. The second emphasizes the existence of a natural and universal order of some kind, such that obedience to moral and political authority is an expression of a fundamental characteristic of the human personality. In this theory, people are by nature social, and the fulfillment of the potential that lies nascent in all human persons can be promoted only through social activity, which in turn can be guided in a commonly beneficial direction only by some authority, however variously constituted.[3]

With regard to the first response, Hobbes argued, for example, that obligation proceeds entirely out of fear of the consequences of not obeying, that is, out of a fear of anarchy. Unconditional obedience is enjoined, therefore, even in cases in which particular actions might be unjust, on the plausible assumption that the evil caused by obeying the unjust order of a ruler would be far less pernicious in its ultimate consequences than the anarchy that would almost certainly follow if every citizen took it on himself to decide which orders should be obeyed and which disobeyed. To Hobbes there could be no such thing as divided loyalty. The implications of this doctrine are perhaps more obvious to us in the twentieth century than they were to him. We now know that under certain circumstances, such as Nazi Germany or Soviet Russia, some things can be done in the name of order that make anarchy look positively charming by comparison.

Proponents of this Hobbesian doctrine, or variations on its theme, are satisfied that a ruler ought to be obeyed merely by virtue of his position as head of state. In other words, they are interested in the legality of obligation, which proceeds entirely from the will of the sovereign, and not in legitimacy, which incorporates standards of evaluation other than the will of the sovereign, usually some transcendent standard of right and wrong. Suppose, for example, that one were to disobey a ruler for failing to provide for the welfare of the people. In that case, one would be making a judgment that the welfare of the people (apart from, or above and beyond, that already provided for by the mere existence of a ruler and the order that his existence will produce) is a moral good that ought to be the final object of a ruler's actions. Inability to provide for the public welfare would then be grounds for asserting that the ruler's legitimacy had been correspondingly called into question. This appeal to a transcendent value involves a standard for evaluating political obligation different from the one used by Hobbes. It is possible to argue that political thought in the West has greatly benefited from the tension between these two modes of evaluating political obligation, the one concentrating on legality, the other on legitimacy.

The danger of relying too heavily on the former, of course, is that the law will become hollowed out and that, as time passes, the moral truths that once animated legal doctrine and gave it substance slip further and further from public consciousness, until finally obedience can be enjoined only by coercion. On the other hand, the danger of relying too heavily on the latter is that, no matter how simple moral truths may be in their formulation, they are notoriously messy in practice, with the result that two perfectly conscientious people, both in the service of the same moral beliefs, can and often do decide on separate courses of action that conflict with each other. When this happens, the result is chaos, and the cooperative action necessary for the health of society is jeopardized. And so in the West the dialogue between law and justice never ends, and probably never should. But for the most part we have been able to assert that a given law ought to be obeyed even if it is not always a just law. In this view, reform ought to take the form of changing the law to bring it into accord with our changing standards of justice, not that of disobeying the law. Socrates chose not to flee Athens, and thus to suffer an unjust execution, in defense of this very principle.

It is important to note, however, that, even though these two solutions to the moral dilemma discussed above continue to dominate the prevailing mode of thinking in the modern age, they represent a substantial departure from the tradition of medieval natural law that preceded them. This subject will be treated further in chapter 6. Suffice it here to say that those who held to a medieval understanding of natural law affirmed the existence of absolute moral values that transcended the positive laws of any particular ruler and thereby opposed claims to absolute authority put forth by European rulers in the seventeenth and eighteenth centuries. At the same time, however, natural law theorists freely admitted the ambiguities of moral choice and made no attempt to deny them.

But what precisely was the context of authority within which this moral dilemma existed? Since the significance of this study will not become fully apparent without a clear understanding of the meaning of the term *authority*, it would be desirable to turn our attention for a moment to a brief consideration of what is a very complex concept indeed. The modern social sciences are far from unanimous in their definition of the term *authority*.[4] Most observers, however, seem to argue that it represents a form of "legitimate power," an acknowledgment by the governed that the government has the right to rule and be obeyed.[5] That legitimacy may, according to the social scientists, derive from several possible sources. Max Weber believed that there were three: legal-rational, traditional, and charismatic.[6] For these thinkers, heirs of the developments in Western political theory from Hobbes through Locke to the nineteenth-century utilitarians and liberals, authority in government is understood to be entirely the result of a voluntary compromise —a social contract—entered into between the citizens of a state and a "ruler" in order to protect certain rights. It is not a natural but a contrived relationship.

To the extent that such a view of authority made it a function of the human will, in the form of either a legal-rational, a traditional, or a charismatic formulation, it departed from previous Western tradition, which regarded the world, both natural and human, as inherently and fundamentally hierarchical. Hannah Arendt has perhaps best expressed this traditional understanding. Writing in the 1950s, she argued that authority is not to be mistaken for coercion or persuasion and that it is intimately connected with a hierarchical interpretation of the social order:

> Since authority always demands obedience, it is commonly mistaken for some form of power or violence. Yet authority precludes the use of external means of coercion; where force is used, authority itself has failed. Authority, on the other hand, is incompatible with persuasion, which presupposes equality and works through a process of argumentation. Where arguments are used, authority is left in abeyance. Against the egalitarian order of persuasion stands the authoritarian order, which is always hierarchical. If authority is to be defined at all, then, it must be in contradistinction to both coercion by force and persuasion through arguments. (The authoritarian who obeys rests neither on common reason nor on the power of the one who commands; what they have in common is the hierarchy itself, whose rightness and legitimacy both recognize and where both have their predetermined stable place.)[7]

Arendt concludes that the egalitarian assumptions about the nature of man prevalent in the last few centuries in the West and the belief that history is a progressive unfolding of freedom have made it difficult for the modern mind to see the dif-

ference in kind, not just in degree, between the total loss
of freedom in totalitarian government and the limitations on
freedom in authoritarian government. It has become equally
difficult for us to understand how an "authoritarian" government, which restricts freedom, must to a certain extent also be
committed to the preservation of freedom,[8] and indeed cannot
survive without it (without becoming a tyranny), while a totalitarian government must, equally in order to survive, destroy
freedom and spontaneity altogether. What in fact is the difference between a tyranny and an authoritarian government? A
tyrant rules by means of the arbitrary exercise of whatever
means of power he may have at his disposal, legitimate or
otherwise. In authoritarian governments, however, the source
of authority "is always a force external and superior to its own
power; it is always this source, this external force which transcends the political realm, from which the authorities derive
their 'authority,' that is, their legitimacy, and against which
their power can be checked."[9]

Dennis Wrong has argued that power is the "capacity of
some persons to produce intended and foreseen effects on
others" and may or may not be (but usually is) backed up by
the threat of coercion.[10] Authority, on the other hand, refers to
the right by which power is exercised. It is itself, in a sense, a
form of power because it also influences other people's behavior, although without the threat or use of coercion or persuasion. Coercion is unnecessary because authority grows out of an
acceptance by all members in a particular community of certain fundamental values. Obedience is enjoined by consent,
not coercion; it is voluntary, although also mandatory. Authority may take three forms: legitimate, competent, and personal.[11]
It is "legitimate" authority when it is simply accepted as a natural and unquestioned part of the universe; it is "competent," as
when we speak of the "authority" of a doctor or a sea captain,
when it arises from a particular knowledge or skill possessed by
a certain person; and it is "personal" when based on particular
qualities in a single individual, aside from mere competence.

What then is the relation between power and authority?
Assume for the purpose of argument that authority is one kind
of power because it represents one way that A influences B. In
the case of authority, B accepts A's right to issue commands

without question on the basis of an acceptance of A's legitimacy (an acceptance based on habit, or religious belief, or tradition), or competence, or some personal quality. An interesting situation arises when someone may be in a position of "authority," such as an emperor in Japan, or a constitutional monarch in Europe, or a member of the Senate in imperial Rome, while the seat of actual "power" lies elsewhere, in the person of the shogun, or the prime minister, or the emperor, as the case may be. What are we to make of this? How can someone who has no "power" have "authority," which is a kind of "power"? How can he have it and not have it at the same time? A plausible response to this paradox is to make a distinction between the "position" of power and the actual person who may happen to occupy that position. The actual person in "authority" may or may not be able to influence B's actions, but someone else, acting in the name of that person or position, can and may influence B's actions. The distinction between the actual person and the position is thus crucial (especially for understanding the political thought in the Sung, when—I believe—Confucian thinkers promoted the authority of the emperor even as they hoped to divert some of his power into their own hands).

There can be few who would deny the importance of having a standard of moral reference against which actions and beliefs can be measured and that can command the allegiance of the intellectual leaders of any particular age. In fact, it is only in terms of such reference that freedom and obedience have any meaning. The British historian of philosophy Peter Winch put it this way:

Authority . . . is not by any means a curtailment of liberty but is, on the contrary, a precondition of it. The liberty in question is the liberty to choose. Now choice, as Hobbes (though in a misleading way) emphasized, goes together with deliberation (*Leviathan*, Ch. 6). To be able to choose is to be able to consider reasons for and against. But to consider reasons is not, as Hobbes supposed, to be subject to the influence of forces. Considering reasons is a function of acting according to rules; reasons are intelligible only in the context of the rules governing the kind of activity in which one is participating. Only human beings are capable of participating in rule-governed activities, hence other animals cannot be said to deliberate and choose, though Hobbes, consistently with his premises, maintained otherwise. Thus it is only in the context of rule-governed activities that it makes sense to speak of freedom of choice; to eschew all rules—supposing for a moment that we understood what that meant—would not be to gain perfect freedom, but to create a situation in which the notion of freedom could no longer find a foothold. But I have already tried to show that the acceptance of authority is conceptually inseparable from participation in rule-governed activities. It follows that this acceptance is a precondition of the possibility of freedom of choice. Somebody who said that he was going to renounce all authority in order to insure that he had perfect freedom of choice would thus be contradicting himself (a conceptual version of the man who thought that he could fly more easily if only he could escape the inhibiting pressure of the atmosphere).[12]

The Chinese Context of Neo-Confucianism

Having sketched briefly the general problem, let us turn now to a consideration of its relevance to Chinese political thought and further to the subject of this study. The theme of this work is that the full significance of the neo-Confucian advocacy of obedience to the ruler in Northern Sung China (960–1127) emerges only after we place it in the context of a simultaneous advocacy of obedience to absolute moral values that transcended the interests of any particular ruler and to which the ruler himself could be held accountable. The importance of those absolute values, in turn, can be fully comprehended only by placing them in the context of the metaphysical and cosmological explanation of the universe that was the hallmark of the neo-Confucian movement. The assertion that political thought becomes fully intelligible only when the metaphysical assumptions on which it is based are made explicit has not, as I have suggested above, commanded general assent in the twentieth century. On the contrary, the Western (and particularly the English and American) tradition of empiricism has rejected the relevance of metaphysics altogether, simply by denying the possibility that the human mind is capable of arriving at any form of absolute or transcendent moral truth. This, combined with the modern Western views of individualism, egalitarianism, and freedom that have exercised such a profound influence on modern Chinese intellectuals as well as their Western colleagues who study Chinese history, has done much to cloud our understanding of the authoritarian political ideas and ideals of the Confucian tradition.[13]

The key to understanding how moral values might have been perceived as exercising such profound influence on the levers of political power lies in the hierarchical relation between what Romeyn Taylor refers to as the "three perduring domains of the orthodox Chinese worldview: the cosmos, the official pantheon, and human society."[14] K. C. Chang goes so far as to argue that the very origins of Chinese civilization itself are fundamentally different from the origins of civilization in the Middle East. Whereas political, religious, and economic institutions in the Fertile Crescent rose in some ways autonomously from each other, in China all those functions were fulfilled by one institution—the kinship group. The head of the family was the chief priest, the head of the clan, the CEO of all economic ventures, the generalissimo, and the ruler of the state, all rolled into one.[15] If true, then the doctrine of the mandate of heaven is merely a later expression of what began as a basic characteristic of Chinese civilization—the complete integration of political and religious power. Although this assumption of the interpenetration of the cosmic and political orders required obedience to the ruler as one of its essential features, it also required the ruler to obey the moral laws of the cosmos.[16]

In a partial reaction to the overly idealistic and exaggerated claims put forward by many traditional Confucian scholars, there has been something of a rush in the twentieth century to demonstrate how far short of their noble ideals the Confucianists fell in actual practice. The May Fourth generation of Chinese intellectuals consistently blamed Confucianism for China's weakness.[17] The prejudices of that generation— expressed most dramatically in Lu Hsün's scathing indictment of Confucianism in "Diary of a Madman"—set the tone for much of the twentieth century, persisting even to the end. Lu Hsün's views have been echoed in more recent times by the Taiwan writer Bo Yang, whose 1984 speech at the University of Iowa, entitled "The Ugly Chinaman," was subsequently published in Hong Kong and Taiwan and stimulated much discussion. In his speech, Bo Yang concluded that Chinese culture as a whole is to blame for China's predicament:

> In the last 4,000 years, China has produced only one great thinker: Confucius. In the two and one half millennia since his death, China's literati did little more than add footnotes to the theories propounded by Confucius and his disciples, rarely contributing any independent opinions, simply because the traditional culture did not permit it. The minds of the literati were stuck on the bottom of an intellectually stagnant pond, the soy-sauce vat of Chinese culture. As the contents of the vat began to putrefy, the resultant stench was absorbed by the Chinese people.[18]

These views continue to be voiced in China as well, even (or especially) by those who have lived through the totalitarian decades of Maoism. A new generation of Chinese intellectuals appears to have rekindled the May Fourth flame of condemnation of the Confucian heritage. Like Hannah Arendt and Karl Wittfogel in the West, who were galvanized by Hitler to spend their lives searching for the origins of totalitarian power, many Chinese are also searching for the sources of autocratic power in China, and finding them in the Confucian heritage. The television miniseries "River Elegy" *(He shang)*, for example, which appeared in China in 1988 as a documentary on the Yellow River, was a devastating attack on Chinese culture, once again blaming it for China's continuing backwardness.[19] Many scholars from China now in the United States are equally suspicious of Confucianism. Zhengyuan Fu, who is certainly no stranger to the abuse of total power, having spent twenty years in labor camps in China, asserts that in Sung neo-Confucianism "the subordination of the subjects to the ruler must be absolute and unqualified" and that, moreover, "the enhanced autocracy since the Song dynasty was to a large extent inseparable from Neo-Confucianism."[20]

American scholars have continued the venerable May Fourth tradition. Arthur Wright has argued that neo-Confucianism developed the concept of loyalty into "an imperative to unquestioning and total subordination to any ruler, however idiotic and amoral he might be. The new Confucianism was

more totalitarian in intent than the old had been, in that it
gave the monarch authority to police all private as well as
public morals and customs."[21] The foremost contemporary
American scholar of democracy in China, Andrew Nathan, has
written that the Confucian tradition did not provide moral
restraints on the power of the ruler: "Confucians did not see
the moral order as limiting the power of the ruler. . . . So while
the Chinese tradition like any other had its own sense of what
was naturally right, neither Legalism nor Confucianism saw
moral laws or individual rights as limiting the power of the
state."[22]

The accusation that Confucianism was used to stunt the
development of pluralistic institutions may very well be true.
Rulers in China as elsewhere around the world have frequently
manipulated doctrine to suit their own purposes. Nevertheless,
Confucianism was a house of many mansions and also served to
limit the central power whose expansion it is accused of fostering. In rejecting Confucianism, modern detractors may well be
turning their backs on a lifeboat that could offer them at least
temporary refuge, if not transportation to some more sheltered
harbor in the future. The danger is that, by dwelling on the
authoritarian uses to which Confucianism has been put by centralizing governments in the past, some contemporary scholars
may have come greatly to underestimate the beneficial role
that Confucian ideas have played through the long course of
Chinese history.[23] Confucianism may have been used to expand
the power of the state, but it also provided moral limits to that
power (limits, it is worth noting, that its totalitarian successors
have ruthlessly ignored).

Chinese thinkers and practical statesmen, in fact, have wres-
tled with the dilemma of conflicting loyalties to authority from
very early times. One of the earliest classical examples appears
in the *Shu-ching*, where it is recorded that the pillar of Confucian virtue, the great duke of Chou himself, executed his own
brother Kuan Shu in order to suppress a rebellion against King
Ch'eng. This has been taken to imply the primacy of loyalty to
the state over loyalty to family relations. Later, however, under
differing circumstances, Confucius took a position that subordinated loyalty to the state to filial piety: "The Governor of She
said to Confucius, 'In our village there is a man nicknamed

"Straight Body." When his father stole a sheep, he gave evidence against him.' Confucius answered, 'In our village those who are straight are quite different. Fathers cover up for their sons, and sons cover up for their fathers. Straightness is to be found in such behavior.' "[24] These two examples illustrate the complexities of moral choice and the impossibility of arriving at a definition that would apply to all cases. Each particular situation embodied a unique configuration of costs and benefits, the final moral decision being reached by a process of elimination in which the appropriate course of action was by no means clear.

Confucius believed that society was best ordered in conformity with certain principles that were hierarchical in nature. In the early Han, this belief was harnessed to the purposes of a centralized bureaucratic state to elevate the position of the emperor to a higher level of importance than ever before.[25] The ruler's authority, however, was understood to be, not absolute, but contingent on the bestowal of heaven's mandate *(t'ien-ming)*. Heaven, perceived in the early Chou as theistic and only gradually becoming viewed as naturalistic, was thought to grant or withdraw this mandate in accordance with whether the welfare of the people was being properly served.[26] In the words of the *Shu-ching*, "Heaven sees as my people see; Heaven hears as my people hear."[27] Mencius, who affirmed Confucius' conception of society as inherently hierarchical, had said that, "if the prince have great faults, they [his ministers] ought to remonstrate with him, and if he do not listen to them after they have done so again and again, they ought to dethrone [*yi-wei*] him." He also said that "those who accord with heaven are preserved, and they who rebel against heaven perish."[28] Although Hsün Tzu was regarded by some as leaning toward Legalism because of his emphasis on the importance of the ruler, he did not minimize the importance of the people. He argued that, "when the people are satisfied with his government, then only is a prince secure in his position. It is said, 'The prince is the boat, the common people are the water. The water can support the boat or the water can capsize the boat.' "[29] These ideas were not rejected by later Confucianism but incorporated into it, as we shall see.

Confucianism became the dominant ideology of the Chinese

state in the Former Han dynasty (206 B.C.–A.D. 8), partly because its emphasis on the natural hierarchy of the social order
was attractive to rulers concerned about the legitimacy of their
own authority. But Han Confucianism was not simply an ideological justification for the ruler's authority. The most important of the Han scholars, Tung Chung-shu (179–104 B.C.), attempted to curb the arbitrary exercise of the ruler's power by
threatening the intervention of heaven in the form of natural
portents and disasters should the ruler stray too far from the
path of righteous and responsible behavior. Such a theory, of
course, was based on an assumption that heaven and earth
were very closely related. This belief in the interaction of
heaven and earth *(t'ien-jen kan-ying),* however, became discredited in the Later Han (A.D. 25–220), when sycophantic scholars
used the theory not to limit the power of the ruler but to enhance it (by interpreting natural portents as indications of
heaven's favor toward a particular ruler).

The breakup of China following the end of the Han,
together with the growing influence of Buddhism and Taoism
on Chinese scholars from the Six Dynasties period (A.D. 222–
589) to the T'ang (618–906), greatly affected the content of
political thought. During the Wei-Chin period (220–317), for
example, Lao-Chuang Taoist thought, which emphasized either
a passive role for the ruler or no ruler at all, was the dominant
influence on political thought.[30] Even later Confucian scholars
were greatly influenced by this Taoist current. Wang T'ung
(584–617) took nonaction as the keystone of his political
thought and, following Mencius, placed great emphasis on the
importance of ministering to the needs of the common people.
Han Yü (768–824), the T'ang Confucian praised by the early
Sung thinker Ou-yang Hsiu (1007–1072), tended to exalt the
ruler and downplay the importance of the people, adhering
more closely to the ideas of Hsün Tzu than Mencius.[31] Such a
position was understandable in someone born not long after
the An Lu-shan rebellion (755–757) had demonstrated the devastating consequences of weakened central rule and civil war.
But the destruction of civil order that caused Han Yü to reassert
the importance of a strong ruler caused others to return once
more to the solace of Lao-Chuang Taoism, and indeed the
dominant influence on political thought during the troubled

times from the An Lu-shan rebellion to the end of the Five
Dynasties period (907–960) was Taoism.[32]

When we bring the story down to the Sung, what changes
do we find? What is new in the political ideas of the neo-
Confucians? Have they simply renovated an old tradition, or
have they added any striking innovations? The answer is a composite one. It arises from the observation that change in history
is often the consequence, not of the introduction of a radically
new ingredient to a given set of circumstances, but of an alter-
ation in the relative proportion of the ingredients, an increase
or adjustment in the importance of one at the expense of
others, such that the old ingredients act on each other in a
novel and unpredictable way. The major categories of thought
that formed the currency of early Sung intellectual and political speculation grew out of ideas that had already had a long
history. There were of course many concepts that underwent
changes in definition as they were called on to perform new
tasks, but for the most part the children bear a remarkable
resemblance to their parents. The concept of principle, or *li*,
for example, which was one of the most significant ideas of the
neo-Confucian movement, owes its importance more to a shift
in emphasis than to a radical departure in definition.[33]

The same is true of neo-Confucian attitudes toward the
ruler. There is a change in emphasis, an elevation of the ruler
to a degree of importance that was unprecedented. On a practical level, this change was due to a desire to avoid the anarchy
that had prevailed before the Sung and originated not with the
intellectuals but with the first Sung emperor, T'ai-tsu (reigned
960–976). Having once been a general himself in the Later
Chou dynasty (951–960), the last of the Five Dynasties, and having himself usurped the throne, T'ai-tsu was more than moder-
ately aware of the need to reduce the power of the military and
reassert the authority of a strong central ruler. There were also
plenty of powerful men in his service who traced their ancestry
to military governors in the T'ang or to royal families during
the Five Dynasties period.[34] Their loyalty could never be completely assured. The first emperor consolidated his position by
retiring his own top generals on generous terms, replacing
them either with civilian officials or with military men whose
jurisdiction over nonmilitary matters such as tax collection was

carefully circumscribed. In general, the best troops were moved to the area around the capital where they could be carefully supervised (unless of course they were involved in a specific military campaign, which was in any case closely directed by the emperor). The examination system was gradually revived and expanded, and supplemented by a program of sponsorship, so that by the middle of the eleventh century the governing bureaucracy was dominated by civilians trained in the Confucian classics and owing their positions to a system presided over and controlled by the emperor himself. The aristocracy of the T'ang dynasty (618–907) had for the most part disappeared, removing one of the previous checks on the ruler's (and the officials') own power. Thus, both the ruler and the officials found themselves in possession of a degree of power that had not been enjoyed by their counterparts for many centuries.

Beginning in the eleventh century, neo-Confucian political theory emphasized the importance of revering the ruler *(tsun-wang)*, both for the reasons just outlined and because from the very beginning the Sung was menaced by the threat of invasion from two barbarian peoples in the north, the Khitan Liao in the northeast and the Tangut Hsi-hsia in the northwest. The threat was not an idle one, and, after a century and a half of intermittent fighting, the Northern Sung was ultimately brought to an end at the hands of a third northern tribe from Manchuria, the Jürchen, in 1127. This preoccupation on the part of the Northern Sung thinkers with expelling the barbarians *(jang-i)* inclined them to favor a strong centralized state.

At the same time, however, the ruler's authority was integrated into a rational view of the universal order that clearly transcended the position of the ruler and to which in fact the ruler himself was made subordinate. The contribution of the neo-Confucians to the history of Chinese political thought, in fact, lay in the way in which they incorporated their views on political authority into a metaphysical explanation of the universe. Such a conception as they developed of the nature of the universe, in which moral values were held to be absolute and unchanging, but in which the ruler nevertheless played the role of an indispensable intermediary between heaven and man, could serve only to intensify, not to repudiate, the fundamental moral dilemma alluded to above.

In endeavoring to grapple with this dilemma in their effort to integrate the often conflicting demands of life and thought, the neo-Confucians returned to the classics for guidance, especially to the *Ch'un-ch'iu* (the *Spring and Autumn Annals*), a chronicle of events covering the period 722–479 B.C. and considered at the time of the Northern Sung to have been compiled by Confucius himself. This ancient classic had been revered from early times as the quintessential handbook for those interested in putting Confucian political principles into practice. The views of three Sung commentators on the *Ch'un-ch'iu*, Sun Fu (992–1057), Ch'eng I (1033–1107), and Hu An-kuo (1074–1138), exercised a profound influence on their contemporaries and later generations.[35] Because of this influence, their commentaries have been selected to serve as the major focus of this study. For reasons that will become more apparent in chapter 2, which deals with the background of the neo-Confucian movement, the Northern Sung neo-Confucians, spearheaded by Sun Fu and followed by others with more metaphysical inclinations such as Ch'eng I, all shared a basic optimism in their ability to change the practical order. They also shared an assumption that the ultimate ends to be served by the political order were moral, not material. As suggested above, their fundamental concern was to form a view of authority that would constitute a basis for civil order and national unity but would also contain within it an acknowledgment of the moral purposes of human social life, serving indirectly to restrain the arbitrary exercise of imperial power and prevent government from degenerating into tyranny.

Organization of This Study

This study is intended to be a history of political thought, which takes as its principal focus the way in which certain fundamental, even universal, political and moral questions were interpreted in the light of the most important political problems of, in this case, the Northern Sung. Because of the emphasis by the neo-Confucians on synthesizing classical thought and practical problems, and because a full understanding of their ideas must take into account how they reflected the conditions of their times, the body of this study has been divided into two main parts. The first part concentrates on providing the historical background of the neo-Confucian movement and of Sung *Ch'un-ch'iu* studies. The second part then moves on to consider the content of the commentaries themselves and their relation to the fundamental question of political authority and ultimately to the question of whether the Confucian assumption of a universal moral order might become the basis of a new doctrine of human rights in China that incorporates Chinese as well as Western ingredients.

Chapter 2 is devoted to a consideration of the main social, political, economic, and intellectual forces that formed the backdrop of Northern Sung neo-Confucianism. The consideration in this chapter of forces that, taken individually, did not always directly influence neo-Confucian ideas on authority is deliberate. Taken as a whole, these various forces integrated Chinese society and fostered social mobility to a degree never before achieved in Chinese history. Of course, in comparison with its Western counterparts, Chinese society was always relatively single centered, with the vast preponderance of power gathered into the hands of the state. Nevertheless, within the last two or three millennia of Chinese history, there have been some periods in which society was more open and optimistic than others. The Sung, especially the Northern Sung, was one of those periods, and this had a profound impact on Sung attitudes toward political authority. Thus, the way in which authority is understood in any society, that is, whether it is seen as the instrument of an oppressive government unresponsive to the real needs of the people or as a necessary and potentially beneficial means of organizing the activities of the community to a mutually agreed on common goal, will be greatly influenced by the conditions of any given thinker's own time. Writing with the echo of the English Civil War reverberating in his mind, Hobbes took a dim view of man's ability to govern himself and used the doctrine of natural law to justify absolutist government. On the other hand, writing just a few years later, and after the Glorious Revolution of 1688 had marked the gradual and peaceful ascendancy of Parliament over the monarchy in England, John Locke took a much more optimistic view of human nature, using the doctrine of natural law to justify not absolutist but constitutional government.

Contemporary affairs also exerted a profound influence on late nineteenth-century intellectuals in Russia, who, for a variety of reasons feeling estranged from their own society and utterly powerless to influence the course of practical affairs, and confronting the apparent impossibility of ever realizing their ambitions, were driven to the brink of despair and beyond (in a manner not unfamiliar to dissidents in China today). According to Mikhail Gershenzon writing in *Vekhi* in 1909, for those Russian intellectuals life and thought "had almost nothing in common."[36] The result of this separation was to push the intelligentsia, in a misguided effort to compensate in one realm for weakness in the other, to extremities of theory and practice that were destructive both to themselves and to Russian society. Some, like Mikhail Bakunin, dispensed with authority altogether and became anarchists; others, indeed the majority, turned to the other extreme and embraced socialist doctrines of one form or another. This example is not intended to show that ideas are simply the product of their times; rather, it is intended to demonstrate that the circumstances in which a given thinker lives will often predispose him to look favorably on some ideas and unfavorably on others. Thus, the approving way in which the Sung thinkers discussed authority stems in part (and only in part) from the relatively open society in which they lived, and, conversely, the disapproving way in which thinkers in the late Ming and Ch'ing (and the present!) discussed the same subject is influenced by the very different— and much more restrictive—conditions in which they found themselves.

Turning to the second part of the work, the ideological dimension, chapter 3 then presents a brief sketch of *Ch'un-ch'iu* studies from the late Chou down to the Northern Sung in order to place the Sung commentators in the context of the classical exegetical tradition. Chapters 3 and 4 demonstrate how Northern Sung commentators on the *Ch'un-ch'iu* sought to unify the disparate worlds of knowledge and action (*chih-hsing ho-yi*, to borrow the felicitous term of the Ming neo-Confucian Wang Yang-ming [1462–1529]). These chapters utilize a category of literary analysis that was first clearly stated in the West by Thomas Aquinas and Dante Alighieri in the late thirteenth and early fourteenth centuries. Adopting a system of interpretation that had grown out of biblical hermeneutics and had probably been fully developed already by the fifth century, they believed that there were several levels on which a work of art could be interpreted. Of these, according to Dante,

> The first is called literal, and this is that sense which does not go beyond the strict limits of the letter; the second is called the allegorical, and this is disguised under the cloak of such stories, and is a truth hidden under a beautiful fiction. . . . The third sense is called moral; and this sense is that for which teachers ought as they go through writings intently to watch for their own profit and that of their hearers. . . . The fourth sense is called anagogic, that is, above the senses; and this occurs when a writing is spiritually expounded which even in the literal sense by the things signified likewise gives intimation of higher matters belonging to the eternal glory.[37]

The last phase, the anagogic (or the metaphysical), seeks then to say something universally true and has often been associated in the West with specifically religious issues. It was believed, and still is by some, that a well-integrated work of art lent itself to meaningful interpretation on several of the above levels. This belief arose out of an implicit assumption that the truth about man and nature was to be found not in one narrowly limited category of action or existence but in an attempt to understand them as a whole, recognizing the value of each part but refusing to become fixated on any one of them to the exclusion of the others.

It seems to me that these categories of literary analysis offer a most fruitful way to understand the place of the *Ch'un-ch'iu* both in the history of Chinese political thought in general and in the Northern Sung in particular. As a result, I have devoted one chapter, chapter 4, specifically to a consideration of the literal level on which the *Ch'un-ch'iu* can be interpreted. This chapter concentrates on the practical imperative of obedience to the ruler *(tsun-wang)*, which in part reflected the desire to avoid the reappearance of the decentralization of the late T'ang and Five Dynasties periods. It focuses on Sun Fu, who was very concerned about the chaos of the pre-Sung period, and shows how Sun integrated his concept of authority with the absolute moral values expressed by the term *li* (ritual). Sun's

commentary, written in the late 1030s and entitled *Ch'un-ch'iu
tsun-wang fa-wei* (An exposition on the subtle concept of exalting the ruler in the *Ch'un-ch'iu*), was regarded even in the
Northern Sung as the single most important commentary of
the period.

Chapter 5 then turns to a combination of the moral and anagogic levels (the allegorical level is not considered separately
since the whole *Ch'un-ch'iu* was thought to have allegorical
overtones conveying moral messages), by which means the significance of the literal level is fully revealed. It is in this chapter
that the shift in emphasis from a concentration on *li* (ritual) in
the earlier *Ch'un-ch'iu* commentaries to a concentration on *li*
(principle) in the later commentaries is discussed. In doing so,
I deal first with the commentary by Ch'eng I, written a generation later and entitled *Ch'un-ch'iu chuan* (Commentary on the
Ch'un-ch'iu), and argue that those neo-Confucian thinkers
whose political attitudes were integrated into a cohesive metaphysical system were likely to have a highly complex and ambivalent attitude toward centralized political authority. This chapter also includes a discussion of the commentary written by Hu
An-kuo in the early years of the Southern Sung and shows how
the ideas of Sun Fu and Ch'eng I were carried forward to the
Southern Sung (and the Ming as well since Hu's commentary
became the orthodox text for the examinations at the beginning of the Ming). Indeed, according to the Ch'ing editors of
the *Ssu-k'u ch'üan-shu tsung-mu t'i-yao*, Hu's commentary was so
popular that for centuries students stopped reading the *Ch'un-
ch'iu* itself (somehow one imagines that they didn't need too
much encouragement) and read only Hu's commentary.[38]

Chapter 6 then puts the neo-Confucian ideas on obedience
to authority in the context of a similar body of thought in late
medieval Europe. Here I discuss how the conduct of politics—
statecraft—among natural law theorists carried forward the
Greek assumption that politics and morality formed a seamless
whole, adding to it a theologically based assertion of a universal
moral order that infused both the natural world and the
human world, which rulers as well as subjects were enjoined to
obey. The universality of this doctrine was the basis for the later
development in Europe of a doctrine of natural rights, known
in its present form as human rights. Such a doctrine not only

implied limits on the power of the ruler but confirmed them, and for that reason the European experience is relevant to the issue considered in this study, in spite of the differences that also exist between the Chinese and the European context (which I discuss in this chapter).

Chapter 7, the conclusion, then shows how Sung ideas on political thought, in particular the concept of *tsun-wang jang-i,* were revived in Meiji Japan to justify proposals for sweeping institutional reform. Indeed, the rallying cry used by the samurai intellectuals to bring down the Tokugawa shogunate—*tsun-wang jang-i,* known to the Japanese as *sonnō jōi*—thus setting in motion the modernization of Japan, was lifted directly out of Sun Fu's commentary, where the two terms appear for the first time together. The Japanese modernizers then proceeded to do precisely what the Sung Confucianists had hoped, in vain, that they could do—increase the authority of the emperor while taking his power into their own hands. This chapter also shows how in China many other ideas embodied in the Sung commentaries were revived in the reforms advocated by New Text scholars such as K'ang Yu-wei and Liang Ch'i-ch'ao in the closing years of the Ch'ing dynasty. There was life in the old horse after all, and may still be. A strong case can be made, I believe, for the proposition that any modern attempt to synthesize Chinese political thought with Western notions of democracy and human rights ought to begin with the same assumptions of a universal moral order that animated the thought of the leading neo-Confucian political thinkers considered in this study.

Finally, it is also my hope that this study will stimulate others more knowledgeable than I am to give greater attention to the crucial role played by the *Spring and Autumn Annals* in Chinese political thought. From the early Han to the end of the nineteenth century, the *Annals* were a source of guidance for scholars in need of inspiration in confronting the most fundamental political problems of their day. Their reflections became a river of commentaries that flowed from the distant past to the present and that nourished generation after generation of idealistic scholars. A rebirth of intellectual vitality in China, when it comes, must surely be based on the classics, and the *Spring and Autumn Annals* deserves to be among them.[39]

PART ONE

The Historical Dimension

2

The Background of
Neo-Confucianism

L IKE the high mountains of China's western regions where
the rivers of Asia begin their long and circuitous descent,
the Northern Sung was the origin of the major currents of Chinese thought from the eleventh to the twentieth centuries.
Some of those currents were beneficial, providing a common
language of discourse and a common foundation of moral
understanding, and others were harmful, submerging alternative modes of thinking that might have added a welcome diversity to a sometimes excessively homogeneous intellectual landscape. Beneficial or harmful, they marked a major turning
point in China's intellectual history.

In its role as a shaping force, as well as in the content of its
ideas, the Northern Sung has remarkable affinities with the
period of the Renaissance in Europe. One of the earliest formulations of this parallel was made by the Japanese scholar
Naitō Torajirō (1866–1934) to justify his theory that the Sung
represented the beginning of the "modern" period in Chinese
history. His student Miyazaki Ichisada made the connection
even more explicit in an article published in 1940.[1]

There were, of course, many differences (among them differing views on the individual and on the role of the state).
Nevertheless, we may infer from the similarities that they play a
significant role in defining the central characteristics of the two
periods. Both shared similar qualities of secularism, humanism,
rationalism, and classicism.[2] Both periods also possessed an

energetic self-confidence born of new and significant developments in a variety of realms: in society, in the economy, and in
political life.[3] In Europe, the Renaissance went on to stimulate
a veritable explosion of creative achievements. Although those
achievements were obviously the product of individual genius
at work under widely varying circumstances, they would not
have been possible had those new developments not provided
the conditions (necessary but not sufficient) in which individual genius could be challenged and nourished. Increased trade
in Europe stimulated the growth of a money economy and
fostered the migration of population from the countryside to
newly emerging urban centers. The expansion of capital available for investment and consumption was conducive to the arts,
whose creators found a livelihood in producing objects of
beauty for the urban market. (The aristocracy in Italy, where
all this began, was an urban phenomenon, unlike its counterparts in England or France, which were based on rural estates.)
Sweeping changes in social and political institutions, not the
least of which were the dismantling of feudalism in the face of
the Commercial Revolution and the beginnings of what would
eventually become the nation-state system, prompted thinkers
to take a new look at certain fundamental problems having to
do with authority, obedience, power, and legitimacy and to
redefine those problems in terms of the new developments. A
wide range of institutions was in a state of rapid change, and
the leading intellects were filled with a new sense of mission
and with a new faith in their ability to influence those changes
through the use of reason.

    With the exception of feudalism (which the Chinese never
had), the above remarks would apply to China almost as readily
as they do to Europe. Intellectuals were responding to a new
and dynamic set of challenges, and when they turned to politics, their ideas—in time-honored fashion—were expressed in
the form of commentaries on the *Ch'un-ch'iu.* Just as the neo-
Confucian movement must be understood in relation to the
historical circumstances of the Northern Sung period in China,
the significance of the commentaries on the *Ch'un-ch'iu* written
during the Northern Sung can be fully understood only as they
also reflect, and in turn influence, the wider currents of
thought running through the period. A more complete expla-

nation of the ways in which the commentaries and their times are related will appear in later chapters. It suffices to note here that the *Ch'un-ch'iu* commentators and other major neo-Confucians were driven by a common impulse to place absolute Confucian moral values in a new metaphysical system susceptible to rational apprehension by the properly cultivated human mind. They all understood human nature in such a way that its ultimate fulfillment was perceived to lie in the active pursuit of the common good through public service. Because of this concern for the practical application of Confucian moral values, the Sung thinkers were sensitive to the dilemma of moral choice in an imperfect world. Therefore they turned to the classics, and especially the *Ch'un-ch'iu,* which since the early Han had been accepted as the principal fountain of Confucian wisdom on the subject of political morality, for guidance in these choices.[4] This chapter and the following one will be concerned with defining and clarifying the relation between neo-Confucianism, the *Ch'un-ch'iu* tradition, and the times of which they were a part.

The political history of the Sung is generally characterized by historians as manifesting two related qualities, a civilian form of government and a centralization of the institutions of governance in the hands of an increasingly autocratic ruler. What was the purpose of these two developments, and what means were employed to achieve their realization? Broadly speaking, the early emperors wished to avoid the military challenges to central authority that had carved up China like a melon into a number of military satrapies from the time of the An Lu-shan rebellion in 755 to the establishment of the Northern Sung in 960 (or, more precisely, until the final defeat or surrender of all the rival states in 979).[5] They were also worried that the continual threat of invasion from the Hsi-hsia tribesmen in the northwest and the Khitan Liao in the northeast would cause local military commanders to acquire too much power and again undermine the central authority of the emperor, as they had done in the T'ang. These two phenomena, the regionalism of the late T'ang and the Five Dynasties period and the threat of foreign invasion from the north, were also largely responsible for the preoccupation of Sung *Ch'un-ch'iu* scholars with the concepts *tsun-wang* (revere the ruler) and

jang-i (expel the barbarians), as we shall see in the following
chapter.[6]

The manner in which the Sung state responded to these
problems greatly influenced the evolution of social and economic institutions in the Sung and helped create the conditions in which the revival of Confucian thought took place. In
some respects, the Sung was as creative in its foreign policy as it
was in its metaphysical speculation. Although conventional
wisdom holds that the Chinese state considered itself superior
in its relations with foreign governments, the Sung government
was much more flexible. It signed treaties with "barbarian"
states—such as the Treaty of Shan-yüan in 1005 with the Khitan
—in which both parties negotiated as equals.[7]

The interrelation of all these factors, which for the sake of
analysis are considered separately, will become more apparent
in the following sections of this chapter. Suffice it to say that the
important role of the state in Sung dynasty affairs was in part
both a response to certain social, economic, and political conditions and a cause of others. Insofar as a study of intellectual
history, in this case one focusing on political thought, seeks to
understand the relation between ideas and the society that gave
birth to them, this chapter shows how the integration of China
on the political level, in response to both internal and external
threats, was paralleled by equivalent integrating trends in both
the society and the economy. Some of this change was guided
by the state, some the result of trends already under way before
the Sung.

The appearance of these new forces and the way in which
they now exerted their various influences on each other at the
national level called for, or created a need for, an intellectual
synthesis capable of relating the new parts to the new whole.
Political thought in the T'ang and the Five Dynasties period,
such as it was, had been influenced more by Buddhist and
Taoist than by Confucian ideas. Now China was entering a new
period of economic prosperity and social integration, centralized under a strong ruler and governed by a bureaucracy that
promised (partly because of the demise of the aristocracy and
partly because of the civilian policies of the early emperors) to
give new and unprecedented opportunities to the scholar-
officials. The otherworldly preoccupations of Buddhism and
the concept of nonaction associated with Taoism could hardly

provide a persuasive stimulus in the face of these new responsibilities and opportunities that now confronted the scholar-officials. Some new statement of principles was required that would serve as a guide to purposive action, on the one hand, but that would also answer the intellectual needs fulfilled for so many centuries by Buddhism and Taoism, on the other hand. The neo-Confucian synthesis, which began in the Northern Sung and culminated in the grand synthesis of Chu Hsi (1130–1200) in the Southern Sung, arose in response to this demand. Just as the revival of learning in the European Renaissance took a variety of forms, including the fine arts and literature as well as science and philosophy, Sung neo-Confucianism flowed principally in three divergent currents: politics, metaphysics, and aesthetics.[8]

Such a broad interpretation of neo-Confucianism goes beyond the traditional Chinese definitions and beyond the definition of some contemporary scholars. The problem of terms is an important one, treated in some detail by Hoyt Tillman.[9] Some scholars have used the English term *Neo-Confucianism,* which has no counterpart in classical Chinese, to refer only to the school of principle *(li-hsüeh)* or to the school of the Way *(tao-hsüeh)* associated with the Ch'eng-Chu school of philosophy.[10] Others have used the same term to apply to the entire movement reviving Confucianism in the Sung. Tillman himself prefers to use the term *Sung learning* to designate the broad range of "the Confucian renaissance during the Sung."[11] In this work, I have employed a compromise term, an uncapitalized *neo-Confucianism* meant to designate the whole spectrum of the renewal of Confucian thought and action in the Sung. Like the legs of a tripod, metaphysics, aesthetics, and politics all play a part, it seems to me, in supporting the Confucian revival of the Sung. But, before dealing with these substantive aspects of neo-Confucianism itself, it is necessary to review the major political, economic, and social conditions of the Northern Sung that set the stage for this major rethinking of the Confucian tradition.

Sung Government

We have already noted that the Northern Sung emperors sought to preserve the unity of the state from internal rebellion by concentrating power in their own hands. This object was

pursued in two major ways—by curtailing the authority of the
military, both in the field and in the government bureaucracy,
and by reducing the power of the grand councilors *(tsai-hsiang)*
over the routine administration of Sung government.[12]

The first challenge was to control the military. A number of
policies implemented by Sung T'ai-tsu and continued for the
most part by his successor and younger brother, T'ai-tsung
(r. 976–997), had as their goal the domestication of the military
establishment.[13] One of their first priorities was to profession-
alize the officer corps and put it under the bureaucratic control
of civilian officials.[14] In general, the first emperors followed two
principles. One was "to emphasize the civil, deemphasize the
military" *(chung-wen ch'ing-wu)*. The other was "to strengthen
the trunk and weaken the branches" *(ch'iang-kan jo-chih)*. Care
was taken to concentrate the best troops at the capital (which
may partially account for the poor performance of some Sung
troops in the field against the Liao and the Hsi-hsia). Commanders were rotated frequently from post to post (although
border commanders enjoyed much longer tenure in the early
years) and from the field to the capital, diminishing the effect
of personal ties between the troops and their commanders.
Measures were adopted to acquire control of local revenue,
which had fallen into the hands of local military leaders, by
sending out officials from the central government *(ch'ang-ts'an
kuan)* to local areas, both at the provincial level (where they
were known as *chuan-yün shih*) and at the prefectural level and
below (where they were known as *p'an kuan*), to take over
direct control of taxation and transportation of goods to the
capital. Military promotions were gradually centralized in the
hands of the emperor. After 962, cases involving the death pen-
alty were ordered to be forwarded to the capital for final review,
and, in the same year, the office of sheriff *(hsien-wei)* was reestablished, removing responsibility for law and order from the
hands of the local garrison commanders. The authority of the
military in the central government was also undermined by a
deliberate policy of removing from the office of the *Shu-mi yüan*
the authority over the civil functions of government that it had
enjoyed during the Five Dynasties period and confining its
responsibilities to military matters only. In the second half of
the tenth century, it was placed officially on an equal footing
with the civilian bureaucracy.[15]

As the authority of the military declined, that of the civilian arm of government increased, especially after the examination system was reestablished by T'ai-tsung and rapidly rose to become the principal means of entry to positions of power in the bureaucracy. In fact, the annual average number of *chin-shih* degrees conferred between 1020 and 1057 was larger than in any other comparable period in Chinese history, and, as we have noted above, the total number of civil officials staffing the government bureaucracy rose dramatically during the eleventh century.[16]

This development is significant for reasons that go far beyond the topic of civil administration. I have stressed above the theme of integration and synthesis that runs like a common thread through much of Chinese life and thought during the Sung. I have also stressed the confidence displayed by early Sung thinkers, who believed that they were indeed entering a new world of opportunity to implement the moral principles of which they felt themselves to be the guardians. While the social and economic forces promoting such integration will be covered in more detail below, the role of the examination system in that same synthesizing enterprise is one of the most important aspects of Sung political institutions. While it is true that not all positions in government were filled with examination graduates and that there were generally only about twelve to nineteen thousand actual positions out of a total pool of about forty thousand individuals in the Sung civil service at any given time,[17] nevertheless the examination system may have done more to integrate China than any other single institution. Winston Lo compares the Chinese system with that other historical tradition that has become synonymous with bureaucracy—the Byzantine—and concludes that, by drawing its ruling elite from all over China and from the major social elite, the Chinese system succeeded in integrating state and society more successfully.[18] John Chaffee concurs and in his study of the Sung examination system concludes that "the cultural unity created, in large part, by schools and examinations was an important contributing factor to the political unity of late imperial China."[19] Peter Bol has further argued that in the Southern Sung, when a national elite had given way to a more locally based elite, the examination system continued to validate membership in the influential class of literati *(shih-ta-fu),* not only for

those who passed the examinations, but also for those who
merely stood for the exams.[20] Moreover, the tremendous sense
of confidence in their own ability to influence events displayed
by the major figures of the Northern Sung would appear to
be justified by the fact that there were twice as many degree
holders (as a percentage of officials who entered public service
through the examination system) in 1046 than 1213.[21] As the
Sung drew to a close, that early confidence had disappeared,
no doubt in part because the competition to take the exams
had heated up considerably. Whereas there were about seventy-
nine thousand candidates participating in the exams at the end
of the eleventh century, by the end of the Southern Sung that
number had grown to 400,000.[22] The total number of civil service personnel increased as well, from 12,700 in 1046 to 19,398
in 1213.[23]

While the body of the civil bureaucracy was expanding, its
head, in the form of the office of the grand councilor, was
shrinking.[24] Military affairs, over which the grand councilors
had once exercised authority in the T'ang, were now (following
the precedent of the Five Dynasties period) controlled by
either the *Shu-mi yüan* or the emperor himself. The emperor
now took an active role in drafting edicts, instead of merely ini-
tialing those that had been drawn up by the grand councilors.
The first and second emperors further clipped the ministers'
wings by withdrawing their authority to issue executive orders
that did not meet the prior approval of the emperor. Assistant
grand councilors *(ts'an-chih cheng-shih)* were appointed with the
intention of diluting the power of the office by spreading it
more thinly among more people, so that the total number of
grand councilors varied from five to nine. Financial affairs,
which were more centralized in the early Sung in the hands of
the Finance Commission *(san-ssu)*, were also taken out of the
control of the prime minister and made the direct responsibility of the emperor. Personnel decisions relating to the higher
level of the bureaucracy were shifted to another office. Censors
and policy-criticism officials, once under the exclusive authority of the prime minister, were also made more independent
and often directed their criticism at the very offices to which
they had once been subordinate (thereby serving the interests,
of course, of the emperor).[25]

Other institutional devices were established to foster the emperor's own control of the government. A spy system, known as the *huang-ch'eng ssu,* was established within the imperial palace as a means of obtaining information from sources completely outside official channels. Even ritual was used to enhance the authority of the emperor, so that prime ministers who had been accustomed to chatting about affairs of state with the emperor over a cup of tea were now required to stand in the emperor's presence. The city of Kaifeng, rebuilt by the Sung as its central capital, was designed in such a way as to emphasize the ritual functions and importance of the emperor as the bearer of heaven's mandate.[26] Nevertheless, the scholar-officials of the Northern Sung (and the Southern Sung as well) were fortunate in that the emperors under whom they served actively supported the Confucian intellectual tradition and treated them with respect (as exemplified by the phrase "[the emperor] does not kill the literati," *pu-sha wen-jen*).

What was the significance of these political developments, both to later political history and to the rise of neo-Confucianism? Politically speaking, they set in motion an institutional trend toward autocratic power that was to accelerate during the Yüan, Ming, and Ch'ing dynasties (not only because of these Sung precedents but also because of later factors unrelated to these precedents). This movement did not, however, advance through time in an uninterrupted series of stages until finally the entire population was reduced to a state of blind obedience. There were many false starts and much slippage. The power of the grand councilors, for example, always tended to increase when the emperor was personally weak or uninterested in affairs of state, and in fact this was the case during much of the Sung dynasty. Nevertheless, many of the centralizing changes implemented by T'ai-tsu and T'ai-tsung became institutionalized, with the result that the potential for the exercise of autocratic power was always there, although sometimes dormant. More important to our topic, these changes set the stage for and provided a partial stimulus to the rise of neo-Confucianism, whose ideological tone was in many ways a response to the forces discussed above. They influenced both the practical programs of reform and the metaphysical speculations of the eleventh-century neo-Confucians.

Sung Economy

Economically, China had reached a level of development in the eleventh and twelfth centuries that was not equaled in Europe until about the eighteenth century.[27] There were a number of reasons for this, among the most important of which was a sudden increase in population following two hundred years of political unrest and intermittent warfare. Ho Ping-ti has calculated that by the end of the eleventh century the population had grown to about 100,000,000.[28] Kang Chao has estimated that the population grew from approximately thirty-two million in 961 to 121 million in 1109, an almost fourfold increase in 150 years.[29] This increased population permitted the cultivation of formerly neglected land, approximately doubling the amount of arable land in the north and greatly increasing the acreage devoted to crops such as rice, tea, and mulberry trees in the south (especially in the Yangtze delta).[30] New strains of more rapidly maturing rice were introduced from Champa (now central Vietnam), beginning in the eleventh century, which made it possible to plant two (and, in the south, three) crops in areas previously able to support only one (in the south, two).[31] The stability of the dynasty permitted the repair of dikes and other water control projects, so that land once abandoned was again brought under irrigated cultivation. Technological improvements such as the *yang-ma* (a device used in wet rice cultivation for the transplanting of rice seedlings) and the *yün-chua* (for weeding) also made their appearance.[32]

An increase in regional trade was made possible by the peaceful conditions of the early Sung and was further encouraged by the repair of old and the construction of new inland water routes and the growth of maritime shipping, so that goods traveled from one area to another more inexpensively and more quickly than before.[33] This, in turn, was one of the factors responsible for the greater regional specialization in crops that took place in the early Sung.[34] Farmers whose ancestors had been compelled to be self-sufficient in order to survive could now plant crops better suited to their own climate and soil and supply their other needs with cash earned from selling the crop to middlemen who participated in a nationwide market network.[35]

This growth of regional specialization and the rise of a national market system was further enhanced by a number of additional developments, including the growth in importance of merchant and craft guilds *(hang)*,[36] which were no longer restricted, as were their T'ang counterparts, to certain sections of the capital but spread throughout all the major cities and served to protect the commercial interests of their members against outside interference (except, of course, interference by the government, which was sometimes considerable and often ruinous). Restrictive regulations, which had the effect of discouraging interregional trade, were mitigated, especially as the government gradually came to realize that a flourishing commercial trade could be a promising source of tax revenue.[37] Thus, no official measures were taken to inhibit a growing trade with other countries, which consisted of exporting Chinese tea, silks, salt, porcelain, lacquerware, and books and importing products such as Japanese sulfur, Vietnamese garnwood, Arabian frankincense, Javanese sandalwood, Malayan sappanwood, spices, Indo-Chinese and African ivory, Indian pearls, camphor from Borneo and Sumatra, and Korean ginseng.[38] A favorable balance of trade during the Northern Sung made the government sympathetic to trading interests since it acquired a lucrative source of tax revenue while at the same time bolstering its currency with increasing reserves of precious metals.[39] It was not until the middle of the twelfth century, in the early part of the Southern Sung, that international trade was actively discouraged by the government in order to preserve a stable value for domestic currency, which it linked, rightly or wrongly, with the vagaries of foreign trade.[40]

Paper currency in China reached its highest level of development during the Northern Sung after the government started issuing paper currency in 1024 and backed it up with reserves of precious metals.[41] During the eleventh century, the system worked successfully, but confidence in the currency was later eroded when, acting under the pressure of increasing expenditures and decreasing revenues, the government printed more than could be supported by metal reserves. Thereafter, China returned in the main to the use of minted coins as the most common medium of exchange, a custom that lasted until the end of the Ch'ing dynasty. During the Northern Sung, however, the adoption and widespread use of paper currency greatly facilitated the transfer of goods and services from region to region and further encouraged the regional specialization and capital investment in agriculture that contributed to the general level of prosperity in the Northern Sung.

During the early Sung, the state became much more involved than before in a wide variety of economic activities. It continued a practice already instituted during the T'ang of encouraging specialized training of government officials in economic matters. Financial expertise was made the condition of appointment and promotion in certain assignments.[42] Agencies of the central government concerned with economic questions were brought together under one roof by the reforms of Wang An-shih (1069–1085), so that policies could be more efficiently formed and executed. The government actively promoted agricultural development, sponsoring the publication of agricultural treatises that were then disseminated among the owners of larger landholdings, who were not only literate but also in a position to afford both the capital investment and the risk of experimentation involved in introducing new equipment and techniques. Former classics on agriculture, such as Chia Ssu-hsieh's *Ch'i-min yao-shu* (Essential techniques for the common people), written in the sixth century, were reprinted.[43] The new seeds from Champa mentioned above were introduced as a result of government initiative. The central government did not always confine itself to advice on how to increase production in various industries, however, and exercised a monopoly over at least the sale if not the production itself of staple commodities such as porcelain, textiles, wine, tea, and salt.[44] In some of these enterprises, the central government in the Northern Sung significantly increased its control over all administrative aspects, with the result that by 1178 salt revenue amounted to 37 percent of the government's cash income and wine 20 percent.[45] Technological advances in these industries as well as in agriculture also played an important role in increasing production.

The state was not the only vehicle of industrial development, however. Robert Hartwell has documented the remarkable rise of the coal and iron industries in the northern provinces of Honan and Hopei during the eleventh century and their subsequent decline.[46] A number of favorable circumstances appeared, including innovations in ferrous metallurgy, the growing use of coal to feed the blast furnaces used in making steel (owing to the scarcity of wood resulting from the deforestation of much of northern China), and the rapidly rising demand emanating from the urban centers of the north, particularly Kaifeng. In fact, the growth of the city of Kaifeng, presenting a tremendous stimulus for economic development in the form of an easily accessible market, was probably the most significant stimulant to this industrial spurt, and it was the decline in population of Kaifeng following the loss of the north to the Jürchen in 1127 that brought an end to the prosperity of the coal and iron industry. At its height, however, iron production in the Northern Sung increased by seven times and amounted to 125,000 tons per year.[47] Shipbuilding is another example of an industry that remained principally in private hands and underwent a period of considerable prosperity in the Northern Sung.[48]

Many of the factors mentioned above, including population growth, commercial development, improvement of communication and transportation facilities, and increase in agricultural production, contributed to the rise of major new urban centers in the Sung. Comparisons with Europe point up the significance of urban development in China. By the thirteenth century, the Southern Sung capital at Lin-an—present-day Hangchou in Chekiang province—had a population of 2.5 million (swelled in part by refugees from the north). The largest cities in Europe at the time were Florence and Venice, each with about ninety thousand. In fact, no city in Europe reached a population of 2.5 million until London did so at the end of the nineteenth century.[49] This urbanization in China was made possible by the agricultural surplus produced in the rural sector and by improved transportation facilities.[50] It was accelerated by the migration of rural people who were either escaping the growing burden of taxation and corvée services levied on the small landholder or who had lost a crop to some natural disaster and no longer had the resources to sustain themselves until the next harvest.[51] The major Sung cities such as Ch'in-chou, Ch'ien-chou, Chen-chou, Ch'eng-tu, Ch'u-chou, Hang-chou, Kuang-chou, Su-chou, and Yang-chou, differed from the promi-

nent T'ang urban areas in that the Sung cities owed their rapid
growth to commercial rather than political factors.[52] While the
T'ang had prohibited the growth of markets outside administrative centers, those restrictions were ended during the Sung,
and small market towns began to appear in large numbers.[53]
Although many may have originally come into existence as centers of administration, it was their position as transportation
and communication nodes in the emerging national market
network that accounted for their explosive growth in the Sung.

The economic conditions touched on briefly thus far have
been cast in a favorable light. Indeed, their influence on what is
now, in the parlance of the times, called the "quality of life" was
largely positive. There was greater scope for individual initiative; fewer people suffered under the unpredictable ravages of
war and natural disaster; there was a greater variety and accessi-
bility of the material resources of pleasure and enjoyment, such
as food. It was, all things considered, a good time to be alive
and doing business in China. But the clouds of future misfortune were already beginning to gather on the horizon by the
middle of the eleventh century. As their implications became
more apparent, they became the focus of attention of most of
the scholars whom we now refer to as neo-Confucians. In many
cases, the problems grew paradoxically out of developments
that are normally regarded as a mark of success and prosperity.
Not only was the growth in population, for example, the natural consequence of a restoration of peace and stability, but it
also contributed greatly to the economic prosperity of the early
Sung period. There was a point, however, when this growth
in population exceeded the capacity of the economic and political institutions to absorb it, so that what was once a sign of
affluence gradually came to assume the form of a burden.
Land, once relatively plentiful, became scarce and was therefore divided into smaller and smaller units.[54]

Other changes were also taking place in the conditions of
land tenure during the Northern Sung. Whether the changes
were in the direction of a free peasantry and were a consequence primarily of population growth, as argued by Kang
Chao,[55] or were produced by conditions of an exploitative and
absentee landlordism is a matter of some scholarly dispute.
Adherents of the former position stress the freedom of action

available to tenant farmers in the Sung, while those of the latter (scholars like Mark Elvin) stress the manorial form of ownership that had grown up during the last years of the T'ang and continued into the Sung. They argue that by the end of the eleventh century a large percentage of land was owned by officials, monasteries, or merchants in the form of manors *(chuang-yüan)* and was managed by bailiffs *(chuang-li).*[56] One trend is clear, however. Beginning in the Sung, and then continuing into the Ming and Ch'ing, more and more tenant farmers were converted from a system of share tenancy (when the normal practice was to divide the crop fifty-fifty with the owner if the farmer provided the livestock, forty-sixty if the owner provided the livestock) to one of fixed-rate tenancy. This trend shifted the burden of risk from the landlord to the tenant and resulted in more hardship on the tenant during lean times.

Moreover, landowners frequently found it convenient to manipulate connections in order to avoid their share of the tax load, and one scholar has estimated that, by the middle of the eleventh century, 70 percent of the cultivated land in China was not taxed.[57] Although this situation may have helped agricultural productivity, it certainly did not do much to balance the budget.[58] Nor did it have much to offer the farmers who did have to pay taxes since they had to shoulder a disproportionately greater amount of the tax burden. Government revenues declined from 150,850,000 units of cash in 1021 to 116,138,405 units in 1065.[59] The consequence of population growth and concentration of land was that the well-being of many farmers began to decline by the end of the eleventh century.[60] Dissatisfaction sometimes erupted in the form of open revolt, as in the Wang Tse rebellion of 1047–1048 and the Fang La rebellion in 1120–1121.[61]

By the middle of the Northern Sung, the declining income and rising expenditures of many tenant farmers were duplicated at the national level, where shrinking revenues—the result of a declining rural tax base—were accompanied by an alarming increase in government expenditures.[62] This was due principally to the cost of maintaining a huge standing army whose appetite for money grew even faster than its size and ultimately came to absorb more than 75 percent of the total budget.[63] In 1064, for example, the scholar-official (and great

calligrapher) Ts'ai Hsiang (1012–1067) estimated that 60–70
percent of government revenue was spent on support of active
and old soldiers alone, not including other military expenditures.[64] In addition, the civilian bureaucracy expanded throughout the eleventh century, requiring a progressively larger piece
of the fiscal pie.

There is no doubt that the favorable circumstances for
economic growth that obtained in the early Northern Sung
resulted in an increase in the total wealth of the country.[65]
Some have noted that this wealth tended to gravitate into the
hands of an increasingly smaller number of landowners (often
members of the imperial household or court officials) and
merchants. But this development may not have been a uni-
formly bad thing. Often it was the availability of large amounts
of capital that made it possible for the more enterprising landowners and merchants to invest in innovative techniques and
new (and therefore risky) projects. Certainly this was the case
in seventeenth- and eighteenth-century England, where the
enclosure movement consolidated landholding in the hands of
a much smaller group of people than before, which made the
land much more productive (generating in the process the capital used to finance the Industrial Revolution) but also displaced many marginal farmers, who thereafter sank into abject
poverty (whereupon they moved to the cities and provided
cheap labor for the new factories).

In general, however, the overwhelming impression of the
Sung economy is one of prosperity. The importance of this
growth and prosperity for neo-Confucianism lies in the degree
to which it helped integrate China as never before. Peace, prosperity, and economic cohesion were the outward, visible supports for the synthesizing edifice built by the great Sung
thinkers. The relation was certainly not so strong that economic forces constituted in themselves a sufficient condition of
neo-Confucianism. It is enough to say that, taken with other
considerations, they encouraged the important thinkers of the
time to believe that life and thought could be brought into
some measure of harmony. One does not have to claim, for
example, that the intellectual creations of the Renaissance
were caused entirely by the vast changes taking place in the
European economy in order to demonstrate that the Renais-

sance cannot be fully understood without considering to some degree the Commercial Revolution. To put it simply, all these developments were closely related.

Sung Society

Such sweeping changes in the economic landscape of the country were bound to have important social consequences, one of which was the growth of a class of merchants whose influence was much greater than that of their counterparts in the T'ang dynasty and the Five Dynasties period. The reasons are complex.

There are a number of developments in the early Sung that, although they did not make the rise of the merchant class inevitable, greatly facilitated it. One of the most important was the decline of the old aristocracy. The aristocratic families, the cultivation of whose support had once been indispensable to the very existence of the emperor's power, had been decimated by the revolts and sporadic but destructive wars in the late T'ang and Five Dynasties period.[66] By the end of the tenth century, it was possible for the emperor to act independently of the great families; officials, even those who were descendants of those families, increasingly owed their position to the discretion of the emperor, not to their pedigree. For their part, the emperors filled the vacuum left by the demise of the aristocracy with a new generation of officials. The actual figures for the growth in the total number of officials can only be estimated. One source cites a doubling every four years before Shentsung's reign (1067–1085).[67] The important point is that a significant increase in numbers had in fact taken place and was frequently remarked on by commentators of the period as representing something of a problem. In terms of Sung society, the departure of the aristocracy opened up social mobility, and merchants took full advantage of the new opportunities in both urban and rural life.

Another development that aided the growth of the merchants was the abolition of the restrictive system of dividing urban areas into separate walled enclaves *(fang)* with access and egress limited to certain periods of the day and with a large number of regulations regarding commercial transactions.

Cities such as Kaifeng became more open, and both business
and people were able to flow more freely in response to their
own inclinations and the needs of the city. Guilds, which had
previously existed in prescribed areas of a city as informal
monopolistic associations, grew in geographic scope and in the
services that they provided to their members (to become the
prototype of the later *hui-kuan*).[68] They were not, however, as
free from government control as their European counterparts
and often suffered dearly (as well as prospered) as a result of
their close association with the state bureaucracy.

The attitude of the government toward the merchants during this early period was somewhat ambivalent. The traditional
contempt for the commercial occupations in general did not
change, and the state was not always quick to realize the potential advantages that might result from a prosperous commercial
economy. The welfare of the merchants was almost always
thought to be subordinate to that of the peasants, and when
foreign trade began to be frowned on at the end of the eleventh century, it was partly because of a perceived threat to the
stability of agricultural prices from that trade. Nevertheless,
during the early Sung, the government pursued a permissive
policy toward the merchants, and many of the former sumptu-
ary laws were rescinded, or simply not enforced, so that the outward appearance of the merchants began to correspond more
accurately with their increased share of political and social
prestige.[69]

This development was paralleled by the tremendous growth
in number and importance of the civilian bureaucracy in the
Northern Sung. The reasons for this are partly political and
partly social. Politically, it was the result of a deliberate policy
on the part of the first emperors to curtail the potentially
disruptive power of military commanders. Sung emperors
wanted to consolidate appointive powers in their own hands,
continuing a process that originated in the Five Dynasties
period. Ultimately, military officials were replaced by civilian
officials whose selection and promotion were controlled by the
emperors themselves.[70] Socially, the civilian officials, together
with the merchants, merely stepped in to fill the vacuum
created by the decline in the aristocracy.

The degree to which the bulk of the literati, or *shih-ta-fu*,

were composed of representatives of certain powerful families
that maintained their influence over time, or were chosen
through the examination system from families of which no previous members had been literati, has been the subject of a good
deal of scholarly attention.[71] For some time the latter view,
based on the research of Ho Ping-ti and Edward Kracke, has
been dominant. Ho Ping-ti, for example, concluded that 46.1
percent of the officials in the Northern Sung (whose biographies were included in the *Sung-shih*) came from humble
origins *(han-tsu),* as opposed to only 13.8 percent in the late
T'ang (of those whose biographies appeared in the two T'ang
histories).[72] Robert Hartwell and Robert Hymes, however,
reject Edward Kracke's conclusions that the majority of the officials who passed the examinations and entered the civil service
were "new men," with no previous family background in the
literati.[73] Hartwell and Hymes argue that Kracke failed to consider relatives other than father, grandfather, and great-grand-
father and that in fact families were able to perpetuate their
power through a wide variety of stratagems. Hartwell believes
that the real watershed in terms of the ruling elite in China was
not between the T'ang and Sung, when the aristocracy was supposed to have been replaced by a new elite chosen on the basis
of merit, but in the transition from the Northern Sung to the
Southern Sung, when the bureaucratic elite oriented toward
the nation as a whole was replaced by representatives of local
gentry whose loyalties were more regional than national.[74]
Hartwell also sees something of a paradox in the Naitō formulation of an increasing tendency to despotism in the Sung.
On the local level, according to Hartwell, the exact opposite
was taking place—the influence of the central government
was declining in proportion as the influence of the local elite
was increasing.[75]

Richard Davis and Thomas Lee, on the other hand, believe
that the bureaucracy in the Sung was indeed a meritocracy and
that new opportunities for education and for advancement
brought a significantly wider body of talent into government
service than before. Davis in particular notes that kinship
groups rose and fell regularly.[76] John Chaffee and Umehara
Kaoru see complications with both positions, and Patricia
Ebrey concludes that, in spite of all the ways in which families

could manipulate the system to gain official positions for their sons, "most of the common generalizations about the differences between the T'ang and the Sung elites still hold true."[77] Final consensus on this issue remains elusive. Suffice it to say that the confidence placed by the neo-Confucians in education as a road to public service had a substantial basis in fact and was not merely a product of their own wishful thinking.[78]

The rise and fall of social classes must also be seen in relation to other changes taking place in the Sung, some of which have already been mentioned in passing, and all of which might be made to fit under the category demographic change. Among these was a shift in population from the northern plains to the area south of the Yangtze River, concentrating particularly around the mouth of the Yangtze and along the coast.[79] This dramatic shift had of course been under way for some time before the Sung and in fact was stimulated in large part by the political uncertainties and physical destruction in the north that prevailed from the An Lu-shan rebellion until the rise of the Sung. In 650, the population south of the Yangtze valley was estimated to contain only 40–45 percent of the nation's population, but by the end of the thirteenth century it had risen to between 85 and 90 percent.[80] The advent of advanced techniques in wet rice cultivation and the use of the new seeds from Champa also encouraged rapid population growth in the south. This shift in population was accompanied by a shift in wealth and influence, with the result that the nouveaux riches of the Yangtze delta began to overwhelm their more conservative counterparts in the north by sheer numbers, giving rise to friction and jealousy, which sometimes crystallized in the form of political cliques within the bureaucracy.

Sung people were on the move, not only south, but to the cities as well. Urbanization proceeded apace, in both the north and the south, as we have already seen. Sung cities were much more lively than their T'ang ancestors. Suburbs grew helter-skelter outside the walls of the old cities; the restrictive *fang* were abolished; merchants were allowed to organize themselves to protect their own interests, and their guilds added a new dimension to Sung urban life. The constant ebb and flow of merchants, artisans, scholars, and farmers between the countryside and the city accentuated a process of cultural integration that was already under way in the cities themselves. New forms of entertainment were encouraged by the large potential audiences now gathered in the urban centers. Professional storytelling, for example, which had probably grown out of oral exegesis of difficult texts delivered by Buddhist proselytizers in the colloquial language, known as "transformation texts" *(pien-wen)*,[81] grew into a fully developed art of great literary richness and originality. While in the T'ang storytellers had remained relatively faithful to written versions of their plots, during the Sung they added their own innovations freely, and their collective efforts became the core of such novels (written down during the Ming) as the *Shui-hu chuan* (Water margin) and the *Hsi-yu chi* (Journey to the west).[82] Storytelling became one of many developing channels of communication between the Confucian literary tradition and the common person and was important in encouraging a greater homogeneity of values in the Sung, one of the hallmarks of the modern age.[83]

The same phenomenon was taking place in Europe during the Middle Ages, as traditional tales such as the *Song of Roland* were written down and new works such as those produced by Chaucer in England or Dante in Italy were written in the vernacular and thus made available to a much wider audience than before. Indeed, as European historians delve more thoroughly into the social history of the Middle Ages, many are discovering more of a reciprocal relation between the "high" culture of the educated classes and the popular culture. Carlo Ginzburg, for example, posits a theory of "circularity," which holds that "between the culture of the dominant classes and that of the subordinate classes there existed, in pre-industrial Europe, a circular relationship composed of reciprocal influences, which traveled from low to high as well as from high to low."[84] Much the same phenomenon applies to China as well.[85]

In China, the phenomenon of Confucianism trickling down the social pyramid was further enhanced by the great changes taking place in Sung education and scholarship. Among the most important developments was the vast increase in the number of schools funded both by the government and by private donations.[86] Fan Chung-yen (989–1052), for example, was responsible for the establishment of many private educational institutions. He was also responsible for the government establishing a system of local schools that ultimately spread to every county and prefecture in China. They were supported through the income generated by the rental of land donated to the school (normally from seventy to 140 acres) and were open to children from all backgrounds.[87] But, as time passed, the official schools gradually became limited to preparing students for the civil examinations and by the twelfth century had declined in terms of offering a rigorous program of general instruction. That function came to be performed by the private academies *(shu-yüan)*, which were supported by either wealthy officials, landlords, or merchants. These are where the greatest teachers and best students in the Southern Sung were to be found, and the best known was the White Deer Grotto *(Pai-lu tung)* on the south side of Mount Lu in what is now Kiangsi province, built up by Chu Hsi to become a model for academies in China and throughout all East Asia.[88] This tremendous growth in the field of education, made possible by many of the social and economic conditions sketched above, brought Confucian values to a wider audience and broadened the scope of advancement for those who took advantage of the opportunity to go to school.[89]

This process was aided also by the full exploitation of the printing technology that had been developed in the T'ang dynasty and the appearance in the early Sung of major encyclopedic works, among the most important of which were the *T'ai-p'ing yü-lan,* the *T'ai-p'ing kuang-chi,* the *Wen-yüan ying-hua,* and the *Ts'e-fu yüan-kuei.*[90] Making the Chinese literary and philosophical tradition available on such a massive scale and at a much lower cost than ever before possible could not fail to exercise a profound impact on the educational system and on the transmission of ideas.[91] Instead of being exposed merely to the standard commentaries, students and scholars now had much greater access to a wide corpus of scholarship and literature. These technological innovations form one more ingredient, together with those economic and social factors mentioned above, in the rise of the syncretic neo-Confucian movement, to which we now turn.

Metaphysical Neo-Confucianism

The neo-Confucian interest in metaphysics is traditionally thought to be a response to the attraction of Confucian scholars after the Han to Buddhism and philosophical Taoism. Traditional Confucian doctrine had largely ignored metaphysical questions, and, for many literati, the collapse of the Han had called into question the efficacy of Confucianism in fostering a stable political order. Moreover, there were many elements in Buddhism and Taoism incompatible with Confucian beliefs. In Wing-tsit Chan's words,

> Generally speaking, the Neo-Confucians attacked the Buddhists for looking upon the world as illusory, for regarding everything as the mind, for failing to understand the nature of life and death and trying to undermine them, for their inability to handle human affairs, for escaping from the world and public responsibilities, for failing to fulfill human relations, for deserting parents, for leaving family life and thus eventually terminating the human race, for being lazy and selfish and aiming only at rebirth in Paradise, and for frightening people with transmigration.[92]

From the Buddhist point of view, the written record, on which the Confucian tradition placed so much emphasis, is little more than a catalog of dreams, the imperfect reflection of a material world that is fundamentally illusory, a chronicle of false appearances that are an actual impediment, not an aid, to the search for the "true" reality.

In spite of these differences, however, there are also many elements of both Buddhism and Taoism that appealed to intellectuals moved by the spectacle of human suffering to ask spiritual questions. They were also attracted to the rational elements in Buddhist and Taoist metaphysics. In this regard, the Hua-yen and Ch'an sects were particularly influential. The term *li,* "principle" (in Hua-yen Buddhism referring to "noumena," as opposed to *shih,* "phenomena"), has been defined as "pattern, reason, truth, discernment, analysis, . . . being, reality, the principle of organization, that which is full of truth and goodness, the transcendent and normative principle of moral action." In neo-Confucianism, it came to be placed in relation to *ch'i,* "breath, ether, vital force, matter-energy, . . . the concrete, material, differentiating principle of things, that which together with *li* constitutes all beings, that which gives life to things."[93] This focus on *li* had earlier been given metaphysical dimension by Neo-Taoists in the Six Dynasties period, particularly Wang Pi (226–249) and Kuo Hsiang (d. 312).[94]

In addition, the concern for the cultivation of the mind-and-heart *(hsin),* which came to occupy such a prominent place in neo-Confucianism, owed much to the Taoist pursuit of tranquillity and the Ch'an Buddhist emphasis on calmness and concentration.[95] The neo-Confucians modified this by reemphasizing the Confucian virtues of *ch'eng* (sincerity) and *ching* (reverence, seriousness) through the practice of quiet-sitting *(ching-tso).* Differing interpretations as to precisely what *hsin* consisted in ultimately led to a later split in metaphysical neo-Confucianism. This is seen in the polarity between those who adhered to Chu Hsi's emphasis on *li,* which implied that moral understanding was reached partly through a knowledge of the principles inherent in all things (hence the necessity to investigate things, *ko-wu*), and those who, following Lu Hsiang-shan, concentrated more on *hsin,* the mind, as an avenue to enlightenment, arguing that the mind, already full of *li,* was sufficient unto itself. As de Bary has noted, however, this polarity was not present in the orthodox neo-Confucian tradition until well after the synthesis achieved by Wang Yang-ming (1472–1529) in the Ming dynasty, which stressed the importance of the mind.

It remains in this brief overview to consider one more fundamental concept of metaphysical neo-Confucianism, the quintessential Confucian virtue of benevolence, *jen. Jen* was integrated into the neo-Confucian system by identifying it with the basic nature of heaven itself and by regarding it as representing the creative, productive force of nature. By elevating this virtue to the level of a cosmic principle, it no longer became merely an ethical goal but rather a fundamental quality of human nature itself inherent in man by virtue of his being a creature of the larger universal order. The pursuit of *jen* thus became a natural consequence of human beings striving to fulfill their basic nature.

These ideas were advanced in the Northern Sung by five philosophers since regarded as the founders of neo-Confucianism. All the Northern Sung neo-Confucians were preoccupied, in a way reminiscent of the pre-Socratic philosophers of Greece, with the problem of the one and the many—how to find in the bewildering confusion of constant change an underlying principle of order and meaning. Since the Confucian tradition had not previously emphasized this question, the Northern Sung thinkers were forced, in their search for a Confucian metaphysical explanation of the universe, to draw on many schools, not only Taoist, but the early *yin-yang* school, the Five Elements school, and the *Book of Changes,* as well as Buddhist philosophy. The first two philosophers (of the five Northern Sung founders) were particularly indebted to Taoism for many of their ideas, although they frequently modified the Taoist nature of certain concepts in order to make them fit into a fundamentally Confucian framework.

Chou Tun-yi (1017–1073), who is generally regarded as having been the first of the neo-Confucian metaphysical thinkers, explained the creation of the material world and the phenomenon of change within it by borrowing from the Taoist use of diagrams. His book the *T'ai-chi t'u-shuo* (Diagram of the supreme ultimate) begins with a statement positing the unity of *t'ai-chi* (supreme ultimate) and the Taoist *wu-chi* (nonbeing). In order to explain how they are related to each other, Chou draws on the *Book of Changes* and incorporates the principles of the movement of the *yin* and the *yang* and the five agents.

Shao Yung (1011–1077), second in the line of transmission established by later neo-Confucians, located his principle of unity in a theory of images and numbers that he borrowed from Taoist cosmology and used to explain the origin and workings of the cosmological order. Again the parallels with the pre-Socratics, especially the Pythagorean school, are striking. Shao was, incidentally, a great admirer of the *Ch'un-ch'iu,* and that text is said to have been, together with the *Book of Changes,* the most influential text in the formation of his own theories.[96]

The third great thinker, Chang Tsai (1020–1078), found his unifying principle in the concept of *ch'i,* which he argued was synonymous with the supreme ultimate, *t'ai-chi,* in which capacity it constituted the physical structure of the universe as well as the principles by which the universe operated.[97] Because *ch'i* had a material as well as a nonmaterial form, Chang provided a metaphysical explanation for the reality of the universe to contrast with the Buddhist belief in the illusory nature of the world perceived by the senses. The "Great Void" of the Buddhists was explained as "undifferentiated" *ch'i.*[98] In so far as benevolence *(jen)* partook of the supreme ultimate, it was universal in scope and inhered in all things.

This *ch'i* was regarded by the fourth and fifth of the five

thinkers, the brothers Ch'eng I and Ch'eng Hao, as merely the
material manifestations of certain external principles, which
they called *li*. Although the two brothers were in agreement as
to the central place occupied by *li* in their philosophical
system, their differing emphases resulted in the formation of
two different schools of neo-Confucian thought. Ch'eng Hao
believed the mind *(hsin)* and principle *(li)* to be identical, thus
making it possible to apprehend principle by concentrating on
cultivating the mind. This produced a tendency to philosophical idealism that was carried on and developed later by Lu
Hsiang-shan and led to Wang Yang-ming, as already mentioned. Because, however, of Ch'eng I's emphasis on the investigation of things *(ko-wu)*, he produced a rationalistic strain that
culminated in the synthesis of Chu Hsi in the Southern Sung.[99]
When Chu Hsi's commentaries were made the basis of the civil
service examination after 1313, they came to constitute one of
the major shaping influences on all Chinese political thought
in the last three dynasties.

Aesthetic Neo-Confucianism

The aesthetic mode of neo-Confucianism expressed itself in
prose, poetry, and painting. Prose and poetry have usually been
regarded as part of a wider development known as the Archaic
Literature Movement *(ku-wen yün-tung)*, which was itself, among
other things, another manifestation of the general neo-Confucian drive to reconcile moral theory and practical application.
The *ku-wen* movement sought to use literature in order both to
apprehend the *tao* and to put it into practice *(wen yi te tao, wen yi
hsing tao; ming tao chih yung)*.[100] It was partly the result of a reaction in both the T'ang and the Sung, led by Han Yü (786–824)
in the T'ang and Liu K'ai (947–1001) in the Sung, against the
aridity of the prevailing form of textual criticism and the super-
ficiality of the flowery form of literary composition known as
parallel prose *(p'ien-wen)*.[101] But the *ku-wen* movement was more
than a revival of a simple and direct literary style. De Bary,
for example, has formulated five major contributions of Han
Yü to later neo-Confucianism.[102] Han attacked Buddhism and
Taoism, revitalized Confucian ethical standards, rejected ideas
that he regarded as stemming from non-Chinese cultural traditions, formulated the idea of the orthodox transmission of the

Confucian *tao* (*tao-t'ung*), and, finally, asserted the importance of upholding this orthodox tradition even in the face of strenuous opposition from contemporary political forces.

In general, the *ku-wen* scholars felt confined by the prevailing methods of classical exegesis and sought to dispense with them and return to the classics themselves, even going to the extreme of doubting the authenticity of some classics (*yi-ching*). The Sung spirit of criticism was thus an outgrowth of a similar spirit in the T'ang, as we shall see in greater detail in chapter 3. The concern on the part of the participants of the *ku-wen* movement with the question of orthodox transmission in a wide variety of activities is illustrated by various terms in common use at the time. *Tao-t'ung* came to refer to philosophical orthodoxy and *cheng-t'ung* to political orthodoxy. Both were different manifestations of the same driving impulse to relate the essence of the Confucian tradition to the practical world. The greatest figure in the *ku-wen* movement in the Northern Sung was Ou-yang Hsiu (1007–1072),[103] and in fact six of the eight prose masters of the T'ang and Sung all belonged to this period of revival in the Northern Sung: Ou-yang Hsiu, Su Hsün (1009–1066), Su Shih (1036–1101), Su Ch'e (1039–1112), Tseng Kung (1019–1083), and Wang An-shih.

Sung poetry has been described by one scholar as representing "a new departure, not only from the poetry of the T'ang, but from all the poetry of the past."[104] Among other things, poets in the Sung developed a new genre, the *tz'u,* or "songs," that employed lines of unequal length and new tone rhymes.[105] This departure lay in the degree to which Sung poetry concerned itself with social and political issues, philosophical theories, and descriptions of common, everyday life. It was also illustrated by the fact that Sung poets were much less preoccupied with sorrow as a theme for their poetry than were their T'ang predecessors; they were, on the whole, a more optimistic lot, perhaps reflecting their times.[106] Su Shih, the optimist's optimist, wrote about history, philosophy, and morality.[107] Mei Yao-ch'en (1002–1060) wrote that "the basic purpose of literature is to aid the times."[108] In other words, poetry was intended by the Sung poets to convey in an aesthetic mode an integrated view of the intellectual, moral, and practical worlds of human life.

Sung painting also underwent a major transformation in the

Sung. In the eleventh century, painting began to be equated with poetry as an expressive device for the artist's inner vision. Su Shih became the leading exponent of this idea, the first to use the term *shih-jen hua* to refer to paintings by scholars who were amateurs, not professionals. He was also the author of that famous phrase describing a painting by Wang Wei, "When one savors Mo-chieh's poems, there are paintings in them / When one looks at Mo-chieh's pictures, there are poems."[109] The purpose of painting thus became not merely to represent nature accurately, as it had been in the T'ang, but to pass along insights into the *tao* of nature acquired by the painter in ways that had nothing to do with the technical skill of painting itself. Painting, along with prose and poetry, became something in the nature of a bridge between life and thought, over which it was possible to travel at will from one realm to another.

Practical Statecraft

Practical statecraft *(ching-shih)* is the third leg of the neo-Confucian tripod.[110] The Northern Sung paragons of practical statecraft were generally uninterested in metaphysical questions. One must keep in mind, however, that, although men of action are not often men of profound philosophical insight, it does not follow that men of thought are somehow congenitally unaware of the practical limits under which men of action are constrained to operate. Nor does it follow that intellectual assumptions are any less important because they are not fully understood by the people who entertain them. In the case of the Sung statesmen, therefore, it is important to remember that, although they were not philosophers, their actions can be understood only in the light of their adherence to ideals that were given intellectual substance by their more metaphysically inclined colleagues. As James T. C. Liu has put it, "Many of them [Sung statesmen] came up from modest circumstances, remained true to their social origin, and served the empire only in accordance with their Confucian principles, often at great personal risk. Without such a fine crop of idealists in any given period, the Chinese bureaucracy, instead of maintaining an appreciably high standard of government administration, could hardly have functioned at all." The attitude of these scholars was best characterized by Fan Chung-yen's famous maxim, "A scholar should be the first to become concerned with the world's troubles and the last to rejoice in its happiness."[111] Fan was the driving force behind the Ch'ing-li governmental reform of 1043–1044, which became a model for the reforms later introduced by Wang An-shih under the emperor Shen-tsung in 1069–1085. Among other contributions, Fan was instrumental in establishing educational institutions (through the founding of the charitable estate, *yi-chuang,* and the charitable school, *yi-hsüeh*) and revitalizing the familial clan system. All of them became major institutions through which the Confucian value system was brought to bear on the daily living habits of an increasingly larger portion of the population than ever before.

These ideals were further developed by the scholar-officials of the utilitarian *kung-li* school, of which the most notable were Ou-yang Hsiu, Li Kou (1009–1059), and Wang An-shih.[112] These scholars were more frankly interested in pursuing the wealth and power *(fu-ch'iang)* of the state (although still directed to Confucian, not Legalist, ends) and argued that only in such a way could the welfare *(li)* of the people be permanently secured. They generally refuted Mencius' criticism of the hegemon *(pa),* believing that the hegemons ought to be praised for the contributions to unity and stability that they did make, whatever their motives may have been. Harkening back to Legalist precedents, they tended to emphasize the primacy of law and institutions in governing rather than moral cultivation. In Wang An-shih's words, "That which harmonizes the people is wealth [*ts'ai*]; that which manages wealth is law [*fa*]."[113] Both Li Kou and Wang An-shih turned to the *Chou-li.* Not everyone, however, agreed with them. Ou-yang Hsiu, for example, was a great admirer of the *Ch'un-ch'iu,* which he regarded as possessing great practical value.[114]

After having surveyed the political, economic, social, and intellectual threads that composed the fabric of Northern Sung life and witnessed the rise of the scholar-officials to unprecedented political and social prominence, and after having noted the greater availability of the tools for disseminating the Confucian ethic to the common man (such as printing and educational institutions), one can now appreciate more fully than before the almost limitless faith that the early neo-Confucians placed in their own power to influence the moral development of "all-under-heaven." Since many of the conclusions reached by this study rest on the belief that Sung metaphysical thought and the problems of practical politics in the Northern Sung were intimately connected—indeed, were regarded as inseparable—it has been necessary to present the wider framework in which these problems were encountered.

It is this peculiar sympathy between ideas and action in the early Sung that prompts me to give to the term *neo-Confucianism* the widest possible interpretation and that, in a larger sense, frames the small canvas of human experience sketched in this work. This impulse to reconcile theory and practice led the neo-Confucians, metaphysicians and reformers alike, to the classics, in much the same way that all questioning men turn to the record of the accumulated wisdom of those who have gone before them—partly as consolation and justification for actions already taken or beliefs already held, partly as inspiration, as a guide in learning to deal with questions that are so fundamental to the human condition that they transcend the barriers of time and place and are never answered with finality but only understood with greater profundity. These motives are not always as comfortably discrete as scholars sometimes make them out to be, and one can safely assume that in most individuals they are, and always have been, mixed.

The precise manner in which the neo-Confucians came to understand the overriding practical issue of obedience to the central ruler in terms of their long study of the *Ch'un-ch'iu* is taken up in chapter 4. Chapter 5 considers how the question of central authority was then fit into a cohesive and rational conception of the moral universe. First, however, we must turn our attention to a brief history of the *Ch'un-ch'iu* textual tradition itself, without which it would be difficult to understand why the *Ch'un-ch'iu* became such an important vehicle in the Northern Sung for the discussion of these immensely complex practical and philosophical questions.

3

Background of the
Ch'un-ch'iu Commentaries

THE *Ch'un-ch'iu* (Spring and autumn annals) occupies a
place in the history of Chinese political thought entirely
out of proportion to the scale of the work itself. From the early
Han to the late Ch'ing, a period of more than two thousand
years, it has been the single most important reservoir of ideas
about politics in all classical literature. For questions of self-
cultivation Chinese have gone for inspiration to the *I-ching* or
the corpus of Confucian dialogues (the *Lun-yü*, the *Ta-hsüeh*, or
the *Chung-yung*), but for questions of government they have
usually gone to the *Ch'un-ch'iu*. It was common for scholars to
view the *I-ching* and the *Ch'un-ch'iu* as complementary to each
other. Chu Hsi, for example, wrote that "the *I-ching* goes from
the hidden to the manifest, while the *Ch'un-ch'iu* goes from the
perceptible to the hidden. . . . The *I-ching* explains what is
within form by what is above form; and the *Ch'un-ch'iu* explains
what is above form by what is within form."[1] More commentaries were written on the *Ch'un-ch'iu* in the Sung dynasty, for
example, than on any other classic.[2] Yet, stripped of its embel-
lishments in the form of numerous commentaries, the work
itself presents a barren prospect indeed, especially to those
whose interest is first stirred by its profound impact on Chinese
political thought and who expect the cause to be as readily
apprehensible as the effect. It is not. The *Ch'un-ch'iu* possesses
about as much intrinsic literary merit as the New York City tele-
phone book.[3]

The text itself is basically a chronicle of events pertaining to the state of Lu in the 242 years between 722 B.C. and 481 B.C. It is divided according to the reigns of the rulers of Lu, of which there were twelve. It contains in its present form about sixteen thousand characters and for the sake of analysis has been broken down by various commentators into various categories, into at least one of which all the events in the *Ch'un-ch'iu* can be made to fit, albeit occasionally with a little pushing and squeezing. One of the most useful such efforts was done by Mao Ch'i-ling (1623–1716), who compiled a list of twenty-two categories: changing of the first year of a ruler, the accession of a new ruler, the birth of a son to a ruler, the appointment of a ruler in another state, court and complimentary visits, covenants and meetings, incursions and invasions, removal and extinction of states, marriages, entertainments and condolences, deaths and burials, sacrifices, hunting, building, military arrangements, taxation, notation of good years and bad, ominous occurrences, departures from a city or state, arrivals at a city or state, notation of thieves and murderers, and punishments.[4] Another traditional listing, which is more concerned with the method of analysis than with the classification of content, breaks the *Ch'un-ch'iu* into the following eleven subjects: main purposes *(chih)*, way *(tao)*, specific purposes *(chih)*, method *(fa)*, system *(chih)*, precepts *(yi)*, conventions *(li)*, incidents *(shih)*, writing style *(wen)*, diction *(tz'u)*, and moral instruction *(chiao)*.[5] Other states of the period also possessed annals, with either the same name *(Ch'un-ch'iu)* or other names, such as the *Sheng* of Chin or the *T'ao-wu* of Ch'u; these were regarded as raw records only, not having been altered by the hand of any later historian. These other annals are no longer extant.

The *Ch'un-ch'iu* has traditionally been studied in conjunction with three commentaries, the *Tso-chuan*, the *Kung-yang*, and the *Ku-liang*, which provide greater historical background to the events listed in the *Ch'un-ch'iu* itself and speculate in some cases about the meaning of the wording of certain events. Of these three commentaries the *Tso-chuan* is the most voluminous (about 196,000 characters). However, the evidence now suggests that it was not originally written as a commentary to the *Ch'un-ch'iu* at all; rather, it was meant as a separate historical chronicle drawn from the historical records of the states of

Chin, Ch'u, and Wei as well as other sources.[6] The text appears
to have been written around 300 B.C.,[7] much later than the traditional Chinese interpretation, which ascribed its authorship
to Tso Ch'iu-ming, a disciple of Confucius'. The *Tso-chuan* ends,
not with the appearance of the unicorn in 481, as do the *Ch'un-
ch'iu* and the two other commentaries, but with the assassi-
nation of the count of Chih in 463. The *Tso-chuan* did not
become an integral part of the *Ch'un-ch'iu* corpus until Liu
Hsin (53 B.C.–A.D. 22) divided it up according to the chronol-
ogy of the *Ch'un-ch'iu* and used it as a commentary on the
Ch'un-ch'iu. It is in this form that it has come down to the
present. While it does contain moral judgments, the *Tso-chuan*
is primarily a narrative history and frequently describes in great
detail events that are alluded to only briefly in the *Ch'un-ch'iu*
itself. Since it did not lend itself so readily to the kind of interpretation favored by court scholars, the *Tso-chuan* did not
receive in the Han dynasty (except very briefly) the formal
blessing of the official academic institutions. But by the end of
the Later Han it had been adopted by the scholarly community
as the most important of all the commentaries, primarily
because of its value as a historical document. This position was
to remain unchallenged until the middle of the T'ang, when
the *Kung-yang* rose in stature,[8] for reasons that are discussed in
greater detail below.

Both the *Kung-yang* and the *Ku-liang* commentaries are products of different schools of Confucianism that originated in the
differing interpretations of Confucius' students. Both commentaries trace their pedigree back to Tzu-hsia (520 B.C.–?), a student of Confucius', but then split. The *Kung-yang* has been
identified with the state of Ch'i and may have influenced Mencius.[9] The school of Ch'i emphasized the interaction of heaven
and man, and texts were interpreted to show that heaven punished man's improper deeds. For example, numerology and
divination were used to interpret the *I-ching,* geomancy and *yin-
yang* to interpret the *Li-chi,* the five periods *(wu-chi)* to interpret
the *Ch'i-shih,* and calamities and prodigies *(tsai-yi)* to interpret
the *Ch'un-ch'iu*.[10] Hu-mu Sheng, a native of the state of Ch'i,
is credited with being the first to commit the teachings of
the *Kung-yang* school to writing, in the early years of the Han
dynasty. Its first influential supporters were Tung Chung-shu

and Kung-sun Hung (200–127 B.C.). Tung was the first to refer
to the *Kung-yang* text as a commentary and is supposed to have
supported the *Kung-yang* and argued successfully against the
Ku-liang scholar Hsia-ch'iu Chiang-kung in debates conducted
before Emperor Wu.[11]

The *Ku-liang* is slightly shorter than the *Kung-yang*.[12] There
exists some dispute as to whether the *Ku-liang* is older or
younger than the *Kung-yang*, but the preponderance of evidence suggests that it is the more recent.[13] Because it has traditionally been thought of as having descended through the
school of Confucius' disciples in Lu, it has been regarded by
many scholars as representing a more authentic version of
Confucius' teachings than the *Kung-yang*.[14] But it has always
been overshadowed by the *Kung-yang*, partly because it did not
attract the support of the early giants of Han Confucianism,
Tung Chung-shu, Kung-sun Hung, and Hu-mu Sheng. Its brief
triumph came during the reign of the Emperor Hsüan (73–49
B.C.), who was fond of it and supported *Ku-liang* scholars such
as Wei Hsien (148–60 B.C.) and Hsia-hou Sheng. The *Ku-liang*
was established as a part of the orthodox canon in the meetings
at the Shih-ch'ü pavilion held from 53 to 51 B.C.[15] The *Ku-liang*
has also been more closely associated with Hsün Tzu than the
Kung-yang,[16] suggesting to some a more authoritarian interpretation of the *Ch'un-ch'iu*.

The tremendous importance attached by Chinese political
thinkers to the *Ch'un-ch'iu* rests on two fundamental assumptions. Neither of these assumptions can be verified beyond all
doubt, with the inevitable consequence that each has had its
own proponents and detractors. The controversy has not yet
been resolved, and probably never will be, unless new evidence
of some incontrovertible nature is unearthed in the future. The
first assumption is that Confucius himself compiled the *Ch'un-
ch'iu*. Indeed, this was the standard belief from the time of
Mencius in the fourth century B.C. and was not brought into
question until Tu Yü (222–284) in the third century A.D.
claimed that it was compiled according to principles established by the duke of Chou and that Confucius did not add or
subtract anything. In the early twentieth century, the wave of
skepticism with regard to the authenticity of classical texts that
swept through the Chinese scholarly community caused such

scholars as Ku Chieh-kang and William Hung to reject any tradition of authorship that could not be conclusively proved, including the attribution of the authorship of the *Ch'un-ch'iu* to Confucius. Archaeological evidence in the past several decades, however, has lent considerable support to the accuracy of many traditional interpretations, hitherto unproved, of classical texts. It now seems more reasonable to accept the traditional interpretation of the authorship of the *Ch'un-ch'iu,* recognizing that we are never likely to have complete unanimity among students of the work.[17]

The second assumption is that Confucius conveyed judgments of praise and blame *(pao-pien)* indirectly, by selecting certain evidence, presenting it in a certain way, and omitting other evidence. Confucius' real points were understood to reside in subtle twists and turns of the narrative, which expressed the great principles of the kingly way, *wei-yen ta-yi* (sublime words with deep meaning). If the title of a particular official, for example, is mentioned on one occasion but not on another, this may be interpreted as conveying Confucius' censure of that individual for unethical behavior.

Disagreements over these assumptions have often taken the form of a debate over whether the *Ch'un-ch'iu* is a classic or merely a primary document of history composed of records kept by generations of historiographers at Lu. Advocates of the *Ch'un-ch'iu* as a classic point to the statements of Mencius, who was the first to assert that Confucius compiled the *Ch'un-ch'iu* with a moral message:

> Again the world fell into decay, and principles faded away. Perverse speakings and oppressive deeds waxed rife again. There were instances of ministers who murdered their sovereigns, and of sons who murdered their fathers. Confucius was afraid, and made the "Spring and Autumn." What the "Spring and Autumn" contains are matters proper to the sovereign. On this account Confucius said, "Yes! It is the Spring and Autumn which will make men know me, and it is the Spring and Autumn which will make men condemn me. . . ." Confucius completed the "Spring and Autumn," and rebellious ministers and villainous sons were struck with terror.[18]

Tung Chung-shu also accepted this interpretation, about which more will be said later. The next commentator on the subject was Ssu-ma Ch'ien (145 or 135–? B.C.), who approved of Tung's position and at one point in the *Shih-chi* quotes Confucius as having said, "If I wish to set forth my theoretical judgments, nothing is as good as illustrating them through the depth and clarity of past affairs."[19] In fact, there were no scholars in the Han dynasty who questioned the authorship of Confucius.[20] Indeed, it seems unlikely that Confucius would have remarked that he would be known by the *Ch'un-ch'iu* if all he did was copy the existing records. This is not the place, however, to enter into a discussion of all the arguments that have been raised about this issue. It is enough for us to know that they exist since for our purposes the important point is that the commentators of the *Kung-yang* tradition, which had the greatest influence on the Northern Sung commentaries (for reasons that will become more apparent later), never doubted that Confucius wrote the *Ch'un-ch'iu* and that he conveyed his principles through the device of *wei-yen*.

The precise interpretation of those principles often varied from commentator to commentator and from age to age, depending on the particular problems that dominated each period. But there is general agreement among those who accept Confucius' authorship of the classic that he wrote it as a guide to restore political order and stability to China by returning to an observance of fundamental moral principles. The *Ch'un-ch'iu* was thought to have been written to explain not only the facts of history but their meaning as well. Tung Chung-shu put it this way:

> The *Ch'un-ch'iu*, as an object of study, describes the past so as to illumine the future. Its phrases, however, embody the inscrutableness of Heaven and therefore are difficult to understand. To him who is incapable of proper examination it seems as if they contain nothing. To him, however, who is capable of examining, there is nothing they do not contain. Thus he who concerns himself with the *Ch'un-ch'iu*, on finding one fact in it, links it to many others; on seeing one omission in it, broadly connects it [with others]. In this way he gains complete (understanding) of the world.[21]

It has been argued that as a rule reformers preferred the classics while antireformers preferred historical texts.[22] In support of this assertion, one may note the New Text Movement for reform in the latter half of the nineteenth century, in which Confucius was portrayed as a political revolutionary by reference to certain classical texts. But it was perhaps a testimony to the ambiguity of the *Ch'un-ch'iu* that none of the *Ch'un-ch'iu* scholars of the Northern Sung supported the reforms of Wang An-shih.[23] Clearly, the classic, by itself, does not commend itself either for or against reform, and we would be wise to disabuse ourselves of this misapprehension, at least insofar as the *Ch'un-ch'iu* is concerned (unless, of course, the *Ch'un-ch'iu* is taken to be a history and not a classic; that is not, however, how it was understood by most of its adherents). Regardless of how variously the text may have been interpreted during the last two thousand years of Chinese history, there is, however, universal agreement on its importance in Chinese political thought. This chapter is devoted to a brief survey of the major commentaries on the *Ch'un-ch'iu* from the Han down to the Northern Sung, in order that the significance of the departures from that tradition made by commentators in the Sung can be more fully appreciated.

Commentaries from the Han to the Five Dynasties Period

Since the major commentators on the *Ch'un-ch'iu* in the Northern Sung were more in line with the *Kung-yang* tradition of interpretation than either of the other two (although they claimed to reject all three), I am concentrating my attention on the *Kung-yang.* The first, and perhaps the most influential, of all the writers on the *Ch'un-ch'iu* from the Han to the present was Tung Chung-shu. His work, the *Ch'un-ch'iu fan-lu* (Luxuriant dew of the *Spring and Autumn Annals*), is important, not only because it was a masterpiece of the *Kung-yang* tradition, but because, as Tung's major work, it represented a crystallization of the Former Han belief in the interaction of heaven and man. Although Tung Chung-shu never occupied high political office for a long period of time, the adoption of Confucianism by the Chinese state as its orthodox ideology, officially approved and taught in state schools, probably owes more to the persuasive arguments of Tung Chung-shu than any other single scholar.[24]

If there is one central thread running through early Han

Confucian thought, it is that there is a close and inviolable relation between heaven, earth, and man, a relation characterized
by a powerful underlying unity (expressed by the phrase "interaction of heaven and man," *t'ien-jen kan-ying,* or *t'ien-jen ho-yi*).
Their essential unity is a consequence, not only of their being
connected with each other through the instrumentality of the
sage-ruler, but also of their being governed by the same universal forces. An action in any one of them was believed to pro-
voke a response in the other, so that, in the words of Tung
Chung-shu,

> when the human world is well-governed and the people are
> at peace, or when the will (of the ruler) is equable and his
> character is correct, then the transforming influences of
> Heaven and Earth operate in a state of perfection and among
> the myriad things only the finest are produced. But when the
> human world is in disorder and the people become perverse,
> or when the (ruler's) will is depraved and his character is
> rebellious, then the transforming influences of Heaven and
> Earth suffer injury, so that their (*yin* and *yang*) ethers gen-
> erate visitations and harm arises.[25]

Tung's belief in the mutual interaction of heaven and man
was also manifested in his use of the *Kung-yang* commentary as
a guide to legal judgments. His *Kung-yang Tung Chung-shu chih-
yü* (of which only fragments remain) included 232 legal judgments made by Tung on the basis of the principles of the *Kung-
yang* commentary.[26] Once the essential unity of man, earth, and
heaven was demonstrated and their common essence shown to
be moral in nature, it remained to find a place for the ruler
that would, on the one hand, satisfy the obvious need for an
agency of political stability and moral guidance and, on the
other hand, provide some avenue by which the power of such a
ruler might be restrained within acceptable limits. The solution, taking into account the tremendous power that rulers
after the Ch'in dynasty had unquestionably gathered into their
own hands, was ingenious. Tung argued that heaven established the ruler in order to make men good, to enable them to
fulfill the potential that lies latent in all human beings:

> Heaven has produced mankind with natures containing the
> "basic stuff" of goodness but unable to be good (in them-

selves). Therefore it has established kingship to make them good. This is Heaven's purpose. The people receive from Heaven this nature which is unable to be good (by itself) and conversely, receive from the king the instruction which gives completeness to their nature. The king, following Heaven's purpose, accepts as his charge the task of giving completeness to the people's nature.[27]

The king, for his part, acts as an agency of heaven and constantly subordinates himself to it:

> The king models himself on Heaven. He takes its seasons as his model and gives them completeness. He models himself on its commands and circulates them among all men. He models himself on its numerical (categories) and uses them when initiating affairs. He models himself on its course and thereby brings his administration into operation. He models himself on its will and with it attaches himself to love *(jen)*.

In fact, a ruler should concern himself almost exclusively with this moral mission and not bother himself with the trivial details of everyday affairs, which are better left to his Confucian officials:

> He who acts as the ruler of men imitates Heaven's way, within hiding himself far from the world so that he may be holy, and abroad observing widely that he may be enlightened. He employs a host of worthy men that he may enjoy success, but does not weary himself with the conduct of affairs that he may remain exalted. . . . Therefore he who is the ruler of men takes non-action as his way and considers impartiality as his treasure. He sits upon the throne of non-action and rides upon the perfection of his officials. His feet do not move but are led by his ministers; his mouth utters no word but his chamberlains speak his praises; his mind does not scheme but his ministers effect what is proper. Therefore no one sees him act and yet he achieves success. This is how the ruler imitates the ways of Heaven.[28]

The ruler sets the moral tone; the officials make the decisions. This view was particularly congenial to Northern Sung thinkers, as we shall see. Tung clearly drew on the Taoist tradition for this argument. The *Huai-nan tzu,* for example, contains the following passage: "The craft of the ruler consists in disposing of affairs without action and issuing orders without speaking. . . . Compliantly he delegates affairs to his subordinates and without troubling himself exacts success from them."[29]

Should a ruler disregard his moral responsibilities and abuse his temporal power, heaven would punish him. Now Tung again drew on the *yin-yang* and *wu-hsing* schools to argue that heaven expressed its disapproval in the form of portents and omens, intended as warnings to the ruler to mend his ways. Should those be disregarded, then natural calamities would ensue, announcing that the mandate of heaven had been withdrawn and paving the way for a change in rulers: "The genesis of all such portents and wonders is a direct result of errors in the state. . . . If . . . men still know no awe or fear, then calamity and misfortune will visit them. . . . We should not hate such signs, but stand in awe of them, considering that Heaven wished to repair our faults and save us from our errors. Therefore it takes this way to warn us."[30] This threat, then, gave the officials considerable leverage in influencing the ruler, and they used it often in the Former Han.[31]

Tung Chung-shu was by no means the only scholar to advocate these ideas. He was followed by a century of scholars who found support in Confucian works such as the "Hung-fan" chapter of the *Shu-ching* (for which Hu Yüan wrote an influential commentary in the Northern Sung), the "Yüeh-ling" chapter of the *Li-chi*, and the *I-ching*, as well as the *Kung-yang* and the *Ku-liang*. They included such individuals as Sui Hung (active 80–70 B.C.), a fellow specialist in the *Kung-yang;* Liu Hsiang (80–9 B.C.), whose specialty was the *Ku-liang;* Li Hsün (d. 5 B.C.), an expert in the *Shu-ching;* Meng Hsi (ca. 100–40 B.C.) and Ching Fang (77–37 B.C.), specialists in the *I-ching;* and Yi Feng (first century B.C.), a specialist in the *Shih-ching*, who all had one point in common, "to impose restrictions on the ruler."[32]

By the end of the Former Han, the tide was already turning, and the theory of natural portents was now being twisted by rulers to serve their own interests. Whereas Tung Chung-shu had used portents almost exclusively as a warning that the mandate of heaven was in danger of being revoked,[33] later scholars used them as evidence of heaven's approval of a particular ruler, thus concentrating on the bestowal of the mandate rather than its withdrawal. This was carried to its extremes in the apocryphal literature *(ch'an-wei)* of the Later Han.[34] The attempts of scholars thus to ingratiate themselves with their rulers undermined the usefulness of the theory as a technique to restrain the ruler and provoked a reaction against it by such scholars as Yang Hsiung (53 B.C.–A.D. 18) and Wang Ch'ung (27–ca. 100). It was not to be used to restrain the ruler's power until, as I suggest below, the Northern Sung. What is the significance of Tung Chung-shu to *Ch'un-ch'iu* studies, and what impact did he have on developments in the Northern Sung? First of all, Tung was crucial in establishing classical studies as the focus of Han dynasty scholarly activity and in particular with interpreting those classics as sources of cosmological principles. He evolved a theory in which the hierarchical construction of government and society was tied directly to the fundamental principles of the entire universal order. The microcosm of man's nature was tied into the macrocosm of the universe by the subjection of both to the forces of *yin* and *yang* and the five elements.[35]

Tung thus achieved a major synthesis of Confucian moral principles of government with a developed body of metaphysical doctrine and in the process also provided an instrument of restraining the power of the ruler. This, it should be remembered, took place in a society in which other institutional restraints (such as the feudal aristocracy) on the arbitrary exercise of the ruler's power were being steadily eroded by the centralizing policies of the early Han emperors (continuing those of Ch'in Shih Huang-ti [r. 221–210 B.C.]). By virtue of owing their positions in government to individual merit (in theory if not always in practice), not to an independent power base, scholars were compelled to appeal to a transcendent moral force in order to influence the emperor's conduct of government. But, being men of some experience in practical affairs, they recognized that moral arguments could be more persuasive if they were supported by sanctions that included among them the overthrow of the ruler himself. If that is the case, then, how does one explain the concept "revere the ruler and downgrade ministers" *(tsun-chün yi-ch'en)?*[36] Does it imply that Tung advocated surrendering absolute loyalty to the person of the ruler? From the context of his argument, in which loyalty to the ruler was placed in relation to loyalty to higher universal values, Tung avoided taking what would have been a strictly Legalist interpretation of authority and, as we shall see, established a precedent that was followed in the Sung.

As mentioned, however, the perversion of this theory led rapidly to its being discredited in the Later Han. It is my contention that no replacement for it, that is, no new synthesis of cosmological principles and Confucian political thought of a comparable magnitude and with a comparable effect on the body of Confucian thought, appeared until the Northern Sung. During the Northern Sung, a new effort was undertaken to unify man and heaven according to a rational perception of the natural order, an effort that focused on the ruler as the indispensable link and also subordinated the ruler to heaven and evaluated his behavior in terms of absolute moral standards. After the Sung, the political ideas of neo-Confucianism were manipulated to serve the interests of the ruler in much the same way that Tung Chung-shu's theories had been appropriated by rulers in the Later Han. It is not to be argued here that the two experiences were similar in all respects but rather that the parallels reveal how the ideas of political thinkers are often twisted by later followers in ways that the original thinker never would have condoned.

In the meantime, however, the issue came to be overshadowed by a dispute that arose in the Later Han between the scholars of what came to be known as the "New Text" (*chin-wen*) school and those of the "Old Text" (*ku-wen*) school. The former generally relied on texts that had been committed to writing only as late as the second century B.C., the latter on texts written in a pre-Han form of calligraphy that had allegedly been discovered in the walls of Confucius' home in Ch'ü-fu. Although these texts were discovered in the second century, the differing interpretations did not begin to harden into clearly defined positions until the textual debates that took place at the meeting in the Shih-ch'ü pavilion from 53 to 51 B.C. The *chin-wen* school emphasized the importance of the *yin-yang* and *wu-hsing* concepts in establishing the interaction of heaven and earth and of portents and calamities as evidence of heaven's judgments. The *chin-wen* scholars tended, especially during and after the Later Han, to regard Confucius as an "uncrowned king" *(su-wang)* who received heaven's mandate in the form of the discovery of the unicorn in 481 B.C. The principal *chin-wen* scholar of the Later Han who supported the *Kung-yang* interpretation was Ho Hsiu (129–182), whose major work, the *Ch'un-ch'iu kung-yang chieh-ku,* represents in most respects a continuation of Tung Chung-shu's interpretations, although he tended to become preoccupied with some of the more fantastic notions of natural portents that were current in the Later Han.[37] His claim to a certain amount of originality lies chiefly in his interpretation of the "three ages" *(san-shih)* through which the world was supposed to have passed up to the time of Confucius. His theory, which suggests linear progression, is a departure from the traditional cyclic views of time characteristic of the pre-Ch'in era and the early Han.[38]

Although Chinese historical convention has it that the *chin-wen* school was not revived after the end of the Later Han until the Ch'ing dynasty, there are many similarities between the views on the *Ch'un-ch'iu* expressed by the *chin-wen* school of the Han and those of the Northern Sung.[39] One of the most important of these similarities, which will be considered in greater detail below, is the conviction that heaven and earth form a united whole operating according to principles capable of being apprehended by the use of reason. Another is the belief that classics such as the *Ch'un-ch'iu* contain certain fundamental principles that, when properly interpreted, can serve as a guide to contemporary practical policies.[40]

The *ku-wen* interpretation, stemming originally from the state of Lu (instead of Ch'i, as was the case with the *chin-wen* school), claimed to represent a more pure and authentic form of Confucianism. It emphasized independent etymological research *(chang-chü hsün-ku)* and rejected what it regarded as the frivolous theories of prognostication associated with the *chin-wen* school. It regarded Confucius merely as a teacher, transmitting the knowledge of antiquity without any pretense of applying that knowledge in practical affairs. It emphasized the importance of the duke of Chou, rather than Confucius, and the histories, rather than the classics.[41]

Although there were occasional signs of interest in *chin-wen* ideas, the mainstream of classical scholarship from the Later Han to the Northern Sung flowed from the reservoir qf *ku-wen* interpretation established by such Han scholars, for instance, as Chia K'uei (30–101) and Fu Ch'ien (d. ca. 200), both *Tso-chuan* specialists; Ma Jung (76–166), the first to write commentaries on all five classics; and Cheng Hsüan (127–200), who is still regarded as one of the most authoritative interpreters of the classics.[42] The two principal commentators on the *Ch'un-ch'iu* during the Six Dynasties period were Tu Yü and Fan Ning (ca. 320–ca. 418). Tu Yü's commentary on the *Tso-chuan*, the *Ch'un-ch'iu tso-chuan chi-chieh*, remains standard even to the present day, and his views reflect those of the *ku-wen* school with its emphasis on textual criticism *(chang-chu)* and literary exposition *(hsün-ku)*. He claimed that the *Ch'un-ch'iu* did not contain even one word of praise or blame and that Confucius merely assembled historical records that had already been preserved according to the standards established by the duke of Chou, to whom the real credit for the merits of the *Ch'un-ch'iu* ought to be given.[43] Fan Ning, on the other hand, who concentrated on the *Ku-liang* and whose commentary, the *Ch'un-ch'iu ku-liang chuan chu-shu*, is also the standard commentary on that text today, drew on the *Kung-yang* and the *Tso-chuan* as well in his explications.[44] Generally, however, the unsettled political disunion following the fall of the Han and prior to the rise of the Sui resulted in a spirit of enervating fatalism among the intellectuals, who became increasingly attracted to the consolations of Lao-Chuang Taoist thought and Buddhism.[45]

During this period there were no commentaries on the *Ch'un-ch'iu* that were to exert a powerful influence on later thinkers in the Sung. But the *Ch'un-ch'iu* continued to be a reference point in any discussion of the authority and role of the ruler. In this regard, several thinkers particularly stand out—Wang Pi (226–249), Kuo Hsiang (d. 312), and Ko Hung (ca. 277–ca. 357). According to Hsiao, Lao-Chuang political thinkers were divided into two groups, those advocating non-action *(wu-wei)* and those advocating no ruler *(wu-chün)*.[46] Wang Pi and Kuo Hsiang belong to the former, while Ko Hung attempted to reconcile the Taoist and Confucian positions.

Wang Pi and Kuo Hsiang believed that a king ruled best who ruled least. Almost fifteen hundred years before Adam Smith, Kuo believed that the ruler "who can make the empire be well-governed is the one who does no governing. . . . That is, being well-governed comes from not governing, and action comes from taking no action. . . . Therefore it is he who in every act is with the people who, wherever he may be, can be the world's ruler. To be the ruler in this way is to be innately lofty as are the heavens; that is in truth the virtue of the ruler." The emperor should reign but not rule. In words that must have warmed the hearts of later officials who wanted to get out from under an overbearing emperor, Kuo Hsiang wrote that rulers ought "to remain far away and deeply silent; that is all." Kuo Hsiang is also important because he foreshadows Ch'eng I's emphasis on relating political hierarchy to heavenly principle *(t'ien-li)*. In his commentary on the *Chuang Tzu,* for example, he remarked that "whether one is a ruler or a servitor, a superior or an inferior, and whether it is the hand or the foot, the inside or the outside, that follows from the spontaneity of Natural Principle [*t'ien-li chih tzu-jan*]; how could it be thus directly from man's actions?"[47]

Ko Hung was no Taoist anarchist. On the contrary, having witnessed times of troubles induced, in part, by officials usurping the powers of the ruler, he was inclined to stress the importance of the ruler. Indeed, in language similar to that of Thomas Hobbes, he argued that life in a state of nature, without a ruler, would be violent and short: "Private feuds would be more excessive than public wars, and clubs and stones sharper than weapons. Corpses would be strewed through the fields and blood would stain the roadways. Were a long time to pass without a ruler, the race of mankind would be exterminated." In words that might have been written by Sun Fu 750 years later, he wrote that:

Removing a ruler and installing another is a matter of minor compliance [with duty and virtue] and of major disobedience; it should not be encouraged [i.e., allowed to grow]. . . . For the ruler is as heaven, as the father. If the ruler can be removed then heaven also can be changed, fathers also can be changed. . . . Everything conveyed in the wood and bamboo tablets [i.e., the early Chou documents] supports the elevation of the ruler and the subordination of the servitor, the strengthening of the trunk and the weakening of the branches. The meaning of the *Spring and Autumn Annals* is that heaven must not be taken as one's adversary. The Great

Sage [Confucius] composed the classic to support fathers and serve rulers.[48]

In the early T'ang, the most important commentary on the *Ch'un-ch'iu* was written by K'ung Ying-ta (574–648), whose *Ch'un-ch'iu tso-chuan cheng-yi,* largely following Tu Yü, also rejected the praise and blame interpretation and concerned itself primarily with textual criticism.[49] His subcommentary *(shu)* is added to the commentary of Tu Yü *(chu)* in the *Ssu-k'u ch'üan-shu* edition of the *Tso-chuan.*

But it was not until a century later that there appeared a new spirit of criticism of the *Ch'un-ch'iu* that was to influence greatly the scholarship of the Northern Sung. The first scholar to express this new spirit was Tan Chu (724–770), who, after fleeing the chaos of the An Lu-shan rebellion in 755, spent the last ten years of his life working on a critical review of the *Ch'un-ch'iu* commentaries.[50] Tan was more critical of the *Tso-chuan* than the *Kung-yang* and the *Ku-liang,* which, according to the *Hsin-t'ang shu,* were his favorites.[51] He was more concerned with the meaning *(ta-yi)* of the *Ch'un-ch'iu* itself than he was with textual criticism of the commentaries. He concluded that much of Confucius' teaching had been lost in the process of oral transmission that had preceded the actual writing of the commentaries and that the only way to recover that teaching was to return to the original writings of the great sage himself.[52]

Tan's work was carried out by two admirers, Chao K'uang and Lu Ch'un (d. 806). Very little is known of Chao K'uang, although fragments of his writings have survived.[53] Chao K'uang went further than Tan Chu in questioning the formerly held views on the authenticity of the *Tso-chuan,* saying that there were too many inconsistencies of style and substance for it to have been written by one person.[54] Chao also regarded the praise and blame tradition of interpretation as more fully representing Confucius' intentions and looked on Tung Chung-shu as the foremost commentator of the Han dynasty.[55] Lu Ch'un's writings have survived, however, and include three major works on the *Ch'un-ch'iu,* the *Ch'un-ch'iu chi-chuan tsuan-li,* the *Ch'un-ch'iu wei-chih,* and the *Ch'un-ch'iu chi-chuan pien-yi.*[56] It is Lu Ch'un's writings that exercised a profound influence on *Ch'un-ch'iu* studies in the Northern Sung. Their critical attitude is thought to have inspired such early Sung scholars as Hu Yüan and Sun Fu to use the commentaries as a vehicle to express their own ideas on contemporary political affairs.[57]

There was one additional scholar in the late T'ang, Ch'en Yüeh (fl. 899), who has not been highly rated in the secondary literature but who seems to have kept the critical spirit alive in the late ninth and early tenth centuries. A fragment of his foreword to a collection of the major commentaries to the *Ch'un-ch'iu* (along with his own of course), entitled the *Ch'un-ch'iu che-chung lun,* and parts of the work itself have survived.[58] Ch'en sets out to present all the strengths and weaknesses of the three main commentaries, but in reality clearly supports the praise and blame theory of interpretation.[59] The Yüan dynasty scholar Wu Lai (1297–1340) credits him with having preserved much of the traditional teachings of the *Ch'un-ch'iu.*[60] He also appears to foreshadow Sun Fu's emphasis on revering the ruler,[61] as well he might since he lived at a time when the once-unified T'ang state was in the last stages of disintegration. The importance of a strong ruler in preserving the state was overwhelmingly apparent.

Nevertheless, even considering the rise of a more critical spirit in the T'ang, which has been described above, Wang Ying-lin (1223–1296) has written that there were no major changes in classical studies from the Han to the Ch'ing-li period (1041–1048) of the Northern Sung.[62] The mainstream of criticism adhered very closely to the accepted patterns of textual criticism and literary exposition, as reflected in the commentaries of Tu Yü and K'ung Ying-ta, for example. Without really disagreeing, the editors of the *Ssu-k'u ch'üan-shu* say that before the mid-T'ang the *Tso-chuan* was the dominant commentary but that after Tan Chu and Chao K'uang the *Kung-yang* and the *Ku-liang* began to demand more attention.[63]

Northern Sung Commentaries

If there is any single quality that the many varied expressions of early Sung culture share, it is the impulse to unify, to synthesize, to bring together rather than to separate, to discern underlying essence rather than temporary accident. One of the best, certainly one of the most arresting, examples of this impulse is Chang Tsai's "Western Inscription." In the words of de Bary, "Perhaps nowhere else in all Neo-Confucian literature does lofty metaphysical theory combine so effectively with the basic warmth, compassion, and humanism of ancient Confucianism as in this short passage."[64] As suggested in chapter 2, there are many social, political, economic, and intellectual reasons for this effort to integrate the theoretical and the practical.

The parallel between this unified vision in early Sung China and the corresponding worldview of late medieval Europe is apparent. C. S. Lewis, describing the medieval European model of the universe, has written:

> Its contents, however rich and various, are in harmony. We see how everything links up with everything else; at one, not in flat equality, but in a hierarchical ladder. It might be supposed that this beauty of the model was apparent chiefly to us who, no longer accepting it as true, are free to regard it— or reduced to regarding it—as if it were a work of art. But I believe this is not so. I think there is abundant evidence that it gave profound satisfaction while it was still believed in. I hope to persuade the reader not only that this Model of the Universe is a supreme medieval work of art but that it is in a sense the central work, that in which most particular works were embedded, to which they constantly referred, from which they drew a great deal of their strength.[65]

The parallel is worth pointing out not merely because of its curiosity value but because we who live in an age that has lost this same sense of underlying unity are inclined to depreciate its significance in the past as a driving force in thought as well as in action. The parallel is made not in order to suggest a "comparative model" but to deepen our insight into the minds of an earlier age and to remind us that this same vision of harmony was once part of our own civilization.

In political terms, this sense of unity in Sung China was expressed in the doctrine of a strong central ruler capable of controlling local military commanders, on the one hand, and, on the other, of protecting China's borders against the incursions of the northern barbarians. In support of these practical policies, scholar-officials argued that the principal meaning of the *Ch'un-ch'iu* was to revere the ruler and expel the barbarians

(tsun-wang jang-i) and wrote commentaries to expound and justify that argument. Their purpose, as P'i Hsi-jui rightly points
out, was not to promote slavish obedience to the ruler, nor to
expel every last barbarian from China's border (about which
more later), but to warn against the dangers of usurping officials and foreign invasion.[66]

In addition, as suggested in chapter 2, the Sung emphasis on
unity also expressed itself in metaphysical form, and this in
turn influenced political thought, which constituted in the
minds of the neo-Confucians one part of an integrated whole.
In the evolution of *Ch'un-ch'iu* scholarship in the Northern
Sung, this metaphysical interest proceeded in two stages. The
first was represented by Sun Fu's emphasis on *li* (ritual) as
a unifying and absolute moral principle, but still within the
mainstream of Confucian moral thought, and also by Ch'eng
I's emphasis on *li* (principle) and *t'ien-li* in interpreting the
Ch'un-ch'iu, thus bringing the political theory of *tsun-wang*
into line with a new formulation of the cosmic order. The influence of these two developments was very great, and they were
united in the person of the Southern Sung commentator Hu
An-kuo (1074–1138). Since these developments in *Ch'un-ch'iu*
studies will be treated in more detail below, suffice it here
to introduce briefly the other major commentators of the
Northern Sung.

Hu Yüan (993–1059)[67] is often regarded as having led the
first wave of the neo-Confucians[68] and was distinguished for his
conviction, alluded to above, that thought and action form an
integrated whole. Liu I, a student of Hu Yüan's, was once asked
by Emperor Shen-tsung (r. 1069–1085) who was superior, Hu
Yüan or Wang An-shih. Liu replied,

> Our dynasty has not through its successive reigns made sub-
> stance and function the basis for the selection of officials.
> Instead we have prized the embellishments of conventional
> verification, and thus have corrupted the standards of con-
> temporary scholarship. My teacher [Hu Yüan] from the
> Ming-tao through the Pao-yüan periods [1032–1040], was
> greatly distressed over this evil and expounded to his stu-
> dents the teaching which aims at clarifying the substance [of
> the Way] and carrying out its function. . . . The fact that
> today scholars recognize the basic importance to govern-

ment and education of the substance and function of the
Way of the sages is all due to the efforts of my Master.[69]

Hu required his students to demonstrate proficiency in two
areas, the meaning of the classics *(ching-yi)* and practical affairs
(chih-shih), and they were admonished to clarify substance in
order to put it into practice *(ming-t'i ta-yung)*. He exercised
great influence as an instructor in the newly revived National
University (which, incidentally, adopted Hu's curriculum) during the 1050s, and it was said that, out of every ten candidates
who passed the official examinations, four or five were former
students of his.[70] His writings reflect the catholicity of his interests. He wrote commentaries on the *I-ching* (entitled *Chou-yi
k'ou-yi*) and the "Hung-fan" chapter of the *Shu-ching* (entitled
Hung-fan k'ou-yi), which survive, and one on the *Ch'un-ch'iu*
(entitled *Ch'un-ch'iu k'ou-yi*), which has been lost.[71] His most
influential students were Sun Chüeh (1028–1090) and Ch'eng
I, and it is principally through their commentaries on the
Ch'un-ch'iu that Hu's ideas on that text have been perpetuated.

Among the other principal commentators on the *Ch'un-ch'iu*
in the Northern Sung, the most famous was Liu Ch'ang (1019–
1068),[72] whose extant writings on the *Ch'un-ch'iu* are numerous.[73] Liu Ch'ang was an active administrator who received his
chin-shih degree in 1046 and reached in the course of a relatively short life (he died at the age of forty-nine) the high positions of academician of the Academy of Scholarly Worthies
(chi-hsien tien hsüeh-shih) and supervisor of the Censorate in
Nanking *(nan-ching yü-shih-t'ai p'an-kuan)*.

He was highly regarded for his knowledge of ritual *(li)*, and
in fact his commentaries are basically expositions of how the
political problems raised in the *Ch'un-ch'iu* were infractions of
ritual and how attention to ritual would have solved the problems then and could also resolve them in contemporary life.
Ch'ing scholars, who looked with considerable disfavor on Sun
Fu's tendency to invest the classic with what they regarded as
his own unsupported opinions, had a much higher estimation
of Liu Ch'ang's scholarship. Although he too was not innocent
of the charge of introducing his own views in the commentary,
he did not dispense with the previous exegetical tradition
(actually, neither did Sun Fu, but he had a reputation for doing

so) but based much of his analysis on the *Kung-yang* and *Ku-liang* commentaries.[74]

Liu's commentaries are not masterpieces of clarity. He himself seems to have derived some perverse pleasure in making things difficult for his readers, running as much of his text together as possible instead of breaking items down according to the passages in the *Ch'un-ch'iu* itself. He even announced once that no one in the world would be able to understand his book.[75]

Liu Ch'ang's commentaries are reflective of the main ideas of the first wave of Northern Sung commentators on the *Ch'un-ch'iu*. As with Sun Fu's commentary, judgments of blame are everywhere couched in terms of the violation of ritual *(fei-li)*. This is exactly the way in which Sun Fu also conveyed his judgments. Furthermore, as was also the case with Sun Fu, Liu continually emphasized the subordination of the ruler to the will of heaven, as when very early on in his *Ch'un-ch'iu chuan* he stated, for example, that "the king receives his mandate from heaven; the feudal lords receive their mandate from the ruler."[76] This passage, incidentally, is not without relevance to contemporary issues in the Northern Sung—notably the debate surrounding the appointment of local officials by the emperor. The passage might well have been intended to support the principle that local officials should receive their positions from the emperor, not from their more immediate superiors. Efficiency would dictate local appointment; control would dictate central appointment. Uppermost in the minds of early Sung commentators, of course, was the fear that local officials would build a network of their own appointees who would be more loyal to them than to the central government, à la late T'ang. The operative principle underlying all these particular views toward appointment was to "strengthen the trunk and weaken the branches" *(ch'iang-kan jo-chih)*.

Liu also condemned, as did Sun Fu, those states that made treaties with the barbarians on their own, as when the duke met the Jung barbarians at Ch'ien in 721.[77] Liu's impact as a scholar on the *Ch'un-ch'iu* derives from his enormous erudition and from his emphasis on ritual as a unifying moral framework that transcends the authority, and power, even of rulers and against which the actions of all men were held up for judgment (and usually blame). In this, Liu followed directly in Sun Fu's footsteps.

Another *Ch'un-ch'iu* scholar whose commentary has been preserved, and whose significance derives from his having followed the iconoclastic tradition of the T'ang scholars Tan Chu and Chao K'uang, was Wang Hsi. Very little is known about Wang Hsi's life.[78] In his attitudes toward the *Ch'un-ch'iu*, Wang is said to have continued the tradition established by Tan Chu and Chao K'uang in the T'ang and also the tradition that influenced the commentaries of Sun Fu. Unlike Sun Fu, however, he did not believe that the *Ch'un-ch'iu* contained all blame and no praise.[79] Nor did he refrain from introducing his own opinions into the commentary, which again is a characteristic of many of the commentators of his age. He also takes the problem of revering the ruler as the central problem of the *Ch'un-ch'iu*, arguing that it began with the reign of Duke Yin in order to condemn the usurpation of the throne (via the duke's murder) by his brother, who became Duke Huan.[80]

But the issue of the "kingly way" is always paramount. Wang wrote that heaven expressed its dissatisfaction with a ruler who was not following the kingly way by sending down natural disasters: "The ruler of men should fear the occurrence of unusual phenomena or frequent disasters; rulers ought to grieve, because the purpose [of those phenomena is to point up the need for] virtuous government."[81] With Wang, as with Liu Ch'ang, the purpose of the *Ch'un-ch'iu* was to exalt the authority of the ruler, but always in the context of a higher authority, to which the ruler was clearly subordinate. The people should fear their ruler, but their ruler should fear the power of heaven. Although he freely introduced his own ideas (rather too freely, according to Ch'ing scholars), his commentary was not focused effectively on those contemporary issues that were regarded as of fundamental importance by Sung scholar-officials.

For those commentaries that did focus on the critical problems of their times, we have to return to the mainstream begun by Hu Yüan and Sun Fu, exemplified best by the two most famous of Hu's students, Sun Chüeh (1028–1090)[82] and Ch'eng I. Sun Chüeh was a student of Hu Yüan's and pursued an active political career. He passed his *chin-shih* exam with honors and in public office ascended to the position of vice censor–in–chief *(yü-shih chung-ch'eng)*, the second in charge of the Censorate. He is said to have incurred Wang An-shih's disfavor by attacking the *ch'ing-miao* (green sprouts) reforms as harmful to the people.[83] In his commentary on the *Ch'un-ch'iu*, the *Ch'un-ch'iu ching-chieh,* he concentrated on the issue of criticizing the hegemon and revering the ruler *(yi-pa tsun-wang)*. In supporting his conclusions, he drew from all three commentaries, but particularly from the *Ku-liang*, and he emphasized the praise and blame method of interpretation. When he departed from those commentaries, he was most likely to borrow from the Tan, Chao, and Lu commentaries of the T'ang or directly from Hu Yüan.[84]

From the point of view of subsequent influence on the development of neo-Confucianism, unquestionably the most important Northern Sung commentator on the *Ch'un-ch'iu* after Sun Fu was Ch'eng I (1033–1107).[85] The precise manner in which he synthesized the Confucian hierarchical view of political authority traditionally embodied in the *Ch'un-ch'iu* with his own metaphysical philosophy of principle, *li,* will be considered in greater detail in chapter 5. Suffice it to say that Ch'eng I represents the height of Sung scholarship on the *Ch'un-ch'iu* in the Northern Sung and the wellspring, together with Sun Fu, from which the great Southern Sung commentators, the most important of which was Hu An-kuo (see chapter 5), drew their main themes.

Ch'eng I had two students who were also well known for their writing on the *Ch'un-ch'iu,* Hsieh Shih[86] and Liu Hsüan (1045–1087).[87] Their writings on the *Ch'un-ch'iu* are no longer extant,[88] but Liu Hsüan was closely involved in the preparation of Ch'eng I's writings and sayings on the *Ch'un-ch'iu.*[89]

In addition, there are three other important *Ch'un-ch'iu* scholars (other than Hu An-kuo) who were educated in the Northern Sung but who spent their mature years in the Southern Sung. They are Ts'ui Tzu-fang,[90] Yeh Meng-te (1077–1148),[91] and Lu Pen-chung (1084–1145).[92] Ts'ui Tzu-fang lived most of his life in retirement from active affairs, and his books were not published until the Southern Sung. He generally relied on the *Tso-chuan* and to a lesser extent on the *Kung-yang* and *Ku-liang*, but he did not concentrate on the *Ch'un ch'iu* text itself. In this regard, he represents a departure from the main-stream of Sung commentaries on the *Ch'un-ch'iu*.[93]

Yeh Meng-te relied more on the *Tso-chuan* than Sun Fu, but in most respects followed Sun's rejection of the commentaries and reliance on the text of the *Ch'un-ch'iu* itself.[94] According to the Southern Sung scholar Ch'en Chen-sun, Lu Pen-chung's commentary was just a composite of the ideas of Lu Ch'un and the major Northern Sung commentators, without adding anything new.[95]

The Sung dynasty thus represented a major departure from the mainstream of classical exegesis on the *Ch'un-ch'iu* from the late Han to the end of the Five Dynasties period. In many cases, it was a response to the particular configuration of internal and external threats that confronted the Sung dynasty. In their attempts to relate the importance of revering the emperor to the higher code of absolute moral law held to govern the entire universe and to formulate this moral law in terms of a rational metaphysics that incorporated many Buddhist and Taoist ideas, Sung *Ch'un-ch'iu* scholars were also returning to principles first enunciated in *Ch'un-ch'iu* scholarship by Tung Chung-shu in the early Han. Belief in the interaction between heaven and man, disregarded or repudiated by scholars who were pre-occupied with problems of etymological research, was again asserted and again fulfilled the dual function of both legitimizing and limiting the authority of the emperor, as we shall see in the next three chapters.

PART TWO

The Ideological Dimension

4

Sun Fu's Views on
Obedience to Authority
The Literal/Moral Levels

FROM very early times, the belief that Confucius wrote the *Ch'un-ch'iu* in order to expound the kingly way *(wang-tao)* to future generations was commonly accepted. Since according to Confucius good government could be realized only when the ruler conformed to a prescribed set of moral principles, the *Ch'un-ch'iu* was understood to serve the dual purpose of defining those principles and demonstrating how they should be implemented in particular circumstances. In the Northern Sung, China had just passed through a period of disunion reminiscent of the period in which Confucius himself had lived, and Northern Sung scholars were not unaware of the parallel. But the parallel was not always applicable. The position of the ruler in imperial Confucian ideology had already been raised in Han times to a higher level of importance than had originally been envisioned by Confucius. By the time of the Sung it had also become apparent to many scholars that even rulers of dubious moral character, who were nevertheless still able to unify China, performed a valuable service to the common good and deserved credit for it, quite apart from the question of their own personal moral conduct.[1] The problem in the Northern Sung, as suggested earlier, had become one of incorporating the obvious need to obey the ruler into a system of moral values that would transcend the personal interests of the ruler and thus curb the impulse to abuse power that was inherent in a highly centralized form of government. This chapter and the

next are intended to show how the *Ch'un-ch'iu* was used to
arrive at a new and deeper understanding, and a partial resolu-
tion, of this problem.

The historical circumstances that led to the policy of centralization implemented by the emperors T'ai-tsu and T'ai-tsung,
and that attracted the support of even the most idealistic
scholar-officials, have been sketched already in chapter 2. The
emperor was concerned with consolidating his own power and
the scholar-officials with preventing a recurrence of the anarchy that had prevailed in the late T'ang and the Five Dynasties
period. T'ai-tsu's policy was pursued on two fronts, by transferring power from military officers to civilian officials *(chung-wen
ch'ing-wu)* and by gathering decision-making power into his
own hands ("strengthening the trunk and weakening the
branches," *ch'iang-kan jo-chih,* which phrase is found, incidentally, in Tung Chung-shu's *Ch'un-ch'iu fan-lu,*[2] exemplifying the
way in which practical policies were often expressed in terms
deriving from studies of the *Ch'un-ch'iu*). The first was of course
universally welcomed by the scholar-elite since it brought
with it an increase in their own influence in politics. The
second was generally welcomed by *Ch'un-ch'iu* commentators,
but there were many other neo-Confucians who voiced reservations. Such people, for example, Li Kou (1009–1059) and
Chang Tsai (1020–1078), accused the government of sacrific-
ing efficiency for control.[3] Although their opponents might
in turn acknowledge the truth of the charge, they felt that such
a policy was ultimately necessary in order to achieve a stable
government.

Sun Fu (992–1057)[4] failed to pass the *chin-shih* examination
as a young man and retired to T'ai-shan in Shantung province
(whence his sobriquet T'ai-shan), devoting himself to the study
of the *Ch'un-ch'iu* for ten years. After being recommended
by Fan Chung-yen and Fu Pi (1004–1083), he was appointed
collator of the Imperial Library *(mi-shu sheng chiao-shu lang)*
and auxiliary lecturer of the Directorate of Education *(kuo-tzu-
chien chih-chiang).* Later he served as executive assistant of the
Department of Palace Services *(tien-chung ch'eng).* Along with
Hu Yüan (with whom he did not get along, incidentally) he
also taught at the National University (T'ai-hsüeh). Sun's
extant writings include the *Ch'un-ch'iu tsun-wang fa-wei* (which

was written at least before the summer of 1040) and a collection of essays on various subjects entitled *Sun Ming-fu hsiao-chi.*[5]

Sun's influence and importance rest on his interpretation of the *Ch'un-ch'iu,* which was recognized even by those, such as Chu Hsi, who often differed with him.[6] Ou-yang Hsiu said in Sun Fu's epitaph that Sun did not pay attention to the commentaries on the *Ch'un-ch'iu* but used the form of a commentary to examine contemporary events (through the medium of the accomplishments and shortcomings of the feudal lords and officials) and that by emphasizing the importance of *wang-tao* in governing he did the most to extract the basic meaning of the classic. The modern scholar Mou Jun-sun argues in fact that the motives of Sun Fu and Ou-yang Hsiu, as expressed in Ou-yang's *Hsin wu-tai shih,* are closely related through their interest in history as a practical moral guide to public affairs.[7]

Sun's purpose was to search in classical studies for insight into the practical problems of his own time. Following Sun's lead, the *Ch'un-ch'iu* commentaries in the Northern Sung focused on two important issues in contemporary affairs. On the one hand, there was the internal threat of disunity and civil war posed by potentially autonomous military commanders, the *fan-chen* or *chieh-tu-shih* (who had destroyed the T'ang). On the other hand, there was the external threat represented by the growing military power of the Khitan in the northeast and the Hsi-hsia in the northwest. In order to confront these problems, the first Sung emperors undertook a policy of centralization that took two forms, a deliberate reduction in the power of the military by replacing military commanders with civilian officials and institutional consolidation of decision-making power in the hands of the emperor or a staff under his direct supervision. The standard interpretation of *Ch'un-ch'iu* scholarship in the Northern Sung is that its primary purpose was to justify those policies by ignoring interpretations in later exegetical literature that did not support *tsun-wang* (thus the so-called rejection of the three commentaries [*i san-chuan*]) and by forming a new interpretation *(hsin-yi)* claiming to have penetrated to Confucius' real intentions. Their new interpretations can be grouped into two categories, in conformity with the centralizing preoccupations of the commentators. The first category attacked (by attributing to Confucius the intention of blame) the accumulation of power in the hands of the feudal lords (read local military commanders) at the expense of the Chou king. The second category attacked the usurpation of power by the class of officials (here read Sung factionalism) who by the end of the Ch'un-ch'iu period had wrested the power of the states out of the hands of the feudal lords.

In the Northern Sung, the question of how to deal with the barbarians *(jang-i)* was regarded by most of the *Ch'un-ch'iu* commentators as subordinate to that of obeying the ruler *(tsun-wang)*. Their preoccupation with moral issues led them to the conclusion that, if the goal of a moral and centralized government were realized in China proper, the barbarians would not have the military strength to threaten China and in any case would most likely become sinified as they came to recognize the superior qualities (as they must) of Chinese civilization through a long period of peaceful contact. In the long run, barbarians were more likely to be pacified by the benevolence and majesty *(en-wei)* of Chinese culture than by military conquest. The practical consequences of such a view are to be found in the policy of assigning a lower priority to strictly military solutions to the barbarian problems. The extent to which these policies were related to the views of the *Ch'un-ch'iu* commentators would be a fruitful subject for future study, but not one that is directly related to the subject of this work. Exactly how the commentators themselves were preoccupied with these issues will form the substance of the following chapter. It will be considered within the context of *tsun-wang*, which, although it is not synonymous with centralization, was advocated by the *Ch'un-ch'iu* scholars in large part because it would strengthen the centripetal forces within the state.

However, there is more than one level, as mentioned above, on which the *Ch'un-ch'iu* can be interpreted. Echoing the views of the early Han, the Northern Sung impulse to unify heaven and earth, to identify the moral principles governing human action with those governing the universal order, is manifestly apparent in Sun Fu's thought. His selection of individuals who were responsible for the orthodox transmission of Confucianism gives evidence of his interest in synthesizing cosmology and politics: Yao, Shun, Yu, T'ang, Wen, Wu, Chou Kung, Confucius, Mencius, Hsün Tzu, Yang Hsiung, Wang T'ung, and Han

Yü.[8] The metaphysical aspects of Mencius' thought have already been well treated and have prompted Vincent Y. C. Shih to describe Mencius as a bridge between Confucianism and Taoism, claiming that Mencius possessed "a rare insight which discloses the close connection between the metaphysical reality of human nature and its expression in the concrete affairs of the human world."[9] The metaphysical and cosmological implications of Hsün Tzu's concept of *li* (ritual) have not been widely commented on and will be discussed in a following chapter.

Sun's views on Yang Hsiung are outlined in an essay entitled "In Defense of Yang Tzu" *(Pien Yang Tzu)* in which he argues that Yang Hsiung wrote the metaphysical treatise *T'ai-hsüan ching* not in order to correct the *I-ching* but in order to criticize the usurpation of Wang Mang.[10] Apart from the question of whether this argument is valid (it seems that it is not), it does serve to demonstrate Sun's own attitudes toward using classical interpretation of metaphysical principles as a forum for expressing personal political ideas. Sun says that in this essay Yang "greatly clarifies the principle of the beginning and end, the obeying and resisting, of heaven and man, and the distinction between the superior and the inferior, the serving and retiring of rulers and subjects. Those who follow these principles and distinctions will be blessed with good fortune, and those who resist them will be cursed with bad fortune. The basic idea of Yang Hsiung was to warn those who defy heaven, oppose man, slay the ruler, and rob the state."[11] Such a characterization might just as well apply to Sun's own attitudes toward the relation between heaven and man. In another essay entitled "A Discussion of the Institutes of Shun" *(Shun-chih i),* Sun explicitly uses the cosmology of the *I-ching* to describe the relation between politics and the universe: "The utmost principle was [to take] the hexagram for heaven, *ch'ien,* as the *tao* of the ruler, and [the hexagram for] earth, *k'un,* as the *tao* of the subject. They fit together like the upper and lower parts of a garment."[12]

Sun Fu was not the only admirer of Yang Hsiung (although in a diluted manner) in the Northern Sung. Apparently, Yang's writings underwent something of a revival among many neo-Confucians. Shao Yung was an enthusiastic student of Yang's numerology, and, interestingly enough, so was Ssu-ma Kuang (1019–1086), who even composed a numerological work of his own modeled after Yang's *T'ai-hsüan,* entitled *Ch'ien-hsü* (and also edited an edition of the *T'ai-hsüan ching*).[13] Ssu-ma's explanatory passages in the *Ch'ien-hsü* make an explicit identity between the moral values immanent in the conduct of human affairs and the transcendental principles of the cosmological order.[14]

Sun's ideas on metaphysical questions are further developed in two essays on nonaction, "Wu-wei chih shang" and "Wu-wei chih hsia."[15] Sun was greatly attracted to the cosmology developed by the Huang-Lao branch of politically oriented Han Taoists. A very important part of that tradition was the concept of nonaction, to the Taoists an ideal mode of behavior through which the spontaneous (and therefore pure) forces of nature could assert themselves. To Mencius, as to most later Confucianists attracted to Taoism, spontaneity that was not accompanied by strenuous efforts to cultivate the moral faculties of the personality was something to be distrusted. Because of this, *wu-wei* came to mean specifically to the Han Taoists, not nonaction, but rather no action that would run counter to the will of heaven.[16] But just to understand that will of heaven required a vigorous effort of cultivation, and, even after one could claim understanding, in order to obey one's true nature one was further obliged to bring society into conformity with the will of heaven as well, or at least to work toward that goal. Sun follows this line of argument and adduces several examples to show that the sages did in fact take an active part in government. His purpose is to demonstrate the futility of imposing on past events simplistic formulas that fail to take into account the complexities of moral principles when they are applied to particular circumstances. He falls short of advocating that the ruler leave everything up to his officials because he knows that, among other things, the likely outcome would be civil disorder.[17] In this regard, his views contrast with those of Tung Chung-shu quoted earlier and reflect Tung's greater concern with limiting the power of the ruler and Sun's with reducing the likelihood of disunion. Both agree, however, that the ruler is himself subject to a higher law.

Sun Fu, whose commentary is the focus of this chapter, saw the threat of anarchy coming from three sources. The first was from usurping lords, the second from usurping officials, and the third from the barbarians. As a result, he interpreted the history of the Ch'un-ch'iu period as passing through three stages of decline:

> The Son of Heaven began to lose control of the government from the time when he moved the capital east [771 B.C.]. The feudal lords had begun to lose control of the government by the time of the meeting at Chü-liang [556 B.C.]. Therefore from the ascension of Duke Yin [721 B.C.] all the way to the meeting at Chü-liang, the governance of the world and the affairs of the central states were all divided up by the feudal lords. From the meeting at Chü-liang to the meeting at Shen [537 B.C.] the governance of the world and the affairs of the central states were all usurped by the officials. From the meeting at Shen until the appearance of the unicorn [480 B.C.] the control of the governance of the world and the affairs of the central states passed into the hands of the barbarians. Because of this, the regulations, the institutions, the manner of dress, the inherited customs, and the old forms of governance were swept aside. That the central states had all sunk into such a state by this time brought to fruition all that had been said before. Both Chin and Lu were present at the meeting of Huang-ch'ih [481 B.C.]. After that there is nothing more to say on the subject—the feudal lords were in a state of confusion, and the power to give orders was exercised by Wu and was never again restored. This is because the central states and the world were controlled by the barbarians. For this reason the *Ch'un-ch'iu* exalted the Son of Heaven and honored the central states. Because it honored the central states it deprecated the barbarians; because it exalted the Son of Heaven it downgraded the feudal lords. Exalting the Son of Heaven and downgrading the feudal lords [in the *Ch'un-ch'iu*] began with the duke of Yin [721 B.C.], and honoring the central states and deprecating the barbarians ended with the capture of the unicorn. Alas! The essential message of the text is subtle indeed, subtle indeed![18]

This chapter will consider these three stages separately, in order to show precisely how Sun Fu used the past to understand and comment on the present. Examples from the commentary are included as they relate to each of the three stages, so that the richness and variety of human experience covered by the *Ch'un-ch'iu* exegetical tradition can be fully understood and appreciated.

The discussion of Sun's ideas on practical threats to orderly government resulting from a failure to obey the authority of the ruler is followed by a discussion of the moral implications of his views on authority. These are placed in the context of the absolute moral values expressed by the term *li* (ritual) because it is in that context only that Sun's ideas on authority can be adequately understood. So long as authority is defined in terms of its function as guiding action toward greater realization of moral values commonly held to be absolute as well as avoiding certain practical consequences of anarchy, then to advocate authority is not merely to advocate greater personal power in the hands of the ruler and certainly not to make rulers more arbitrary but to serve a moral end. Sun did criticize the actions of rulers, but he did not form his judgments about their behavior on the basis of whether they were unwise, or stupid, or insincere, or unrighteous, or lacking in benevolence or virtue. Rulers were not criticized for being impractical, shortsighted, or narrow-minded. They were criticized for acting in a manner "contrary to *li* (ritual)," *fei-li*. At the same time, obedience to the ruler was enjoined not just because of some compact, or out of fear of the ruler's power, or because of historical tradition, or merely because of the utility of such obedience to the order and stability of the state (although this last factor was hardly absent from the minds of the commentators), but rather because of the imperative of *li*. The obligation of rulers to abide by those standards of *li* was just as forcefully asserted as the obligation of subjects to obey the ruler. Taken together with the interpretation of the main thrust of the *Ch'un-ch'iu* as a decline into anarchy resulting from the failure of all parties to obey *li*, it is abundantly clear that Sun was not in favor of an absolutist ruler subject to no higher authority above himself. In fact, he was as interested in restraining the ruler through *li* as he was in revering the ruler.

Usurpation by Feudal Lords and Obligations of the Ruler

Sun Fu's ideas on this subject reveal themselves in the form of judgments on certain categories of events recorded in the

Ch'un-ch'iu. According to Sun, everything mentioned by Confucius in the *Ch'un-ch'iu* was recorded in order to condemn it.[19] For this he was often criticized by his contemporaries and by later scholars, who claimed that he took unwarranted liberties with the text.[20] For the most part, however, those critics were not objecting to the main thrust of Sun's argument; they merely felt that it was unnecessary to go to such an extreme in order to make his point and feared that he might even alienate some who would otherwise be sympathetic to his position.

Among the many actions criticized by Sun was the usurpation by the feudal lords of the military authority of the Chou king. This usurpation manifested itself in a variety of ways, the most important of which was the attack by one state on another without first having appealed to the king for permission or support. For example, in a passage from the year 720 B.C., in which the ruler of the state of Cheng had attacked the state of Wei without first consulting the Chou king, Sun quoted Confucius' famous dictum:

> When good government prevails in the empire, ceremonies, music, and punitive military expeditions proceed from the Son of Heaven. When bad government prevails in the empire, ceremonies, music, and punitive military expeditions proceed from the princes. When these things proceed from the princes, as a rule, the cases will be few in which they do not lose their power in ten generations. When they proceed from the Great officers of the princes, as a rule, the cases will be few in which they do not lose their power in five generations. When the subsidiary ministers of the Great officers hold in their grasp the orders of the State, as a rule, the cases will be few in which they do not lose their power in three generations.[21]

Sun then noted that the process of devolution of power from the feudal lords to the officials began after the reign of Duke Hsüan (607–590) and Duke Ch'eng (589–572), presumably to illustrate that Confucius' historical generalization was correct —the power of the princes did not last even ten generations. He went on to claim that all further mention by Confucius of one state attacking another was done in order to condemn the parties involved.

Sun's later entries continue to emphasize this interpretation

of Confucius' intentions. He criticized the feudal lords relent-
lessly. For example, in 631 B.C. the state of Chin attacked the
state of Ts'ao and gave over its earl and perhaps some of its territory to the neighboring state of Sung. The hope was that
Sung's acceptance would in turn stimulate an attack by Ch'u,
which would then cause the states of Ch'in and Ch'i to ally with
Chin in an attack on Ch'u, which is what Chin wanted in the
first place.[22] Sun objected to the fact that such wars were pursued by the states entirely for their own temporary advantage in
a bitter struggle for survival, without reference to the Chou
ruler. As it happened, it was in this same year that the ruler of
Chin was granted the title *hegemon* by the Chou king, to whom,
paradoxically, the Chin ruler paid only nominal allegiance. Sun
was very critical of Chin for its cynical maneuvering, and said
so, lamenting the decadence of the times and the lack of a unifying central authority.[23] Again, none of the three commentaries were followed by Sun because none of them focused on the
irrelevance of the Chou king to the unfolding of events, which
to Sun was the central meaning of this and all similar passages.
Force was used to decide all questions, a situation in which the
big states held all the cards and the small states were helpless.

This theme of Sun's work, that the moral foundations of
the political community are undermined by struggles for
power, struggles that might be avoided were there a strong and
able ruler at the center, is not unknown in the West. Writing
just a few decades after the death of Confucius, and having
spent, like Confucius, a lifetime watching his civilization turned
to rubble by war, Thucydides put into the funeral oration of
Pericles a timeless expression of the moral obligation of members of a political community to submerge their own interests
in the larger common good: "Here each individual is interested
not only in his own affairs but in the affairs of state as well: even
those who are mostly occupied with their own business are
extremely well-informed on general politics—this is a peculiar-
ity of ours: we do not say that a man who takes no interest in
politics is a man who minds his own business; we say that he has
no business here at all. . . . When we do kindnesses to others,
we do not do them out of any calculation of profit or loss: we
do them without afterthought, relying on our free liberality."[24]

Another illustration of Sun's condemnation of illegitimate

force concerned the usurpation of the military authority of the Chou king, personified by the formation in 561 B.C. of a third army in the state of Lu. Sun draws on the *Chou-li* to show that Lu was qualified not for three but only for two armies.[25] In 536 B.C., when they disbanded the army, they were again blamed by Sun, this time for not first bringing the matter up with the king and abiding by his decision.[26] Here Sun is not concerned with whether they needed the army in order to survive, simply because that is not germane to his main thesis, which was the need to obey the ruler.

In like manner, Sun also condemned covenants between parties as symptomatic of the loss of the *tao* since they implied the existence of sovereign states, which was not possible if all authority came from the central government. Sun took advantage of the recording of a covenant between the ruler of Lu and the ruler of Ch'u in 721 B.C. to argue that all covenants mentioned in the *Ch'un-ch'iu* were included for the purpose of blaming the participants, as has been noted above.[27] This particular event, however, is praised in the *Kung-yang*.[28] Here again Sun is clearly departing from the traditional interpretation in order to hammer away at his principal theme of obedience to the ruler.

Covenants arrived at between states of China proper were already bad enough, but when they were undertaken between one of the Chinese states and a barbarian state, they were to Sun the ultimate manifestation of degeneracy. In 720, the state of Lu did conclude just such a covenant with the Jung barbarians, and Sun scornfully noted that they had to rely on such uncivilized practices as smearing their mouths with the blood of sacrificial animals in order to compensate for the lack of mutual trust that would have prevailed had they acted in accordance with *li* (ritual) from the very beginning.[29]

Rulers of the state were criticized for usurping the appointive prerogative of the Chou king. This question is especially important because it bore directly on the issue of the appointment of local officials in the Northern Sung. One of the bases of the autonomous military governors' *(chieh tu-shih)* power in the late T'ang had been their control of the appointment of local officials, and Sung political thinkers anxious to prevent the recurrence of these governors were wary of any challenge

to central appointment. Those who argued for greater autonomy on the local level in the name of efficiency were opposed
by others, such as Sun Fu and later Ch'eng I, who argued that
all officials ought to be appointed by the emperor, and numerous examples from the *Ch'un-ch'iu* were cited in defense of
their opinion.[30] In one case, Sun even ignored the *Li-chi* when
he claimed that all officials in ancient times had been
appointed by the Son of Heaven.[31] The *Li-chi* states quite clearly
that the rulers of smaller states were allowed to appoint a certain number of their ministers themselves.[32] But in all cases
where feudal lords attempted to alter the prescribed pattern of
succession within a state, or where officials were not appointed
by the king, or where office was obtained by hereditary right
without petitioning for the king's approval, Sun condemned
the persons responsible for failing to adhere to the proper
ethical standards of *li*. He offered these examples as further evidence of the loss of the *wang-tao*.[33]

Rulers of the states were condemned for exchanging lands,
either as a reward for the spoils of war or as a reward for help in
setting up a ruler in another state.[34] Over and over, whenever
appropriate, Sun repeated the statement that land that was
originally bestowed by the Son of Heaven should not have been
exchanged without his permission.[35] It was his, and his alone, to
dispose of. The parallels between this form of usurpation and
the power of the military governors in the late T'ang and Five
Dynasties period are too obvious to require an explanation.
Sun Fu saw his mission, however, not only as pointing out these
parallels but also as tying them into the general condition of
moral decay that prevailed in the Ch'un-ch'iu period and that
he was trying to warn against in the Sung. Sun was trying to
show how these phenomena were the consequences of a failure
to follow the absolute standards of *li*.

Sun regarded occurrences of natural phenomena as tangible
evidence of heaven's dissatisfaction with the loss of moral harmony in the world. All instances of eclipses are listed by Sun
and interpreted as the consequence of the failure of the Chou
house to rule properly.[36] Floods were visited on the land
because "the rule of the Sage Kings was not followed."[37] Light-
ning striking temples,[38] meteors falling, and fish hawks flying
backward—all were attributed to man's failure to adhere to *li*.[39]

Earthquakes happened because the "earthly *tao* had been lost," and fires were caused because there was "nobody to restore kingly rule."[40]

The murder of ruling feudal lords, or of any heirs to the position of ruler, was condemned, regardless of whether the perpetrators were of the Chou house or were themselves feudal lords. Even though the feudal lords were in many ways usurping epicenters of power, they were still in charge of their state's affairs (having been appointed, after all, by the Chou king) and deserved the respect that should accompany that position. The *Ch'un-ch'iu* is replete with examples of regicide, and in every case they were assumed by Sun to be manifestations of the decline of respect for *li*. In an early example, Sun points out that the decline took place incrementally and led to a gradual escalation in violence until finally even the most basic relationships governed by *li* were infected:

> The phenomenon of officials murdering their rulers, and sons murdering their fathers, does not happen overnight. The underlying factors develop gradually. Because it is difficult to distinguish these factors in their early stages, the sages warned the rulers, and officials, and sons, through their teaching, to take every precaution possible from the very beginning. This is because the evil intentions of officials and sons begin imperceptibly and accumulate only gradually; if they are not stopped over a long period of time, then they will result in the misfortunes of murder and rebellion. . . . Because of this, in the *Ch'un-ch'iu* there were cases of hereditary officials murdering their rulers, of sons murdering their fathers, of younger brothers murdering their older brothers, and of wives murdering their husbands.[41]

In another case, Sun claims that according to the principles of *li* only the Chou king had the authority to put a ruler of one of the feudal states to death. This goes for officials as well since they were also appointed by the king. Sun counted forty-seven cases in the *Ch'un-ch'iu* of officials being executed by their feudal lords, all of whom were thereby considered to be usurping the authority of the Chou king.[42] In some cases, dukes even killed their own sons and heirs. In other cases, patricide was also regicide, doubling the enormity of the offense. How much worse, then, when a ruler was not only killed but used as a substitute for an animal in a sacrifice.[43] In addition, Sun blamed the feudal lords for siphoning off tax revenue from the Chou king and keeping it for their own use.[44] Here again the parallels between the Ch'un-ch'iu period and the unstable and decentralized experience of the late T'ang and Five Dynasties period are clear.

Does the obligation to exalt the ruler imply that rulers do not make mistakes or should not be criticized if they do? Sun's answer is negative. Kings are at fault when they depart from the standards imposed by *li* and deserve to be criticized. In the very first paragraph of the commentary, when Sun explained why Confucius set out to write the *Ch'un-ch'iu,* he said,

> Confucius wrote the *Ch'un-ch'iu* because the world was without a proper ruler. . . . In ancient times the evil kings met with misfortune; King P'ing moved the capital to the east. Since [by so doing] P'ing did not act like a proper king, the *tao* of the Chou house was broken, and its power became weak in proportion as that of the feudal lords increased. The proper *li* of imperial audiences was not cultivated; the responsibilities of sending tribute to the king were not maintained; orders were not attended to; and proper rewards and punishments were not administered. . . . From the time of the accession of Duke Yin on, there was never again a proper king in the Ch'un-ch'iu period.[45]

The obligation of the ruler to walk the straight and narrow "kingly way" was clear and unmistakable, and when he diverged, it was incumbent on his ministers to set him straight. Sun blamed the king for sending an envoy to Lu under circumstances that did not conform to the proper standards of *li.*[46] The king was also blamed in strong terms for personally placing himself at the head of an army sent to suppress a rebellion in the state of Cheng.[47] Sun's argument was that, since in theory the king could have no enemies (he ruled over the whole world), he should not commit his office personally to any particular military campaign. By involving himself in the sordid details of fighting, he was acknowledging his weakness for all to see and further undermining respect for his position. None of the three commentaries have this interpretation of the passage. But most of Sun's readers would have realized that the passage also referred to the mistakes of the second emperor of the Sung, T'ai-tsung, who personally led what turned out to be a disastrous campaign against the Khitan in 979, at the end of which the emperor humiliated himself and his office by abandoning his troops and fleeing for his life. In similar fashion, the king was blamed for leaving the capital in order to escape the consequences of some particular political squabble or another.[48]

The king was also blamed for not coming to the rescue of states that were unjustly set on by other states or by barbarian armies.[49] Presumably, Sun intended the king, not to take command of the situation personally, but to undertake to organize a punitive expedition under the leadership of his ministers still subject to his authority.

Kings were blamed for other infractions of *li*, such as when the Chou king Chuang summoned Duke Chuang of Lu to act as intermediary for him in arranging his marriage to a daughter of the duke of Ch'i while Duke Chuang was still in mourning for the death of his mother. Kings were blamed for trying to do away with heirs to the throne in favor of other sons (usually at the instigation of a favored concubine). Not only did some kings try to get rid of their sons, but they also murdered their younger brothers, and Sun blames them for not acting as proper brothers.[50] Thus does Sun deal with the usurpation of power by the feudal lords, endeavoring to show, by showering the reader with examples from the *Ch'un-ch'iu*, the many ways in which central authority could be eroded gradually over a long period of time and the disastrous consequences to the governing of the state and the preservation of Chinese cultural values (embodied in *li*) that such a process could inflict. In this process, both the feudal lords and the king are held responsible for failing to submit to the absolute moral standards of *li*.

Later commentators continued and further amplified the concept of *tsun-wang* (elaborated by Sun Fu) at some length. Sun Chüeh, for example, went so far as to claim that the heavenly king *(t'ien-wang)* presided over the welfare of all living things, down to the lowliest insect and fish, whose very life flowed from his beneficent influence.[51] He further maintained that the ruler was the basis of the world, the font of all instruction and political order, and that his authority came by natural right, granted from heaven. In fact, his position as a kind of intermediary between heaven and earth endowed him with a very special and crucial role. He embodied the creative power of heaven and earth, which he then used to bestow prosperity on his kingdom.[52] Sun Chüeh even went so far as to say that there was no praise or blame for the king because he rose above it (on the principle that whatever could be praised could by implication also be criticized). He claimed that this meant, not that individual rulers could not make mistakes, but that Confucius did not intend to criticize them as rulers (presumably they could be criticized as individuals, not as institutions). Ch'en Ch'ing-hsin says that this point of view started with Sun Chüeh.[53]

Later, the philosopher Ch'eng I referred to *tsun-wang* as the great principle of heaven and earth, thus raising it to the level of universal principle, about which more will be said in the next chapter.[54] His student Hsieh Shih put it this way: "The ruler and heaven have the same virtue; in their actions they share the same *tao*. . . . If you wish to protect the state, you have to respect heaven; if you wish to respect heaven, you have to exalt the ruler. If the feudal lords had served the ruler as if he were in heaven, then the protection of the state and the prosperity of the people would have been secured." In another passage, Hsieh said, "The mandate of the king is the basis of all under heaven. The people in a state have no right to set up a ruler, and the son of a ruler has no right to be set up by private interests. When the mandate of the king is not practiced, the state will fall into confusion."[55] Thus was Sun Fu's interpretation elaborated by later *Ch'un-ch'iu* scholars in the Northern Sung who placed it in a more metaphysical context. But Sun's message did not stop there. He was also concerned about the potential for usurpation by officials, and he may well have had in mind the danger of imperial sycophants and eunuchs as well as officials appropriating to themselves excessive power over both the bureaucracy and their sovereign.

Usurpation by Officials

Sun believed that the first explicit mention of the rising power of the officials occurred in a passage in 569 B.C., in which it was recorded that a group of officials of the various feudal lords held a meeting of their own soon after one had just been held by the lords themselves.[56] According to the historian Hsü Cho-yün, this process had already started much earlier, at least in the state of Lu.[57] For example, during the reign of Duke Hsi (658–626 B.C.), much of the duke's power was shared with his minister (and brother) Sui, who dominated the next duke, Wen, after whose death Sui engineered the succession of Duke Hsüan by first murdering the two legitimate successors. After that, no duke in the state of Lu ruled except by authorization of the major families, whose members were nominally the ministers of the duke. Fixing the beginning of the trend at any particular time is not as important, however, as identifying Sun's interpretation of the process.

Many of Sun Fu's comments about the usurpation of power by officials are similar to those describing the erosion of the king's power and its passing into the hands of the officials' real rulers, the feudal lords. Officials are criticized, for example, for leaving the state without the permission of the ruler. They are criticized for killing the son of a ruler in order to set up someone else more malleable to their sinister purposes.[58] When officials begin to hold meetings with each other independently of their feudal lords, they are blamed in much the same terms as were the feudal lords when they first began to covenant with each other without regard for the wishes or instructions of the Chou king.[59] The process of usurpation is regarded by Sun as being complete at about the time that the *Ch'un-ch'iu* recorded a meeting of ministers in Sung in 545 B.C.[60] Later on, in 528 B.C., the text of the *Ch'un-ch'iu* itself makes a special point of mentioning that the feudal lords did not attend a meeting of the ministers.[61]

Officials were blamed for not carrying to completion, or for not obeying, the orders of their rulers. They were blamed for offering refuge to officials of other states who were forced to flee because they had become involved in improper activities of one sort or another.[62] Subversive elements were not to be encouraged by the hope of finding safety in nearby states. Nevertheless, no matter how unworthy an official might be, it was not proper for him to be put to death by a feudal lord—

that authority rested only with the Chou king himself. When three officials were executed at the same time in 573 B.C., for example, Sun maintained that this was contrary to the *tao*.[63] In this case, he followed the *Tso-chuan,* a small passage of which is worth quoting because it illustrates how Sun drew from many commentaries to find support for his own interpretations. One of the ministers who was killed, Hsi Chih, had been advised of the ruler's intentions, and when his family urged him to oppose the will of the ruler in order to save his own life, he made the following remarks:

> The things which set a man up are fidelity, wisdom, and valour. A faithful man will not revolt against his ruler; a wise man will not injure the people; a valiant man will not raise disorder. If we lose those three qualities, who will be with us? If by our death we increase the number of our enemies, of what use will it be? When a ruler puts a minister to death, what can the latter say to him? If we are really guilty, our death comes late; if he puts us to death, being innocent, he will lose the people, and have no repose afterwards, however much he may wish it. Let us simply wait our fate. We have received emoluments from our ruler, and by means of them have collected a party; but what offense could be greater than if with that party we should strive against his order [for our death]?[64]

What were the consequences of this devolution of power into the hands of the ministers, according to Sun Fu? Diffusion of power produced anarchy, and anarchy produced lawlessness and needless suffering among the common people. The first appearance in the *Ch'un-ch'iu* of robbers committing murder was attributed to the fact that punishment and governance had been lost. A similar conclusion was reached by Sun when the *Ch'un-ch'iu* recorded in 521 B.C. the murder by thieves of the elder brother of the marquis of Wei.[65] In case after case, Sun sought to drive home the necessity to distinguish between short-term and long-term advantage. He argued that, however compelling the practical reasons might have been to pursue a particular course of action that might result in a diminution of central authority, the long-term consequences were so destructive as to wipe out utterly whatever immediate gain might have been sought or even achieved.

Expulsion of the Barbarians

The threat of invasion from northern barbarian tribes, the Tangut Hsi-hsia in the northwest and the Khitan Liao in the northeast, and in fact the final defeat in 1127 of the Northern Sung by a third tribe, the Jürchen, has already been mentioned in chapter 2. This threat plagued emperors and officials throughout the 150-year period of the Northern Sung. Nevertheless, the problem of the barbarians was subordinated to the issue of centralization in the *Ch'un-ch'iu* commentaries of the Northern Sung. That it never reached the proportions of a fixation until the Southern Sung, when something had obviously gone wrong, is understandable. Officials in the Northern Sung could argue that the barbarians could be bought off or even in the long run gradually assimilated into the Chinese cultural orbit, both of which would tend to reduce the threat of barbarian invasion. Those in the Southern Sung knew better.

One of the first instances of Sun Fu's interpretation of this question in his commentary came as early as 683 B.C., in response to a passage recording an attack on one of the central states by the barbarian state of Ch'u (referred to in its early history as Ching).[66] Sun claimed that the barbarians were able to make inroads into the Chinese states because there were no sagely kings to act. The next treatment came in 655 B.C., on the occasion of the famous covenant of Shao-ling, which was convened after an expedition of the Chinese states led by Ch'i against the state of Ch'u. Both the *Kung-yang* and the *Ku-liang* praised Duke Huan of Ch'i for keeping the barbarians from invading the Chinese states. But although Sun Fu acknowledged that this was indeed a service, he reiterated that this task should have been done by the Son of Heaven and lamented the necessity of having to rely on a feudal lord to do the job of the Chou king.[67] Just five years later, in 650 B.C., commenting on the covenant of K'uei-ch'iu, Sun again praised Duke Huan for his role in expelling the barbarians but at the same time condemned him for not acting properly in relation to the Chou king, for which transgression he was not to be forgiven.[68] Clearly, this offense against the authority of the Chou king was so serious that it could not be justified by whatever temporary benefit the Chinese states might have gained as a result of military campaigns against the barbarians. In this case again, as was often true before, the other commentaries differed from Sun's, the *Kung-yang* praising Duke Huan and the *Ku-liang* praising the covenant.

The primacy of moral considerations is even more forcefully put in response to the battle of Ch'eng-p'u in 631 B.C., in which an army belonging to the state of Ch'u was defeated by armies under the leadership of the state of Chin. Sun again underscored his main point, that this should have been done by the Son of Heaven, not by Duke Wen of Chin, however beneficial the outcome of the military campaign might have been.[69] Sun argued that the fault lay ultimately, not with the barbarians, but with the moral deterioration within the Chinese states themselves.[70] No matter how many times the barbarians are defeated militarily, nothing but a moral rejuvenation of the Chinese states themselves would ever cause the barbarians to exalt the Son of Heaven and adopt the kingly way. In 589 B.C., the first year of the reign of Duke Ch'eng of Lu, when the *Ch'un-ch'iu* recorded that the common people were assigned the task (over and above their normal taxes) of producing military equipment, Sun argued that Confucius intended to blame Ch'eng for not being able to defend the state and ascribed his weakness, not to military circumstances, but to the fact that he was "unable to cultivate virtue."[71]

Even the very definition of a barbarian was based on moral considerations. A barbarian was someone who did not accept the moral standards of the Chinese. In 505 B.C., for example, the ruler of the state of Wu was identified in the *Ch'un-ch'iu* passage by the title *viscount,* normally reserved only for rulers of the central states. According to Sun, this was done in order to praise him for coming to the aid of the central states in their struggle against the barbarian state of Ch'u. Later on in the same year, however, when the same ruler took the mother of the defeated ruler of Ch'u as his wife, both the *Kung-yang* and the *Ku-liang,* and Sun Fu, refer to him as reverting to the status of a barbarian.[72]

The difficulties of this type of interpretation become apparent when one compares this passage with another in 530 B.C., in which the ruler of Ch'u was castigated for his lack of the *tao* in killing the ruler of the state of Ts'ai. Already permanently and irrevocably categorized as being from a barbarian state and here caught in an action manifestly barbarian, the ruler of the state of Ch'u was referred to in the text of the classic by the title *viscount,* and no particular importance was attached to the title in this case.[73] Logical consistency, it seems, was not regarded very highly in this particular genre of criticism. All this does not alter, however, the persistent tendency to interpret barbarian behavior in terms of Confucian morality. In the Southern Sung, for example, even someone as opposed to Sun Fu's method of exegesis as Lü Tzu-ch'ien, who regarded the *Ch'un-ch'iu* purely as factual history, defined the barbarians in terms of their adherence to *li.*[74] This tolerance was not new in the Chinese tradition—it was Confucius who said, "The barbarians of the East and the North have retained their princes. They are not in such a state of decay as we are in China."[75]

Criticism was expressed in other ways as well. When the army of Ch'u occupied P'eng-ch'eng, a city in Sung, and placed a puppet in charge, the *Ch'un-ch'iu* text still referred to it as belonging to Sung. This was taken to instance (in Sun's view) Confucius' unwillingness to countenance the power of a barbarian state to occupy Chinese territory. In like fashion, by subtle choice of words Confucius was said to have made it appear that the states Ch'en and Ts'ai had not been destroyed at all by the barbarian Ch'u (when in fact they had) in order to downgrade Ch'u's importance.[76] In one of the last passages in the commentary, discussing the famous meeting in 481 B.C. at Huang-ch'ih under the auspices of the viscount of Wu, Sun claimed that the state of Chin (also present at the meeting) was now too weak to assert its authority over all the states. He also noted that, ever since the battle of Pai-chü in 505 B.C., control over the central states had passed into the hands of the barbarians, as a direct consequence of the failure of the states to observe the *tao* and restore the rule of the sage-kings.[77] The placement of Wu behind Chin in the passage is supposed to mean that Wu had no right to its pretensions as the organizer of the meeting. The practical consequences of failing to adhere to *li* on the part of the Chinese states are thus regarded by Sun as graphically illustrated by the success of the barbarians and represent the final denouement of the whole process of rejecting *li* begun in the early years of the Ch'un-ch'iu period.

Universal Implications of Li *in the Early Commentaries*

The previous sections have shown how Sun and other neo-Confucians attempted to relate the particular problems encountered in the Ch'un-ch'iu period to those problems that arose during the Northern Sung period. The obvious and not entirely erroneous conclusion to draw from a review of the similarities that they claim to have found is that the commentaries of the Northern Sung were written primarily for the purpose of justifying certain political policies that had been implemented already by the early Sung emperors. A balanced perspective, however, shows that this is only partially true. The greatest significance of the commentaries does not lie solely in this realm but in the way in which they tried to demonstrate the universality of the principles manifested by the particular circumstances of the Ch'un-ch'iu period. In this context, the use of praise and blame should be seen in a slightly altered sense from that in which it is often understood. It is not always intended to be the anachronistic imposition of subjective standards of later political morality on historical events by selecting those facts that easily conveyed a didactic message and rejecting those that did not. Rather, it was the result of a new faith in certain transcendent moral principles, universal in scope but immanent and knowable in history. In fact, it was thought by some that one did not even have to exercise praise and blame explicitly because it was believed that in an honest recording the facts would speak for themselves and convey the message implicitly. Thus could Ssu-ma Kuang, regarded as one of the most conservative of the Sung scholar-officials, say in his introduction to the *Tzu-chih t'ung-chien,*

> Now your servant in his narrative has sought only to trace the rise and fall of the various states and make clear the people's times of joy and sorrow so that the reader may select for himself what is good and what is bad, what profitable and what unprofitable, for his encouragement and warning. He has no intention of setting up standards of praise and blame in the manner of the Spring and Autumn Annals which could compel a disorderly age to return to just ways.[78]

In reading this, it is important to realize that whether he did convey subjective opinions of blame or praise is a separate question from whether he thought that that was what he was doing. The point is that the Sung thinkers believed so strongly in the existence of universal moral principles, and the susceptibility of those principles to rational understanding, that it was not always deemed necessary to state them explicitly.

The term *li* is often translated as "ritual" or "norm" or "decorum." These "rituals" were thought to be the outward manifestation of certain absolute moral principles, and the term *li* was often used to refer to those universal moral principles rather than merely to their ritualistic expression. Because of the complexity of the term (dealt with below) and the inadequacy of any English equivalent, the best solution is simply to use the Chinese term.

Li can be explained as having three different levels of meaning, distinguished from each other by the object that each is designed to pursue. The first aims to cultivate the individual self through the use of ritual and ceremonies, the second to cultivate the order and stability of society through adherence to proper ritual (remembering of course that in all cases the rituals are synonymous with the moral principles that they represent), and the third to bring man into harmony with the laws of the universe. The second is emphasized by those who are most concerned with the practical affairs of government, the third by those who are most concerned with resting their political ideas on a firm foundation of absolute moral principles. Sun Fu used both the second and the third levels in his commentaries, and it is the third level that was later expanded by Ch'eng I to fit into his metaphysical system.

A few examples will suffice to illustrate these three levels of meaning. In the *Analects,* Confucius is recorded as having said, "Respectfulness, without the rules of propriety *(li),* becomes laborious bustle; carefulness, without the rules of propriety, becomes timidity; boldness, without the rules of propriety, becomes insubordination; straight-forwardness, without the rules of propriety, becomes rudeness."[79] Thus, without the judgment that comes from knowing what is proper under the circumstances, even virtuous behavior can be carried to extremes. In speaking of what he had learned from Confucius, one of Confucius' leading disciples, Yen Yüan, said that he "enlarged my mind with learning, and taught me the restraints of propriety,"[80] revealing that for him *li* meant a sense of moral discipline. In the *Tso-chuan, li* takes on a wider connotation, to include the orderly conduct of affairs of a whole community, in other words, of government: "It is propriety which governs States and clans, gives settlement to the tutelary altars, secures the order of the people, and provides for the good of one's heirs."[81] In other passages, according to Burton Watson, *li*

> is expanded in scope until it comes to designate a comprehensive moral standard that embraces all phases of human behavior and extends even to the natural and supernatural worlds. Thus under Duke Chao 25th year we read: "Ritual *(li)* is the constant principle of Heaven, that which is right for the earth, the proper course of the people. . . . Ritual determines the relations between high and low; it is the warp and woof of Heaven and earth and that by which the people are enabled to live."[82]

Hsün Tzu also anticipates the universal significance of *li* that was given to it by the Sung thinkers. According to John Knoblock, Hsün Tzu "transformed the concepts of ritual from an aristocratic code of conduct, a kind of *courtoisie* that distinguished gentlemen from ordinary men, into universal principles that underlay society and just government."[83] In Hsün Tzu's own words,

> Through rites *(li)* Heaven and earth join in harmony, the sun and moon shine, the four seasons proceed in order, the stars and constellations march, the rivers flow, and all things flourish; men's likes and dislikes are regulated and their joys and hates made appropriate. Those below are obedient, those above are enlightened; all things change but do not become disordered; only he who turns his back upon rites will be destroyed. Are they not wonderful indeed? When they are properly established and brought to the peak of perfection, no one in the world can add to or detract from them. Through them the root and the branch are put in proper order; beginning and end are justified; the most elegant forms embody all distinctions; the most penetrating insight explains all things. In the world those who obey the dictates of ritual will achieve order; those who turn against them will suffer disorder. Those who obey them will win safety; those who turn against them will court danger. Those who obey them will be preserved; those who turn against them will be lost. This is something that the petty man cannot comprehend.[84]

The *Li-chi,* now known to have been put together in the Han but once thought to have been of much earlier provenance, also contains some passages that are of particular relevance to our discussion because they extend the meaning of *li* far beyond mere rites or ceremonies. As regards the origin of *li,* it said, "Rules of ceremony must be traced to their origin in the Grand Unity. This separated and became heaven and earth. It revolved and became the dual force (in nature). It changed and became the four seasons. . . . Its lessons transmitted (to men) are called its orders; the law and authority of them is in Heaven." As to the nature of *li* and the consequences of not following its dictates,

> Thus propriety and righteousness are the great elements for man's character; it is by means of them that his speech is the expression of truth and his intercourse [with others] the pro-motion of harmony. . . . They constitute the great methods by which we nourish the living, bury the dead, and serve the spirits of the departed. They supply the channels by which we can apprehend the ways of Heaven and act as the feelings of men require. It was on this account that the sages knew that the rules of ceremony could not be dispensed with, while the ruin of states, the destruction of families, and the perishing of individuals are always preceded by their abandonment of the rules of propriety.[85]

The importance of the interrelation of these three levels of meaning of *li* becomes apparent as one turns to the commen-taries themselves. Although the infractions of *li* pointed out in Sun Fu's and Liu Ch'ang's commentaries are infractions of ritual, their full significance for Sung political thought emerges only when their absolute moral implications are brought out. Violations of ritual are violations not only of the human order but of the universal order as well. The two levels are in fact inseparable, and it was believed that failure to observe the proper *li* would result inevitably in punishment, in much the same way that the people of Judah were taken to task by the prophet Isaiah (Isa. 31:1) for relying merely on the weapons of war to protect themselves from their enemies instead of obey-ing the will of God.[86] The later attack on them by the Assyrians was thus interpreted by Isaiah as just punishment of the Jews for their loss of faith in God.

In Western literature, one of the most powerful expositions

of this theme of the interrelation of the cosmos and the world of human affairs, and the importance of ritual in bringing a tyrant to heel, was the Greek play *Antigone* by Sophocles (495–406 B.C.). In it, two brothers, both sons of Oedipus, the former king of Thebes, led opposing armies that met and fought a battle at the gates of Thebes. In the battle, both brothers died, after which the tyrant of Thebes, Creon, refused to permit the burial of the brother who had attacked the city. Since it was believed at the time that the soul of anyone not granted the proper ritual of burial was condemned to wander the earth forever, a daughter of Oedipus by the name of Antigone buried her dead brother in secret and was discovered. For this she was condemned to be buried alive in a cave, where she committed suicide, followed soon thereafter by her lover, Haemon, who happened to be Creon's son. Meanwhile, the prophet Tiresias had warned Creon that his defiance of the gods would bring about his own downfall and the end of his house, but by the time he sought to undo his actions it was too late, and Antigone, Haemon, and Creon's wife had all died by their own hand.

Sophocles believed that no mortal ruler had the final authority over all things and that the mistaken belief of a tyrant in his own omnipotence would inevitably result in his destruction. *Antigone* was an expression in Greek dramatic form of an identical belief shared by Northern Sung thinkers such as Sun Fu and Liu Ch'ang that ritual is the visible embodiment of absolute moral principles to which even tyrants are subject. The moral of the Greek play would have been perfectly clear to a Chinese audience in the Sung (more clear, one suspects, than it would be to a modern audience anywhere).

The foregoing has traced the main lines of Sun Fu's attitudes toward obedience to authority by concentrating on the three stages of decline that he claimed the Ch'un-ch'iu period had passed through as a result of the failure of its rulers, feudal lords, and ministers to carry out the will of heaven (made manifest through *li*) and exalt the ruler. We have also seen how the concept *li* was used to support a set of moral principles believed to be universally valid and binding equally on rulers and subjects. How influential Sun's ideas were is apparent in the content of later commentaries. For example, Hu An-kuo, echoing Sun, wrote in the Southern Sung that "the unifying theme of the *Ch'un-ch'iu* is to exalt the mandate of the king and deplore the division of authority among officials. . . . The rectification of names [by which a person acts according to the absolute standards that govern those in his position] is the eternal principle of heaven and earth and is the comprehensive principle of righteousness that links the past with the present."[87] Only by obedience to the civil authority of the ruler and to the moral authority of *li* did Sun believe the long-term interests of the people could be properly served.

However, the practical value of centralized rule can be more clearly seen with respect to the threat of internal usurpation than with that of barbarian invasion. No matter how one tries to get around it, the undeniable fact is that a strictly military solution to the problem of the barbarians in the Northern Sung—the Hsi-hsia and the Khitan—would have required the emperor to delegate much of his authority to commanders in the field. Commanders would have had to have the power to appropriate local revenue in order to pay for expenses that could not be anticipated and the power to make on-the-spot tactical (as well as strategic) decisions in order to take advantage of immediate military opportunities. But to do so raised the specter of the autonomous military commanders of the recent past. To avoid that, Sun argued that in the final analysis the long-term benefits gained by sustaining the power of the emperor far outweighed the temporary advantages that might have accrued by allowing local military commanders wide latitude in responding to the military threat of the barbarians. Simply put, he regarded the internal threat as much more serious than the external threat. Policies that implemented this very choice of priorities were in fact pursued by all the Northern Sung emperors, giving the appearance of military weakness that has elicited the condemnation of nationalistically inclined Chinese scholars from the Southern Sung to the present.[88]

I wonder, however, whether such condemnation is fully justified. The more acquainted I become with the *Ch'un-ch'iu* scholars of the Northern Sung, the more inclined I am to the belief that they would have regarded the course of later Chinese history, more particularly the Southern Sung, as a vindication of their ideas rather than an indictment of their failure to protect China from the barbarian military threat. After all, the twin virtues of obedience to a unified state and obedience to the Chinese moral tradition continued to be sustained, albeit on a smaller scale, throughout the period of the Southern Sung and on through the Yüan, Ming, and Ch'ing dynasties. Given their assumptions about the ultimate ends of government, they would have argued, I suspect, that these values would have been placed in far greater jeopardy had the Northern Sung emperors decentralized military authority and delegated it to commanders in the field. The probability that the habits of challenging central authority, so ingrained after centuries of indulgence during the late T'ang and Five Dynasties period, would have reasserted themselves was very great, and as a result China would quite likely have once again lost the benefits of a unified stable government. Fragmented and weakened from within, it would have been in no position to hold off barbarians indefinitely anyway, so the same results would probably have been obtained, but at a far greater cost than was in fact the case.

The *Ch'un-ch'iu* scholars no more deserve the accusation of being impractical than do the early Sung emperors (who in any case were the real authors of the policy of centralizing authority and buying off the barbarians). The point at issue is not one of practicality or impracticality but rather priorities. The Sung scholars were trying to establish a clear set of priorities and standards by which the formation and execution of practical policies could be measured and that would lend unity and direction to those policies.

That they had solid grounds for their fear of decentralizing military power can be illustrated by reference not only to the late T'ang but also to a strikingly similar problem in medieval European history. The Carolingian rulers of medieval France and the Norman rulers of medieval England were also confronted with barbarian intrusions. They also found it expedient to create certain administrative areas on the borders of their kingdoms, called *marches,* that had as their purpose the repulsion of attacks from their less civilized and more warlike neighbors from the north (and, in the case of England, from Wales also). According to Jack Lindsay,

Delegation of power proved from the outset the only way of governing wide areas; and in such a situation there was little or no method of supervising and limiting the local lords who held delegated power. Border-lands in particular created difficult situations where lords needed strong forces and free hands. The policy of Charlemagne with regard to the marches helped to develop the fief, just as both in Anglo-Saxon and Norman England the Welsh marches produced especially warlike and consolidated earldoms. . . . To hold up the fissiparous tendencies a Frankish king might send a count, *comes,* to each city; but in the conditions of the ninth century all local powers tended to grow autonomous. The magnates assumed the right to levy troops or taxes, to exercise police and law administration.[89]

Lindsay adds that "throughout the Middle Ages the marches of north and east produced many challenges to the crown, which, however, had no choice but to allow dangerous concentrations of power there."[90] The point is that the price paid for this protection was high and included both usurpation and dissolution of central rule. For example, Robert the Strong, one of the lords appointed by the Carolingian ruler Charles the Bald (843–877) to protect the Loire valley from the Vikings, spent so much energy consolidating his own power (instead of fighting the barbarians) that his descendants ultimately were able to replace the Carolingians with their own Capetian dynasty.[91]

Of course, the circumstances of the medieval European monarchies were very different from those of the Chinese empire. Among other things, the Chinese benefited from a common written language and long experience in the bureaucratic administration of a large territory. The Europeans lacked those advantages to the same degree (although Latin did serve as a common administrative language) and as a result were more vulnerable to fragmentation than their Chinese counterparts. Nevertheless, the parallel is instructive because in both cases a similar problem led to a similar outcome.

It ought to be clear now precisely how the *Ch'un-ch'iu* was used by Sun Fu and others as a vehicle to express opinions on the fundamental problems of national defense and obedience to the ruler. In order to understand the meaning and significance of those opinions, we must move on to a consideration of the metaphysical level of interpretation in which the duty of obedience is understood not to be imposed from without, in consideration of only utilitarian motives and at the expense of individuality and freedom, but to come from within, from sources that are rooted in the very nature of the human personality and the universe.

5

The Views of
Ch'eng I and Hu An-kuo
The Moral/Metaphysical Levels

W E have now arrived at the major junction in this work, where the hitherto divergent paths of neo-Confucian metaphysical speculation and neo-Confucian political thought intersect and travel for a time along a common route. The immediate cause of their convergence was a mutual interest in the problem of authority. The result was to strengthen the obligation of the subject to obey his ruler while at the same time strengthening the obligation of the ruler to obey universal moral laws, of which the ruler himself was regarded as merely the instrument. The close correspondence held to exist by the neo-Confucian metaphysical thinkers between the nature of man's being (and therefore of political society) and the nature of the universal order, therefore, was intended to be a protection against arbitrary rule rather than a theoretical justification of it. It was the particular contribution of these thinkers to locate traditional Confucian political beliefs within the larger context of a unified body of thought that gave a rational explanation of man, nature, and the cosmos. Those redefined traditional Confucian political beliefs may have supported central authority, but they did not support absolutism.

We have seen that the Sung interpretation of the *Ch'un-ch'iu* developed in the Northern Sung in two stages. The first began with Hu Yüan and Sun Fu and was continued most prominently by Liu Ch'ang. In this stage, the commentators concentrated on exploring the moral and universal dimensions of ritual *(li)*.

The second stage was begun by the philosopher Ch'eng I
(1033–1107), who incorporated the moral and universal concerns of ritual into a unified metaphysical system based on
principle *(li)*, specifically heavenly principle *(t'ien-li)*. His views
were continued in the Northern Sung by his students, among
them Hsieh Shih. Hu An-kuo (1074–1138), who came to maturity in the Northern Sung but wrote his commentary in the first
decade of the Southern Sung, then consolidated Sun's and
Ch'eng's views into an interpretation, focused on heavenly
principle, that was to become the standard commentary on the
Ch'un-ch'iu until the middle of the Ch'ing dynasty. Classical
Confucian views on political authority thereby became integrated into a coherent philosophical system, producing in
China a synthesis on the same order of magnitude, although
with different ingredients, as the synthesis that was being
accomplished at about the same time in Europe by Thomas
Aquinas.

Later scholars have accused both Sun Fu and Hu An-kuo of
being more interested in using their commentaries as a vehicle
for expressing their own ideas about what policies ought to be
followed during the Sung than in pursuing the truth. Hu's
commentary was sometimes referred to as the "Annals of the
Sung" for that reason. The Ch'ing scholars were particularly
critical of them (and even Chu Hsi was not without reservations). While some of those criticisms are probably accurate,
one cannot help but admire the belief of the Sung scholars that
the classics embodied timeless wisdom and that such wisdom
might be of value in confronting the fundamental political
problems of any age, their own included.

Metaphysical Implications of Li *(Principle)* *in Ch'eng I's Commentary*

Ch'eng I's commentary, the *Ch'un-ch'iu chuan,* is a composite of
his own writing (up to the end of the ninth year of Duke Huan,
703 B.C.) and oral explanations recorded by his students.[1] Like
all commentators on the *Ch'un-ch'iu* from Mencius on (and
including Sun Fu), Ch'eng I believed that the basic purpose of
the *Ch'un-ch'iu* was "to make available for all time the means by
which a balanced appraisal of the institutions of kingship might

be acquired."[2] It was, in effect, a manual on how to rule a state in such a way that both the material prosperity and the moral character of the people are fully developed. In a passage referring to an eclipse in 720, Ch'eng I states that "the main principle of the *Ch'un-ch'iu* is to show that when the kingly way is preserved then the principle of man is established." The "kingly way," linking heaven and man, was the natural focus of politics. Echoing the views of Tung Chung-shu, man, nature, and the cosmos were linked in a single interrelated system, in which the actions of people influenced the forces of nature, and vice versa. To borrow Ch'eng I's metaphor, "the ruler is the sun."[3]

That image is a useful one, and not only because of the sun's power or location, for no matter how crucial the sun is to human life on earth, the sun cannot change the rules by which it establishes its dominion over our solar system. It conforms to the same laws of motion that govern its subordinate planets. In like manner, it was not the power of the ruler that Ch'eng I wished to stress in his political theories but the responsibility of the ruler to align his actions with the moral imperatives of a higher authority. In Ch'eng's commentary, that higher authority was expressed in the form of "heavenly principle" *(t'ien-li)*. The term *heavenly principle* was certainly not new to the Sung. It can be found, among other places, in the *Li-chi,* where it was held to be in opposition to the human emotions *(jen-yü)*.[4] Its revival in the Sung appears to have originated with Ch'eng Hao, for whom it meant the natural endowment of principle in human nature (and in all particular objects).[5] As it came to be used on the cosmological level, it referred to "the unity of Heaven and Man, with Heaven understood as that which holds the cosmos together, the fullness of being and goodness."[6]

In time, heavenly principle became the keystone of Sung neo-Confucianism and therefore of orthodox Confucianism in the last millennium. Ch'ien Mu has noted that during the Sung the term *heavenly principle* even came to overshadow the traditional concept of the mandate of heaven *(t'ien-ming)*.[7] For Chu Hsi it became "the core and highest philosophical category."[8] He identified Chou Tun-yi's supreme ultimate *(t'ai-chi)* with the *t'ien-li* of the Ch'eng brothers.[9] He also subsumed the *li* of ritual and propriety under the broader category of heavenly princi-

ple (thus synthesizing both Sun Fu's and Ch'eng I's interpretations of the *Ch'un-ch'iu*). When a student asked Chu Hsi why
the term *rules of propriety* is sometimes used instead of *principle*
(wondering, "Is it because rules of propriety are concrete, have
a finite measure, and are related to an actual situation?"), Chu
Hsi answered, "If you talk only about principle, you will be
abstract. Rules of propriety are the measure and pattern of the
principle of heaven. They teach people to have some standard."[10]

The source of Chu Hsi's inspiration for this was Ch'eng I.
Not surprisingly, in his commentary on the *Ch'un-ch'iu* Ch'eng I
took the concept of *t'ien-li* and applied it to politics. In doing
so, he made the relation between cosmic forces and human
affairs even more explicit than Sun Fu or Liu Ch'ang had done.
In a passage noting an unseasonable snowfall, for example,
Ch'eng commented that "the movement of the *yin* and the *yang*
is regular and without extreme. Whenever it loses its regularity,
then it is in response to human actions. Therefore in the *Ch'un-
ch'iu* it is necessary to record natural calamities. The Han Confucianists transmitted these sayings without understanding
principle *(li)*, so that what they wrote is mostly misguided."
Again, commenting on a *Ch'un-ch'iu* passage (in the year 709
B.C.) noting that "it was a good year," Ch'eng said, "When
human affairs are smooth below, then the material force [*ch'i*]
of heaven is in harmony above. For [Duke] Huan to ascend the
throne by assassinating the prince is [an act] contrary to heavenly principle [*t'ien-li*], which causes the human moral virtues
[*jen-lun*] to become disordered. The material force of heaven
and earth becomes abnormal and perverse [by such behavior].
Floods, droughts, famine, and other disasters are thus the necessary [consequence]. Now the reason [that the *Ch'un-ch'iu*
records] a good year is because [Confucius wanted] to record
how unusual it was."[11]

Following Ch'eng I's lead, later commentators also interpreted the *Ch'un-ch'iu* through the lens of heavenly principle. Hu An-kuo in the Southern Sung took *t'ien-li* as the integrating principle for his own commentary on the *Ch'un-ch'iu*.
Chu Hsi, who was born (1130) just a few years before Hu
An-kuo died (1138), agreed with Hu's views on the *Spring
and Autumn Annals,* writing that "the *Ch'un-ch'iu* [records] the

affairs of a period in disorder and [shows how] the sages regulated everything according to heavenly principle."[12] Even the Southern Sung commentator Yeh Meng-te (1077–1148), who tended to regard the *Ch'un-ch'iu* more as a historical document than a political tract, said that the *Ch'un-ch'iu* "sought heavenly principle through the comprehensive [treatment of] the relations between ruler and subject, father and son, brother and brother, friend and friend, and husband and wife."[13]

Like Sun Fu, Ch'eng I also emphasized the importance of revering the ruler in his commentary, remarking that "the way of preserving the people lay in putting the principle of *tsun-wang* first."[14] Ever aware of the need for a strong ruler to protect China from the threat of invasion from the outside (which was imminent when Ch'eng I wrote his commentary) or rebellion from the inside, Ch'eng I was clearly aware of the need for a strong central government. On the other hand, it is abundantly clear that the main emphasis in his commentary is not on recommending obedience to any passing whim of the ruler but on showing how a ruler ought to bring human affairs into conformity with transcendent moral principles. In his introduction to that work, he notes that "Confucius wrote the *Ch'un-ch'iu* because at the end of the Chou no sages had reappeared and because there was no one to follow [the ways of] heaven in managing contemporary affairs. Therefore he wrote the *Ch'un-ch'iu* in order to provide a great and unchanging norm for a hundred kings."[15] Ch'eng I was forever pointing out that the acts of men in general, and rulers in particular, were linked to the flow of cosmic forces. He frequently mentioned the decline of belief in *li* or *tao-li* that took place in the Ch'un-ch'iu period and the absence of the *tao* in men: "[Belief in] heavenly principle had been destroyed, and the *tao* of men was no more. [When Confucius wrote] the term *heavenly king* [*t'ien-wang*] [he meant] to say that one ought to revere heaven. . . . [Belief in] the principle of men has been extinguished, the motions of heaven have become perverse, and the *yin* and the *yang* have lost their proper order."[16] Whereas Sun condemned everything by claiming that it was contrary to ritual *(li)*, Ch'eng I used several terms connoting a broader context.[17] For example, when the *Ch'un-ch'iu* records a meeting in 721 between the duke of Lu and the Jung people, Ch'eng I claims that it was contrary to righteousness or justice *(yi)*, not *li*, as Sun Fu had done.[18] He also uses the terms *contrary to the* "tao" and *contrary to the heavenly* "tao" as well as *contrary to ritual*.[19]

The relation between the authority of heaven and the authority of the ruler (and the authority of the husband) is explored in the following passage. The incident occurs in the fall of 721 B.C., in the first year of the *Ch'un-ch'iu,* when the king "sent the (sub)administrator Hsüan with a present of two carriages and their horses for the funerals of Duke Hui and (his wife) Chung-tzu."[20] Ch'eng's comment goes as follows:

> The king honors and accords with the *tao* of heaven, [for which reason] he is called the heavenly king [*t'ien-wang*], his mandate is called the mandate of heaven, and his punishment is called the heavenly punishment. What fulfills this *tao* is the kingly way. When later generations used cleverness and power to control the world, [it became] the way of the hegemons [*pa-tao*]. The *Ch'un-ch'iu* relied on [the concept of] the kingly mandate in order to rectify the methods of the kings and used the term *heavenly king* in order to esteem the mandate of heaven. [Thus it is that] the basis of moral relations between husband and wife ought first to be rectified. During the time of the *Ch'un-ch'iu,* wives and concubines misused their authority and caused disorder. The sages were particularly careful in making the proper distinction in names, [so that] in matching men and women there [should be] no changes throughout their lifetimes. For this reason there was no principle [*li*] [by which anyone] could be rematched. From senior officials on down, if within [the home] there was no master, then the way of the family was not established, and for this reason there was no way that there could be [a rule of] *li* [allowing someone] to select another wife. Because the duties of the Son of Heaven and the feudal lords were so all encompassing and their empresses were able to act as regents themselves, there was no *li* [by which they could] select another empress.[21]

Ch'eng I then goes on to say that the wording of the passage under consideration was designed to convey the message that Duke Hui's second wife did not deserve to be elevated to the position of primary wife since to do so was contrary to principle and amounted to a form of usurpation that resulted in dissension between the duke's sons. There are two aspects that are of special importance in this passage. One is the clear and explicit statement of the subordination of the ruler to heaven, which bestows authority on him and punishes him for abusing it. Thus, emphasis is put, not on the ruler's power, but on his obligation to make his actions conform to the will of heaven, that is, to walk "the kingly path." The other is the way in which the problem of authority on the three levels of family, state, and heaven is treated as a unified whole, each linked together in a great chain of moral principle in which the governing order is *t'ien-li.*

To some extent Ch'eng I was carrying out the views of his teacher Hu Yüan. Although Hu's views on the *Ch'un-ch'iu* have not survived, his commentary on the "Hung Fan" chapter of the *Shu-ching* is still extant and reveals a profound concern for restraining the power of an abusive ruler and aligning the actions of all rulers with the higher *tao* of nature. That Hu would choose to focus on the "Hung Fan" chapter already says something about his point of view. That section of the *Shu-ching* is one of the earliest expressions of belief in the interaction of man and nature in all Chinese literature.[22] To be sure, it claims that "the Son of Heaven is the parent of the people, and so becomes the sovereign of the empire," implying that, as one obeys one's parents, so should one obey the Son of Heaven. Nevertheless, that obedience is put in the context of observing the Way, namely, the "way of the ruler," advocating that rulers "without deflection, without unevenness, pursue the royal righteousness; without any selfish likings, pursue the royal way *(tsun wang-chih-tao);* without any selfish dislikings, pursue the royal path; without deflection, without partiality, broad and long is the royal path."[23]

In virtually every passage of his commentary on this chapter, Hu Yüan appeals to the Way, usually the "middle way" *(chung-tao).*[24] When he advocates "revering the ruler," in other words, what he means is, not just subjects revering the person of the ruler, but the ruler himself revering the *tao.* This dual meaning—one political, the other moral—applies to Cheng I's commentary as well. So concerned was Ch'eng I about putting obedience to the ruler in the context of the ruler's obedience to universal moral values that he once wrote, "Don't worry about not respecting the power of the ruler; rather worry that the officials respect it too much, thus leading to a proud heart."[25]

Ch'eng I was forty years younger than Sun Fu and died (in 1107) almost fifty years later than Sun. Since Ch'eng I was working on his commentary to the *Ch'un-ch'iu* during the last years of his life (his preface is dated 1103), it represents his most mature thought on the relation between political life and metaphysical thought. It also represents the observations of a man who spent the bulk of his career in a China in many ways different from that in which Sun Fu had lived. Sun grew up and wrote in the formative period of the Sung, when the dynasty was just beginning, and when the scholar-elite were inspired to a new sense of mission and confidence in their ability to influence practical affairs. Ch'eng I, however, had lived through decades of bitter factional struggle in the central bureaucracy and had suffered much personal anguish at the hands of enemies among rival groups of officials. In fact, Ch'eng spent most of his life in Lo-yang, occupied in scholarship and in various degrees of opposition to the series of institutional reforms introduced by Wang An-shih and his followers (a conflict that began in the early 1070s and lasted to the end of Ch'eng's life). The rarity of his service in the bureaucracy, owed partly to his failure to pass the *chin-shih* examination as well as to the efforts of opposing factions, allowed him more time for intellectual pursuits than his brother Ch'eng Hao, whose shorter life (he died in 1085) was often interrupted by the press of official duties.[26]

Some have been tempted to argue that Ch'eng I's metaphysical ideas in general and his attitudes toward the role of the emperor in particular were motivated primarily by his factional opposition to Wang An-shih's reforms and by the need to counter Wang's reformist ideology (based on the *Chou-li*) with a more persuasive ideology of his own.[27] Certainly, the divisiveness and destructiveness of the factional struggles that took place during the reigns of Shen-tsung (1068–1085) and Che-tsung (1086–1100) must have strengthened Ch'eng's awareness of the need for a strong moral authority. But it would probably be a mistake to explain the metaphysical ideas of Ch'eng I solely in terms of short-term expediency. However disappointed Ch'eng was in his own life, and regardless of how far short of their expectations in bringing about a moral revival

Confucian scholar-officials thought they were by the end of the eleventh century, many of those conditions that inspired the neo-Confucians at the beginning of the century were still present at the end of it. What appeared to be lacking were not the outward conditions of national power but consensus and unity on fundamental questions among the scholar-elite themselves. Ch'eng I's purpose was to restore a degree of unanimity on first principles—then and only then did he believe it possible to expect unified action by high-minded scholar-officials. The fact that such an enterprise propelled him into factional struggles is a consequence of his intellectual efforts; it is not, as some would assert, a cause of those efforts. On the other hand, the destructive potential of factionalism must have contributed some measure of urgency to his desire to locate his theories in the context of unchanging universal principles.

Ch'eng I's contribution was to integrate political and moral obligation into a philosophical system of thought that explained authority not only in terms of the cosmological order but in terms of the basic essence of human nature itself. This was done by identifying heavenly principle *(t'ien-li)* as giving form to the substance of all things, including man.[28] The manifestation of this heavenly principle was benevolence, or love *(jen)*. The hierarchical order of the universe, and of human society, was thought to bring with it certain obligations and responsibilities to those who occupied a given position in the hierarchy. The fulfillment of those responsibilities, through *jen,* was thus the means by which each individual perfected himself as well as the means by which the larger community was brought into line with the principles governing the universal order. To violate heavenly principle, to act without *jen,* was to go counter both to one's own nature and to heaven as well and would invite retribution. This emphasis on heavenly principle was then carried forward into the Southern Sung by Hu An-kuo, through whose commentary it was passed on to the Ming and the Ch'ing dynasties.

Hu An-kuo's Life and Main Ideas

The life of Hu An-kuo (1074–1138)[29] spanned the transition period between the Northern and the Southern Sung dynasties. He grew to maturity in the waning years of the Northern

Sung and wrote his masterpiece, a commentary on the *Ch'un-ch'iu* entitled the *Ch'un-ch'iu chuan,* in the early years of the Southern Sung.[30] As a young man he had studied at the National University *(T'ai-hsüeh)* under Chu Ch'ang-wen (1039–1098),[31] who had been a student of Sun Fu's and a friend of Ch'eng I's. After passing his exam, Hu An-kuo occupied some minor administrative positions but ran afoul of the grand councilor, Tsai Ching (1046–1126), whereupon he retired and devoted himself to studying the *Ch'un-ch'iu.* After the loss of the north, he served the emperor Kao-tsung in various capacities, which included participating in the imperial lecture *(ching-yen).* During his forty-year career, however, he worked as an active official for only six years.[32] His commentary was published in 1136, only two years before he died.

In terms of the traditional categorization of "school," he belongs to that of Sun Fu.[33] But Hu's commentary follows Ch'eng I more than Sun Fu, with Sun a close second.[34] P'i Hsi-jui says that his main principle of interpretation *(ta-yi)* was based on the *Mencius* and his praise and blame on the *Kung-yang* and the *Ku-liang.*[35] During the Yüan dynasty (1279–1368), his commentary became the standard one used in preparation for the official examinations and remained so throughout the Ming until the middle of the Ch'ing. The editors of the *Ssu-k'u ch'üan-shu* claim that Hu's was selected as the orthodox commentary because Chu Hsi had not written a commentary and Ch'eng's was incomplete. Hu's was thought to have been the best surviving commentary that accurately reflected Ch'eng I's views, especially his emphasis on heavenly principle.[36] At the beginning of his commentary, for example, Hu An-kuo claimed that

> the main point of the *Ch'un-ch'iu* is to clarify how [belief in] heavenly principle [*t'ien-li*] weakened as each new generation appeared and how the *tao* declined. Sons killed their fathers and subjects their rulers; concubines and wives inherited positions occupied by their husbands. With the passage of time there were none who could set things right, and [belief in] heavenly principle was destroyed. . . . The unifying theme of the *Ch'un-ch'iu* is to revere the mandate of the king and deplore the division of authority among officials.[37]

Although Hu grew to maturity in the Northern Sung, his interpretation of the *Ch'un-ch'iu* was powerfully affected by the events surrounding the fall of the Northern Sung to the invading forces of the Chin in 1127. Almost from the very beginning of its existence, the court of the Southern Sung emperors was embroiled in controversy between those who advocated military attempts to regain the lost territory of the north and those who advocated a peaceful reconciliation with the Chin dynasty. The emperor Kao-tsung (r. 1127–1162) was of two minds. On the one hand, insofar as he claimed to be the legitimate ruler of all China, he ought to have been committed to the reunification of China, but, on the other hand, since his father, the emperor Hui-tsung, was still alive and a captive of the Chin dynasty in the north, a future defeat of the Chin would place Kao-tsung in the uncomfortable position of having to give up the throne. There thus ensued within the bureaucracy a bitter factional struggle that lasted for decades, reminiscent of cutthroat struggles in the Northern Sung. Hu An-kuo's position as a student and defender of Ch'eng I automatically pitted him against those who followed the legacy of Wang An-shih since Ch'eng I had opposed Wang's reforms. But, more to the point, Hu's devotion to the theme of expelling the barbarians *(jang-i)* in his commentary, inherited from Sun Fu, automatically placed him in the war camp and thus out of favor with those in power associated with the faction of Ch'in Kuei (1090–1155), the powerful official who ultimately became grand councilor about the time of Hu's death and who advocated a policy of dealing with the Chin through diplomacy rather than war.

This problem of the barbarian threat was, of course, a matter of the utmost urgency. For the last decade of Hu's life it was not entirely clear that the barbarians would not overrun the south as well as the north. Kao-tsung did not firmly establish himself in what became the capital of the Southern Sung, Hang-chou (then known as Lin-an), until 1138, the year that Hu died, and it was not until 1142 that a peace treaty was finally signed between the Chin and the Southern Sung, a treaty that came to be honored as much in the breach as the observance.

Hu was understandably preoccupied with the threat of the barbarians, and his commentaries on the *Ch'un-ch'iu* reflected this concern. The theme of "revering the emperor and expel-

ling the barbarians" *(tsun-wang jang-i),* which had characterized
the Northern Sung commentaries, was continued by Hu in the
Southern Sung. As one might imagine, however, Northern
Sung commentaries tended to be more heavily weighted in
favor of revering the emperor, while their Southern Sung counterparts tended to be more heavily weighted in favor of expelling the barbarians. Yet it would be a mistake to regard Hu's
purpose as simply to kick out a specific group of intruders;
much more was involved. One might even say that his purpose
was not so much to root out the barbarians as it was to root out
barbarism, whether practiced by Chinese or by the barbarians.
Only by returning to the civilizing principles of classical Confucianism, as outlined by the Northern Sung thinkers, particularly Ch'eng I, did Hu believe that China could hope to
withstand the threats posed by the present invaders. He was
determined to cure the cause of China's disease, not just treat
the symptoms.[38] In keeping with the underlying principles of
the whole neo-Confucian revival, Hu An-kuo regarded the fundamental problem of government as a moral one, with morality
now understood as having metaphysical dimensions with which
previous Confucian thinkers had not concerned themselves.

Above all, the *Ch'un-ch'iu* "plumbs to the essence of principle
[*li*]." Because of the influence of Wang An-shih, according to
Hu, "nobody reads the *Ch'un-ch'iu* any more to prepare for a
public career, and no one is examined on the *Ch'un-ch'iu* in the
formal examinations. The candidates thus have no way of discovering the proper mean [*che-chung*]. All-under-heaven does
not know what is suitable, and the passions of men increase as
[respect for] heavenly principle decreases. The result is that
the barbarians have caused disorder in China. No one can
expel them. Alas! That it should come to this! Confucius personally edited the words that restrain disorder and restore what
is right in order to put into practice the pleasure of heaven
[*t'ien-tsung*]."[39] Thus, although Hu did attach greater importance to the need to expel the barbarians than to the need to
revere the ruler, it is also fair to say that he attributes the barbarian invasions more to the general decline in the moral faculties of various rulers than to the strength of the barbarians
themselves. Like Ch'eng I, whom Hu invokes in support of his
position more than any other scholar, Hu emphasized the para-

mount requirement that the ruler make his thoughts and actions conform to heavenly principle *(t'ien-li)* and overcome human passions *(jen-yü)*. All the practical issues of the day— even those relating to the loss of the north to the barbarians and the threat of usurpation by officials—should be understood in the light of the universal moral order, that is, heavenly principle.

Hu's Views on the Metaphysical Implications of Li

Samuel Johnson once observed that facing imminent death on the gallows concentrates the mind wonderfully. Something of the same principle must be in operation with regard to great political writings. The collapse of old institutional structures, or the imminent danger that they might collapse, has in the past called forth from certain thinkers prodigious efforts to understand the underlying reasons and to propose remedies. Certainly, Confucius belongs to this category since he wrote in a time of considerable chaos and unrest, as did Mencius and Hsün Tzu.

Hu An-kuo says this rather explicitly in the introduction to his commentary: "Words are only able to record the principles [*li*], while in putting them into practice one can see their use. For this reason Confucius bestowed [to later generations] the history of Lu in order to turn the world away from disorder and back to the right path. . . . Those who know Confucius say that his book curbs the flood of human passions [*jen-yü*], and by planning far into the future preserves heavenly principle [*t'ien-li*], in a world already destroyed, for later generations."[40]

In concentrating on the ultimate loyalty of man to transcendent moral principles, Hu continued the line of reasoning established by the Northern Sung commentators, drawing, in fact, much from both Sun Fu and Ch'eng I. The ruler is clearly subordinate to heavenly principle, which promotes cosmic harmony and which will punish transgressions by the ruler. The purpose of an eclipse, for example, is to warn the ruler not to ignore the phenomena of heaven.[41] The sun represents the *yang* and the invasion of China by the barbarians proof that the *yang* is weak and the *yin* strong. The eclipse is thus a warning of the impending threat of invasion. Rulers are criticized for los-

ing the *tao* of rule. Hu even quotes approvingly from Ch'eng I
that the ruler was created for the sake of the people, not the
other way around.[42] Perhaps this is one reason why P'i Hsi-jui
says that the essence of Hu's commentary follows Mencius.[43]
Actually, Mencius is quoted by Hu with much more frequency
than by Sun Fu. In one passage, Hu quotes from Mencius' discussion of *hao-jan chih-ch'i:*[44] "This is a *ch'i* which is, in the highest degree, vast and unyielding. Nourish it with integrity and
place no obstacle in its path and it will fill the space between
Heaven and Earth."[45]

In another instance, he quotes from Mencius to support his
contention that the root of China's problem lies in the realm of
moral behavior: "Suppose a man [i.e., a 'barbarian'] treats one
in an outrageous manner. Faced with this, a gentleman [i.e.,
the Southern Sung] will say to himself, 'I must be lacking in
benevolence and courtesy, or how could such a thing happen
to me?' "[46] Again and again Hu drives home the admonition
that *t'ien-li* was not being observed and that the failure to abide
by the principles of heaven is the root of the evils recounted in
the text of the *Ch'un-ch'iu*. Like Sun Fu, Hu believed that, if an
incident is recorded in the *Ch'un-ch'iu,* it was intended by
Confucius to be condemned. For example, Hu says very early in
the commentary that, "whenever a covenant is recorded, [the
intention is to convey] blame."[47] He also follows Sun Fu in his
frequent reference to *li* (ritual), as when he says that it was
"contrary to *li*" to grant hereditary offices (but not necessarily
hereditary emoluments). In this same passage, Hu draws on the
Kung-yang commentary for support, as did Sun Fu frequently.[48]

Hu's Views on Usurpation of Authority

Since Hu An-kuo stressed as a principal theme of the *Ch'un-
ch'iu* the moral imperative of revering the mandate of the ruler,
one might naturally expect Hu to incline toward the Legalist
position that the interests of the ruler should take precedence
over those of the people. Such is not the case, however. Regardless of how much Hu, along with his neo-Confucian predecessors in the Northern Sung, emphasized the importance of the
ruler, there was no doubt that it was the people who were ultimately to benefit. Hu stated quite clearly that the purpose of

"kingly government is to look after the welfare and nurturing of the people and to promote the rise of benevolence."[49] In the same passage, he also says that "the *Ch'un-ch'iu* promotes the notion, from the very beginning, from the condemnation of Duke Yin's intentions on, that in order to rectify the hearts of the people it is necessary to give expression to the notion that the empire is for the benefit of all [*t'ien-hsia wei-kung*];[50] one cannot allow disorder motivated by selfish impulses."

The passage that provoked this remark records the unfortunate story of Cheng of the state of Lu. After the death in 722 B.C. of Duke Hui, his oldest son, Cheng, took over as Duke Yin. But the last wife of the late duke, who was not Cheng's mother, naturally favored her own son (the younger half-brother of the duke of Yin) and sought to have him enfeoffed in a strategic location in order to provide a base for a future challenge to the present duke. In order to humor his stepmother, Duke Yin had his brother enfeoffed in a lesser but still potentially powerful location, where he did in fact later revolt, succeeding in killing his half-brother Duke Yin and establishing himself as Duke Huan. Duke Yin in this case is condemned, by the *Kung-yang* and by Hu, because he failed to make the proper choice between loyalty to the state and loyalty to the family. He should have disobeyed his stepmother in order to protect the stability of the state. This example of usurpation of authority on the highest level could not have anything but evil consequences for the people and the state in the long run. But Hu condemns civil disorder not only because it detracts from the public welfare but also because it undermines the moral underpinnings of society and encourages divided loyalties among the people.

Hu An-kuo makes frequent reference to the phrase *t'ien-hsia wei-kung*. Covenants made between states are held as evidence of private interests *(ssu)* predominating over those of the general welfare *(kung)* and are therefore recorded (or so Hu believed) in order to condemn them.[51] This corruption in the body politic was fully evident midway through the Ch'un-ch'iu period—according to Hu "from the reigns of Duke Wen [626–609 B.C.] and Duke Hsüan [608–591 B.C.]."[52] This is about the same time frame given by Sun Fu. But the corruption actually began much earlier. Even during the reign of Duke Huan (711–694 B.C.), the process was already apparent. On one occasion, when the son of a minister of the Chou court visited the state of Lu in 707 B.C., Hu was prompted to write that, "as the Chou became weak, then inferior men took over the court government; titles and offices were dispensed by them to relatives and friends, causing personal rivalries; the dividing up of important positions extended even to the children. Worthy people withdrew to the far corners of the kingdom, older people were not used, and the way of the ruler was not put into practice. As a result the barbarians invaded the various states."[53]

Factionalism was another activity that reflected the preeminence of private interests over the public interest and was also condemned.[54] Hu An-kuo was perhaps more conscious of the disrupting effect of factionalism than Sun Fu had been since it had become a serious problem in the Sung after Sun's time. Very early in the commentary Hu uses the occasion of an unauthorized visit to Lu by the earl of Chi, a minister at the Chou court, to argue that the underlying reason for recording the visit was to warn future generations of the danger of factionalism *(p'eng-tang)*.[55] Another instance of failing to take into account the long-term interest of the community had to do with the question of appointment of officials. Sun Fu had emphasized that they ought to be appointed by the ruler, in order to discourage the rise of local officials who were not entirely dependent on central authority. Hu An-kuo also took this line. He favored giving hereditary emoluments but not hereditary offices and said at one point that "emoluments were to reward accomplishments and offices to revere worth. If a state were not to choose men and to make office hereditary . . . it would be lucky if the state did not decline."[56] There are at least two further reasons for Hu's views on this matter. One is the obvious one of ensuring a high standard of officials, but the other is probably due to the complicated and bloated bureaucracy in the Sung, with many offices granted to people who did nothing and many officials whose titles bore little or no relation to the actual responsibilities that they held. By recourse to the *Ch'un-ch'iu* Hu was thus able to bring Confucius over to his side of the argument to reform the Sung bureaucracy, manifesting once again the practical utility of ambiguity. No doubt this is one of the reasons that P'i Hsi-jui criticized Hu An-kuo for too often injecting his own opinions into his commentary.[57] That was also, of course, the chief criticism by earlier Ch'ing scholars of Sun Fu as well.

Hu's Views on the Expulsion of the Barbarians

In many respects, Hu An-kuo's views on the barbarians were very similar to those of Sun Fu. Neither thinker reacted to the conquest of China by northern barbarians by blaming the barbarians as the real cause of China's distress, as later writers loyal to the Ming, such as Wang Fu-chih (1619–1692), tended to do. If anything, Sun and Hu followed the lead of the *Kung-yang* commentary, which stated that "in the Spring and Autumn Period [the feudal rulers] looked upon their countries as 'that within' and upon all of the other Chinese states as 'that without'; or looked upon the Chinese states collectively as 'that within' and upon the barbarian nations as 'that without.' As a king desired to unify the world, why do we employ the terms 'within' and 'without' in our commentary? What we are saying is that he should commence with the nearer regions" (i.e., distance from the center, not ethnic or cultural difference or political division, should be the fact of importance).[58]

Everywhere the opportunity presents itself, Hu stresses that the troubles that ancient China got into vis-à-vis the barbarians were the result of internal causes, not merely attacks from the outside. In 713 B.C., when a representative from the Chou court arrived at Lu to make friendly inquiries, Hu takes that to indicate the low regard in which the Chou court was held (Ch'eng I made the same remark) since it would normally have been beneath the dignity of the Chou king to send someone to a duke (such as Yin) who had never sent a representative to the king first. According to Hu, the "king was not acting like a king," and "it is because the heavenly king has lost his awesome authority that secondary officials give orders for the country and the barbarians control the Chinese states."[59]

Of greater interest, especially for those familiar with the revival of New Text scholarship by reformers in the nineteenth century in China, is the frequent call by Hu An-kuo for "self-strengthening" *(tzu-ch'iang)*. This is another instance of Sung thinkers adumbrating policies and attitudes that were to characterize the Chinese response to the Western barbarians much later. Perhaps we should not be surprised: it was the same text, after all—the *Ch'un-ch'iu*—that was looked to as a source of inspiration in both cases. In one passage, after detailing all the failures of Duke Yin to pay proper respects to the Chou king, Hu states that the duke was not able "to use ritual to strengthen the state." The *Ch'un-ch'iu* manifests the interrelation between actions and consequences, and "by speaking of the way of heaven [*t'ien-tao*], the mutual interaction [*kan-ying*] of *li* [principle] is made clear."[60] In one breath, Hu thus brings together self-strengthening, the *li* of both ritual and principle, and the cosmic interaction of heaven and earth. But, lest the reader conclude that the lessons of the *Ch'un-ch'iu* are excessively abstract, Hu follows the above passage immediately with a general review of the whole reign of Duke Yin, in which he says that the text embodies "the rules of statecraft, the prescription to end chaos and return to order, and the unchanging laws of the hundred kings."[61]

As if to illustrate the practical utility of concentrating one's moral energy on expelling an invader, Hu makes much of the incident recorded in the *Ch'un-ch'iu* in 677 B.C., when a few remnants of the state of Sui (having been defeated by the state of Ch'i in 681 B.C.) invited the forces sent to guard them to a banquet, got them drunk, and then annihilated them, thereby demonstrating how easy it would be to defeat a larger force with courage and ingenuity: "Their *li* [principle] was sufficient to produce strength."[62] It does not require much imagination to see the obvious lesson for the Southern Sung intended by Hu. As events would have it, the lesson went unheeded.

In many ways, Hu's views of barbarians were similar to those of the *Ku-liang* and the *Kung-yang*. In 482 B.C., in commenting on the meeting between the duke of Lu, the marquis of Chin, and the viscount of Wu, the *Ku-liang* says that "Wu was a barbarian state, in which people cut their hair short and tatooed their bodies. [Its ruler now] wished, by means of the ceremonies of Lu and the power of Chin, to bring about the wearing of both cap and garments. He contributed also from the products of the State to do honor to the king approved by Heaven. Wu is here advanced."[63] But not only are barbarian states considered Chinese if they act properly. Sinified states can be considered barbarian if they act improperly, according to the *Kung-yang*, as in 628 B.C., where the state of Ch'in is supposed to have behaved badly: "What is it that the State of Ch'in should be called? It is to be called barbarian."[64] Such an interpretation (the *Kung-yang* was the first to consider barbarians as such on the basis of behavior, not ethnic origin) enabled later officials like Hsü Heng in the thirteenth century to justify serving a foreign invader, in the hopes that the barbarians could be brought to respect Chinese norms in the future.[65]

Like Sun Fu, Ch'eng I and Hu An-kuo regarded the *Ch'un-ch'iu* as both a handbook for practical affairs and a moral lighthouse to keep rulers on the proper path (i.e., the kingly way). As a guide to statecraft *(ching-shih)*, the commentaries focused on the principal problems of the Northern Sung—the threat of invasion from the northern "barbarians" (and for Hu An-kuo the reality of military defeat) and the threat of usurpation of the emperor's power by officials or generals. It was assumed, as always, that the political integrity of China was a necessary condition for civilized life. As a guide to morality in politics, the *Ch'un-ch'iu* offered guidance to those attempting the always difficult task, not just of separating what was morally right *(ching)* from what was expedient *(ch'üan)*, but also of reconciling two morally justifiable courses of action that happened to be in conflict with each other. Heavenly principle was the fundamental unifying principle, linking the immanent with the transcendent in a single bubble of cosmic harmony. In the words of Hu An-kuo, "The movement of the *yin* and the *yang* has a certain regularity but is not excessive; whatever loses its proper proportion will cause man to be influenced by it. . . . This makes clear the extent of the interaction between heaven and man, the principle of mutual stimulus and response."[66]

With the metaphysical speculations of neo-Confucians like Ch'eng I and Hu An-kuo, politics was tied not just to human ethical principles but also to a vast moral universe operating according to immutable principles. Since the actions of men are merely tangible manifestations of these universal principles, rulers can contravene them only with the gravest of consequences. In practice, of course, subjects must also obey their ruler. Ch'eng I and Hu An-kuo do not ever counsel active disobedience of a ruler by his subjects, but it would be a mistake to

assume that they do not do so merely out of prudence. Thomas
Aquinas, whose views on some of these matters are remarkably
similar, also expressly forbade the individual act of sedition on
the part of a disgruntled citizen, regardless of how pernicious a
particular ruler might be, on the plausible principle that civil
war is more destructive of the common good than a bad ruler
would be. However, when a long train of abuses stimulated a
popular act of rebellion on a massive scale, Aquinas also wrote
that it might not be wrong to take part in such a rebellion,
depending, as always, on the circumstances. Can this be any different from the obligation of the scholar-official to await a clear
sign that the mandate of heaven has been transferred to someone else (in the form of a worthy leader of a popular rebellion)
before transferring his own allegiance to another ruler?

The fact that Mencius figures so strongly in the neo-Confucian commentaries is more than just a hint that the obedience owed to a ruler was not total. It was Mencius, after all, who
told King Hsüan of Ch'i that a bad ruler ought to be removed
from office, or even assassinated.[67] Nor would Huang Tsung-hsi
(1610–1695), the Ming author of one of the strongest statements against despotism in the Chinese tradition, *A Plan for the
Prince* (the *Ming-i tai-fang lu*), have begun his study of Sung and
Yüan philosophy with a laudatory treatment of Hu Yüan and
Sun Fu had he believed that they had contributed to the
growth of despotism in China.

My underlying contention is that the reputation for blind
loyalty to the ruler that seems to have been pinned on the Sung
thinkers should be modified. When Hsiao Kung-ch'üan, for
example, argues that, "since the Sung dynasty, Confucians have
maintained that the minister-servitor had the absolute duty of
total loyalty to sovereign and dynasty and claimed that their
view on this was derived directly from Confucius himself," he
overlooks an important aspect of the neo-Confucian understanding of moral and political authority.[68] Instead of claiming
that minister-servitors owed their total loyalty to the ruler, the
neo-Confucians who wrote commentaries on the *Ch'un-ch'iu*
were much more likely to stress loyalties that were divided
between the ruler and heavenly principle. When they advocated *tsun-wang*, obedience to the ruler was only half the equation. The other half called for the ruler himself to obey the

kingly way *(tsun wang-tao)*. To be sure, the neo-Confucians whose work we have examined did not formulate a doctrine of revolution, but neither did they formulate a doctrine of blind obedience. Above all, they believed that the moral and material welfare of the people was the final measure of any ruler's legitimacy.

6

Statecraft and Natural Law in the West and China

C H'ENG I and Hu An-kuo, and of course Chu Hsi and all subsequent thinkers of the Ch'eng-Chu school, based their philosophical ideas on the assumption that there exist absolute laws of nature, which they referred to collectively as principle *(li)* or heavenly principle *(t'ien-li)*. They assumed, furthermore, that those laws were universal in their scope and application. Having never encountered a non-Chinese civilization as developed as their own, they had no reason to doubt that Chinese standards were universal (all-under-heaven). When China did encounter such a civilization—the West—in the middle of the Ch'ing dynasty, the response ranged from one extreme of rejecting the West altogether, through a middle ground of synthesizing Western concepts with the Chinese tradition (the path followed by K'ang Yu-wei and Liang Ch'i-ch'ao), to the other extreme of rejecting the Chinese heritage altogether in favor of Western science and democracy (the path followed by the intellectuals of the May Fourth Movement).

At the same time that thinkers in Sung China were inching toward a developed doctrine of universal moral laws, their counterparts in Europe were heading in the same direction. The results of their efforts share a good deal in common. To be sure, there are many aspects of the medieval European doctrine of natural law that do not overlap with the Chinese tradition.[1] Nevertheless, the doctrine of natural law in Europe did deal explicitly with the fundamental problem of a potential conflict between two equally compelling obligations—the obligation, on the one hand, to obey the legitimate political authority of the ruler and that, on the other hand, to remain loyal to certain universal moral principles that transcend the person and position of a particular ruler. I believe that Sung political commentators also shared this distinction, although perhaps they did not make it so explicit. This distinction, moreover, is important in showing that the neo-Confucians (at least the ones I am considering in the Northern Sung) did not intend to foster an uncritical obedience to every whim of the emperor when they advocated obedience to him. Certainly, some emperors tried to make believe that that was the case, just as many monarchs in later European history tried to argue, by reference to the theory of the divine right of kings, that, because the institutions of political authority were part of a world created by God, all Christians were therefore enjoined to obey every order issued by that authority. But the Christian position on political authority was a very flexible instrument and contained within it also a good deal of moral ammunition that could be used against the king himself as well as against his subjects. Divine right, in fact, never did receive much theoretical substance (nor did it last very long) and was a cheap justification for the power of rulers who had used brute force to get where they were and were anxious to make their status more legitimate.[2] Similarly, in China, whatever uses particular emperors later made of neo-Confucian political thought must also be understood as a deliberate distortion of neo-Confucian doctrine in order to justify claims to power that exceeded the bounds of traditional authority.

Statecraft in Europe and China

This moral component of authority is vital to a complete understanding of the relation between politics and morality in the Northern Sung dynasty and, indeed, in all Chinese statecraft. It also points up one of the fundamental differences between the way in which statecraft is viewed in China and in recent centuries of European political thought.

The term *statecraft* is in fact a secular term and came into being as the feudal institutions of medieval Europe (and the claims of the universal church) were being replaced by the early ancestors of the modern "nation-state." Statecraft is concerned with power;[3] it is a skill whose purpose is to organize limited resources as effectively as possible in order to enhance the wealth and power of the state. Statecraft is concerned primarily with means. Insofar as it raises the issue of ends, it assumes that the wealth and power of the state itself are the only practical ends toward which the resources of the state ought to be directed.

This preoccupation with the practical exercise of power is certainly understandable when one looks at the history of the "state" in the West. The modern state was forged in the crucible of war between various institutions with competing claims to power, among the most important of which were the church, parliaments, the nobility, free city-states, and the budding monarchies themselves. In the aftermath of the feudal period, and with increasing levels of trade and commerce stimulating rapid changes in military technology, the incentive for ambitious rulers to integrate these institutions into a smoothly functioning and efficient machine was very great. Those who did survived; those who did not perished. In a broader context, of course, the political development of the state was but the capstone of centuries of increasing integration taking place in the economic and social, as well as military, realms.

To a certain extent China also possessed, even earlier in its history than was the case in the West, many of the characteristics of a state: a centralized professional army, a trained bureaucracy charged with administering the state and collecting taxes, and a body of political theory justifying the centralized authority of its governing institutions. The principal characteristic that it lacked, of course, at least by comparison with its European counterparts, was the acknowledgment of the relative equality of states in their relations with each other. In that regard, China thought only in terms of "empire." In China, the "state" grew more gradually, and the contest was not between pluralistic institutions, but usually between China and the encircling tribes of so-called barbarian peoples to the north, and between the central government and regional military commanders charged with the responsibility of suppressing rebellions or repelling barbarian attacks. *Statecraft,* then, refers in the Chinese context almost not at all to international relations. It is a translation of the Chinese term *ching-shih,* which might be more properly, at least to an English-speaking audience mindful of the historical overtones of the term *statecraft* in the West, be translated as the "art of governing" or the "art of politics."

The Chinese term *ching-shih* has more in common with the art of governing discussed by the Greeks since they also, like the Confucians from early times, conceived of politics as preeminently the art of making people virtuous. Aristotle began his discourse in the *Politics,* for example, by asserting that "every state is a community of some kind, and every community is established with a view to some good; for mankind always act in order to obtain that which they think good. But, if all communities aim at some good, the state or political community, which is the highest of all, and which embraces all the rest, aims at good in a greater degree than any other, and at the highest good."[4] This belief of course rests on certain assumptions, the most basic of which is that there exists a code of behavior that all people ought to emulate and that taken as a whole defines and interprets the common good. No ethical relativity here—what is good for me is good for you because human nature is the same. Wants may, and often do, differ from individual to individual, but needs, that is, those particular requirements that identify us as humans and not as some other animal, remain the same for all persons.

For the Greeks, this special quality of being human seemed to reside in the capacity for rational thought;[5] for the Chinese, it resided in the capacity for moral judgment. But in both cases the purpose of government was not, as it has come to be in the West since the rise of the modern state, merely to enhance the wealth and prosperity of either the state itself or of its citizens (although that is certainly part of its responsibilities). More than that, its purpose was to order the activities of its members so that the good of the community as a whole harmonized with the desires and actions of the individuals who made it up; such harmony in fact represented the natural order of things.

"Statecraft," according to the Greeks, was thus a form of "soulcraft" and rested on the assumption that, in order to be successful in governing a state, one must first be successful in governing oneself. The entire *Republic* of Plato, for example, is based on an analogy between the parts of a state and the parts of a soul. In the *Gorgias,* Plato has Socrates assert that "there is the art of politics attending on the soul; and another art attending on the body." Later on Socrates continues, as if he were a Sung commentator on the *Ch'un-ch'iu,* "You [Callicles] praise the men who feasted the citizens and satisfied their desires, and people say that they have made the city great, not seeing that the swollen and ulcerated condition of the State is to be attributed to these elder statesmen; for they have filled the city full of harbours and docks and walls and revenues and all that, and have left no room for justice and temperance."[6] In that view of politics, a person in a position of responsibility must speak with moral authority before he is qualified to speak with political authority. The former is primary, the latter secondary. This view was inherited by the Stoics and then further developed by them into a doctrine of "natural law."

Natural Law in the European Context

Natural law, simply put, is the belief that there exist certain laws or rules of action that are inherent in human nature and that reflect the rationally apprehensible order of the universe. The influence of natural law on Western political thought has been very great, and to understand its significance, and the changes in content that it has undergone in different periods of European history, it is necessary to sketch briefly its origin and development.[7]

Although Aristotle spoke of a distinction between natural law and human law in the *Ethics,*[8] he believed that it was only through the institution of the Greek *polis* that the potential of the individual human being could be fully developed in accordance with natural law. It fell to the Stoics, whose horizons had been broadened by the aspirations of Alexander the Great to world empire, to elaborate on Aristotle's ideas. According to modern scholar of natural law Yves Simon,

> One of the striking features of the Stoics' teaching in ethics is their universalism, their sense of human unity, their belief that human affairs are governed by rules that hold univer-

sally. The Stoics are citizens of the world, citizens of the human republic, and they are strongly inclined to believe in propositions that are equally true and good in all parts of the world. After Plato and Aristotle, they are the main founders of moral universalism.[9]

The Stoics believed—and this was to remain an essential element of natural law—that the human personality could develop itself fully only through life in a community, governed according to rational laws that mirrored the universal order of things. As Richard Hooker (1554–1600) put it much later,

> The laws (of nature) which have been hitherto mentioned do bind men absolutely even as they are men, although they have never any settled fellowship, never any solemn agreement amongst themselves what to do or not to do. But forasmuch as we are not by ourselves sufficient to furnish ourselves with competent store of things needful for such a life as our nature doth desire, a life fit for the dignity of man; therefore to supply those defects and imperfections which are in us living singly and solely by ourselves, we are naturally induced to seek communion and fellowship with others. This was the cause of men's uniting themselves in politic Societies, which societies could not be without Government, nor Government without a distinct kind of Law from that which hath already been declared.[10]

The particular circumstances of the Roman Empire, which contained within its boundaries large bodies of people with widely varying customs and laws, caused the Roman jurists, greatly influenced by Stoic philosophy, to develop three different interpretations of law. The categories of *ius civile* (civil laws, applicable to Roman citizens) and *ius gentium* (laws of nations, applicable to those members of nations under Roman domination), which had been in effect since the third century B.C., were supplemented by what they referred to as the *ius naturale*, held to be above the other two and synonymous with reason itself.[11] According to Cicero,

> True law is right reason in agreement with Nature; it is of universal application, unchanging and everlasting; it summons to duty by its commands, and averts from wrong-doing by its prohibitions. And it does not lay its commands or prohibitions upon good men in vain, though neither have any effect

on the wicked. It is a sin to try to alter this law, nor is it allowable to attempt to repeal any part of it, and it is impossible to abolish it entirely. We cannot be freed from its obligations by Senate or People, and we need not look outside ourselves for an expounder or interpreter of it. And there will not be different laws at Rome and at Athens, or different laws now and in the future, but one eternal and unchangeable law will be valid for all nations and for all times, and there will be one master and one ruler, that is, God, over us all, for He is the author of this law, its promulgator, and its enforcing judge.[12]

Conflicts between, say, the law of nations and natural law were not necessarily considered justifiable grounds for reform. The institution of slavery, for example, was considered to be in violation of natural law but was still retained as a part of the *ius gentium*.[13] These three levels of law remained standard long after the Roman Empire had ceased to exist.

The church fathers added to the Roman heritage the belief that natural law originated in the will of God. One of the last of the Western Latin fathers, Saint Isidore of Seville (ca. 560–636), was responsible for transmitting the idea of natural law to the medieval canon lawyers, and in his encyclopedia, the *Etymologiae,* he wrote, "All laws are either divine or human. Divine laws are based on nature, human laws on custom. The reason why these are at variance is that different nations adopt different laws."[14]

In the twelfth century, medieval canon law underwent a great revival, centering around the appearance of the *Decretum* of Gratian in the 1140s, which began with the words, "Mankind is ruled by two laws: Natural Law and Custom. Natural Law is that which is contained in the Scriptures and the Gospel."[15] In this great compilation of canon law, Gratian dealt with such questions as the relation between natural law and divine law (he held them to be roughly synonymous) and between *ius gentium* and *ius civile* (the former he considered more general than the latter, so that *ius gentium* occupied a position midway between *ius naturale* and *ius civile*).[16] The importance of canon law in the development of natural law was undeniable. It constituted "the principal vehicle, in the Middle Ages, of the doctrine of the law of nature."[17]

But it was a philosopher—Thomas Aquinas—who, in making

the grand synthesis of Aristotelian thought (then undergoing a revival in the thirteenth century) and Christian theology, wove the various strands of natural law into a coherent system. With regard to the relation between positive law and natural law, Aquinas posited three levels—divine, natural, and human. Divine law was held to govern the origin and operation of the cosmos itself, revealed to man in the form of revelation. Natural law was that part of divine law that applied particularly to humankind alone and was made accessible to man through the use of reason. The realm of human law (or positive law) was confined to the application of natural law to the particular problems of everyday living, and it represented the changeable, accidental expression of the changeless, essential nature of natural law. Mulford Sibley has argued that Aquinas united

> in one coherent whole Roman, patristic, Hebrew, and Aristotelian views. Insofar as he accents the need for a definite law-declaring authority he is Roman, as he is also when he stresses the reasonable will. In his consciousness of positive law as subordinate to the law of nature, he combines Aristotelian and patristic positions. Insofar as he looks upon positive law as an externally imposed discipline for the training of mankind, Augustinian and Hebraic elements are present, as they are to the degree that he thinks of legal and political developments as an expression of the will of God in history.[18]

The relevance of this discussion to the subject of this work becomes apparent when we look at how natural law influenced Aquinas' views of obedience to political authority. Because of his recognition of the positive force of custom and of political authority in general (as opposed to the view of Augustine, e.g., who regarded temporal authority as an undesirable expedient necessitated by man's fallen nature), he was inclined to justify obedience even to an unjust ruler.[19] On the other hand, Aquinas was not unaware of the dilemma that was outlined in the first pages of this work. His essential ambiguity on this point is testament to his awareness of the impossibility of forming a theory that would be applicable to all particular situations. Thus it was that he also asserted the primacy of natural law over positive law and the subordination of the temporal ruler to the natural law. Obedience was enjoined, but the possibility of tyranny caused Aquinas to speak also of resistance in the following way: "Man is bound to obey secular rulers to the extent that the order of justice requires. For this reason if such rulers have no just title to power, but have usurped it, or if they command things to be done which are unjust, their subjects are not obliged to obey them, except perhaps in certain special cases, when it is a matter of avoiding scandal or some particular danger."[20] Yet this resistance was considered proper only when in collective form, as opposed to individually initiated sedition, which was expressly condemned.[21]

If Aquinas gave to natural law its finest hour in philosophy, Shakespeare furnished its greatest literary expression in English (as Dante did in Italian). Aquinas lived at the beginning of the age of theistically grounded natural law in the West, while Shakespeare lived at the tail end of that age. His plays contain some of the most powerful and surpassingly beautiful statements of belief in the harmony of the cosmic and human orders in the English language. At the same time, Shakespeare was fascinated with the problems of kingship—the responsibilities and obligations of the king and the limitations that had to be imposed on his power in order to prevent the rise of tyranny.[22]

In many ways, Shakespeare was merely reflecting the prevailing beliefs of his age. The Elizabethan and early Stuart examples of cosmic harmony are often remarkably similar to those employed by the Chinese. Analogies between the king and the sun, for example, were so common in Shakespeare's time as to be almost a convention.[23] They can be readily compared with Ch'eng I's statement commenting on an eclipse in 719 B.C.: "When the kingly way is preserved, then the *li* [principle] of man is established; that is the main point of the *Ch'un-ch'iu.* . . . The sun is the prince, and when it is consumed during an eclipse, it is because the princely way has been proscribed."[24] These parallels are instructive and relevant to the problem at hand because both traditions share a belief in the fundamental unity of man and nature such that the affirmation of hierarchical authority is balanced by a sense of the responsibilities that those in each level in that hierarchy owe to those above and below. This correspondence naturally imposes limitations as well as privileges. Everywhere the responsibilities of the king are emphasized. According to M. M. Reese, "A prince's sins blemish all his people, and always in Shakespeare we find a relationship between the character of the ruler and the moral condition, as well as the actual prosperity, of the governed."[25] Richard II, for example, lost his crown through the weaknesses of his own personality and plunged England into the chaos of civil war (in which the usurpers of the crown suffered dearly for their crime).

By the time of Shakespeare's death in 1616, the great edifice of God-centered natural law had already begun to be dismantled. Starting with Hugo Grotius (1583–1645), who discussed natural law in terms "independent of theological presuppositions,"[26] theories of natural law became intensely rationalistic and antihistorical, thus making possible later assertions that life in a state of nature was "nasty, poor, solitary, brutish, and short" (Hobbes) or characterized by "peace, good will, mutual assistance, and preservation" (Locke). This rationalistic tendency was of course strengthened by the Scientific Revolution.[27] Another strand of natural law was greatly influenced by the Protestant Reformation, which in theory (if not always in practice) emphasized individual interpretation of scripture, thus undermining the notion of objective standards. The Protestants also tended to downplay the importance of reason, drawing on Augustine and William of Ockham, among others, to argue that the world is a direct product of God's will and that man's puny reason can never be sufficient to understand the mysterious will of God. Thus deprived of confidence both in reason and in the objective authority of the church's teachings, this branch of natural law gradually became a tool of individualistic ideas. These two strands of modern natural law, rationalism and individualism, combined to produce a third characteristic—the emphasis on natural rights of the individual procured through the social contract. The contract was taken to be "a manifestation of individual will with the object of establishing a relationship of mutual obligation which would not otherwise exist by the law of nature."[28]

This discursion into the later evolution of the concept of natural law is sufficient to show the wide variety of meanings that are now often invested in the term *natural law.* It is not the modern conception of the term, however, that lends itself to productive comparison with Chinese thought but the medieval understanding. Few people in the modern world believe any longer in an underlying unity between the divine and the human worlds, in a hierarchical world order based on a harmonious balance of privileges and responsibilities, or in absolute moral standards the transgression of which would risk punishment by some transcendent force. But the Chinese thinkers in the Sung most definitely did share those ideas, and it is because of this that many scholars have been tempted to draw a parallel between the terms *li* (principle) and *li* (ritual) and natural law.

Applying Natural Law to Neo-Confucian Political Thought

The leading modern Chinese intellectual and scholar Hu Shih gives a definition of *natural law* that is largely medieval.[29] He believes that *li* (principle), *t'ien-li,* and *tao-li* can all be translated as *natural law* and even quotes from the *Han Fei Tzu* to show how natural law was used to impose theoretical limits on the power of the ruler: "For those who work in accordance with the universal laws of nature *(tao-li),* there is nothing that they cannot accomplish. . . . For those who act foolishly and in disregard of the universal laws of nature, even though they may possess the power and authority of Kings and princes and the fabulous wealth of an I-tun or Tao-chu, they will alienate the support of the people and lose all their possessions."[30]

Hu also mentions the story of the early Sung minister Chao P'u (922–992), who was once asked by Sung T'ai-tsu, the first emperor of the dynasty, what the greatest thing in the world was. Chao replied, "*Tao-li* is the greatest."[31] Hu then goes on to quote a passage from an essay by the Ming scholar and official Lu K'un (1536–1618): "There are only two things supreme in this world: one is *li* (principle), the other is political authority. Of the two, *li* is the more supreme. When *li* is discussed in the Imperial Court or Palace, even the Emperor cannot suppress it by his authority. And even when *li* is temporarily suppressed, it will always triumph in the end and will prevail in the world throughout the ages."[32]

Kenneth Scott Latourette has also noted the similarities between natural law and *li,* saying that *li* was "akin to although not identical with the concept of natural law which was present in the Graeco-Roman world."[33] In addition, Arthur Hummel has written that "government was never regarded as anything more than an instrument for carrying out the will of Heaven, that is to say, the moral law."[34] Herrlee Creel wrote that "the concept of natural law, so important in Europe, is very like the Confucian conception of the Way, as both Leibniz and Wolff recognized." In another passage, he notes a similarity between natural law and "righteousness" *(yi)*.[35] Joseph Needham even "equates" *li* with natural law.[36]

What are we to make of this comparison between medieval European natural law and neo-Confucian concepts of the natural order?[37] What were the similarities and differences? What is their significance? It is clear that there were differences. The Chinese did not make the same distinction, for example, between natural law and positive law as did the West. Although in both traditions positive law was taken to be subordinate to natural law, in the West its tie with natural law (as well as its tie with tradition, which was important for both Roman and English common law) endowed it with much greater authority than was the case in China. The Chinese understanding of natural law differed also from that of its medieval counterpart in that the neo-Confucians did not base their system on belief in a personal God, whose conscious will created the physical universe and all the principles by which it is governed, and who also intervened personally in human affairs. Cosmic principles were not associated with a creator God, and the unity of the cosmic and human order was an ontological, not a teleological, unity.

Nevertheless, for our purpose, which concentrates on that part of natural law in both cultures that dealt with the conflict of obedience to temporal power and obligation to a higher moral law, the parallels are striking and instructive. Both traditions shared the belief that the ultimate ends of government were moral; both were guided by a sense of the underlying unity pervading all the apparent variety of the natural order and by a belief in the harmony of the human and the universal order, proceeding along hierarchical lines; both believed that the principles responsible for change in the world were accessible to understanding by reason; and both believed that temporal authority carried with it heavy moral obligations that acted, given the prevailing assumption that transgressions of absolute moral standards would be punished, as a restraint on the arbitrary exercise of that temporal power. These ideas of universal moral order (and the relation of the ruler to them) were promoted in a number of institutions created or revived both by the Sung state and by early neo-Confucian scholar-officials. The state, for example, greatly expanded the civil service examination system and the bureaucratic recruitment system, as has already been noted in chapter 2. Education was also assigned great importance by the neo-Confucians. Then, as a result of the efforts of reforming Confucians such as Fan Chung-yen during the middle of the eleventh century, the state became more and more involved in setting up public schools.[38] On a higher level, in order to guide (and restrain) the emperor, the institution of the imperial seminar *(ching-yen)* was founded in 1033, in which scholars lectured the emperor periodically on selected topics from the histories and the classics.[39] The lectures took place throughout the lifetime of the reigning emperor and were supplementary to the classical education he received (also at the hands of the scholar-officials of course) when he was growing up.

Another mode of instruction by which the emperor was guided to right action also began in the early Sung and was known as the "learning of the emperor" *(ti-hsüeh)*.[40] The earliest example of this institution is the work entitled *Learning of the Emperor (Ti-hsüeh)* by Fan Tsu-yu (1041–1098), a student of Ch'eng I's who became one of the important collaborators with Ssu-ma Kuang in the compilation of the *Tzu-chih t'ung-chien*. Contained in this work is the distillation of almost eight years of instruction offered to the Che-tsung emperor during the years 1085–1093.

Yet another institution that had classical antecedents but that had not been used in the T'ang was the worship of heaven by the emperor in the Hall of Enlightenment, or *ming-t'ang*.[41] The Sung, in fact, was the only period in which the *ming-t'ang* ritual flourished. The actual worshiping ceremonies took place annually in the Sung, in a temple constructed especially for that purpose, and were devoted not only to heaven but to the founding emperor as well.[42] James T. C. Liu considers the support given these ceremonies by neo-Confucians an example of "how Confucian rationalism was applied to the ideology of absolutism."[43] No doubt the emperors did use the ritual with a view to enhancing their own authority. Nevertheless, insofar as it underlined the importance of bringing heaven and earth into harmony, the ritual could just as easily be regarded as limiting the authority of the ruler. From that perspective, perhaps *absolutism* is not the best term since absolutism by definition acknowledges no limits on the power of the ruler. This is an important point. To be sure, the theory of the divine right of kings in seventeenth-century Europe still held that the ruler was responsible to God, implying that absolutism is not incompatible with acknowledgment of a higher authority. In fact, however, the theory of divine right referred to the will of God alone, not to a body of natural law understandable to all men through reason. Thus, the Chinese understanding of authority is more compatible with medieval natural law than with the later theories of absolutism. According to Fritz Kern, the theory of absolute divine right "changed the moral duty of passive obedience into a legal claim on the part of the king to unconditional obedience. It transmuted the sacramental consecration of the king into a mystical tabu that made the monarch inviolable and a quasi-spiritual person. It exempted him from the authority and disciplinary powers of the Church. . . . It rested finally upon legitimism, the inborn right to rule, which freed its possessor from all human dependence."[44] Absolutism, in short, did not rest on a rational foundation.

It was through such institutional devices that the neo-Confucian scholar-officials sought to inculcate in the educated public and in the ruler an understanding of the principles of natural law that were believed to unite heaven, earth, and man. The notion that moral suasion could act as a restraint on the arbitrary exercise of kingly power stands out as one of the most striking and significant similarities between the medieval European and the Northern Sung concepts of the natural order. In both traditions, morality and politics were unified and expressed in terms of a rational philosophy. The rationality was critical since its moral imperatives could be understood by all men and applied to the ruler as well as the ruled. This assumption that the world was rational and apprehensible by the human mind is one more reason why the Sung thinkers possessed such an enormous reservoir of self-confidence.[45]

The contribution of the major Sung commentators on the *Ch'un-ch'iu* was to integrate traditional Confucian views on statecraft (i.e., "soulcraft") with a unified and rational philosophy (based on *li*) that came to be accepted as orthodox for the next millennium. This philosophy was similar to the medieval European conception of natural law in one crucial respect. Both doctrines were aware of the potential tension between the need for obedience to political authority and the equally valid obligation of all moral men to obey a higher moral code.

It may be true that those who believe strongly in the existence of a transcendent God or a universal moral code are not inclined to rebel against established authority, regardless of its iniquity (not in spite of their fundamental assumptions, but rather because of them). Those who are committed firmly to a belief in transcendent principles of justice are not normally willing to acquiesce in acts of rebellious violence against the state if by doing so they would be forced to adopt means that would violate their allegiance to those absolute principles. However much the two traditions on which I have drawn may differ, in this they are as one, that the right of civil authority to rule, once established, ought not to be questioned (even under the threat of unjust execution). Again, this grows out of a recognition of the necessity of such authority in establishing conditions of peace, security, and unified action, without which civilized life would be unthinkable, and a faith that tyranny, should such arise, in the long run will be punished either by God or by nature without the necessity of individual human intervention.

But such an understanding of obedience did not mean that the power of the ruler was unlimited. Indeed, in China the responsibility for ensuring that the ruler did not become a tyrant rested squarely on the shoulders of the scholar-elite. This responsibility also brought with it certain rights and benefits, namely, a rationally supported argument in favor of their own legitimate claims to political authority, albeit delegated.

If the legitimacy and the long-term success of a ruler depended on his adherence to *li* (either principle or ritual), and if *li* could be fully understood and interpreted only after a long period of classical study, reflection, and self-cultivation, then one would be entitled to conclude that the scholar-officials, in whom exclusively all those opportunities and qualities resided, were the only group qualified to govern (in the name of the ruler of course). These pretensions of the Confucian elite were not new. What was new, however, was, on the one hand, the way in which the legitimacy of their power as a class was made to appear as a natural expression of the universal order of things and, on the other hand, the fact that they really did enjoy a degree of practical authority in government that they had long been denied (for reasons that have been outlined in chapter 2). They now combined the practice of power—or thought they did—with a body of theoretical orthodoxy whose scope went far beyond what had preceded it. These ideas appeared to equip them with ideological claims to political power that the military or the old aristocracy could not possibly have matched. What they did not have, regrettably, was an institutional base to protect that power.

In this way, then, the concept of authority was brought to bear on the problems of limiting the power of the ruler (and of those who tried to usurp that power) and at the same time of buttressing the power of the scholar-officials themselves. They failed to accomplish what they intended, but they also set a precedent that was to provide—and may still—an inspiration for idealistic reformers in modern China. Even nineteenth-century Japan, in search of an ideology to justify overthrowing a moribund shogunate and strengthen the country against a barbarian power, drew its most potent rallying cry—*sonnō jōi*—from the Sung dynasty commentaries on the *Ch'un-ch'iu.*

7

Implications for Modern China and Japan

THROUGHOUT the history of Chinese political thought the need for obedience to authority has been a constant refrain. There are both practical and ideological reasons for this appreciation of the value of a strong central authority. From a purely practical point of view, the presence on China's northern borders of barbarians always willing to invade when China was weak was a powerful incentive to preserve a centralized state. But this practical incentive was also encouraged by the Confucian intellectual tradition, which pursued a stable social order not merely as an end in itself but as a necessary condition for the material prosperity and the moral improvement of all its individual members. Most political thinkers, from Plato and Confucius to the present, would agree that a society in which the lines of authority are clearly demarcated, and obedience to those above oneself is understood to be natural, is likely to be more stable than a society in which those conditions do not apply. Certainly that has been the case in China. In the *Analects,* for example, Confucius linked a hierarchical view of obedience in the family to order in the state: "They are very few who, being filial and fraternal, are fond of offending against their superiors. There have been none, who not liking to offend against their superiors, have been fond of stirring up confusion."[1] This respect for hierarchical authority, part of the Confucian ethic from its beginning, was given further support in the Sung dynasty by the philosophical system of neo-Confucianism, which emphasized, within a cosmological framework, the importance of exalting the ruler.

However, to say that neo-Confucianism lent philosophical credence to an authoritarian view of politics, which it did, is not to say that it deserves to be blamed for the growth of autocratic or absolutist institutions in later Chinese history. On the contrary, as I have tried to show in this study, a review of the political ideas (expressed in the form of commentaries on the *Ch'un-ch'iu*) of many of the leading neo-Confucians of the Northern Sung, such as Sun Fu, Ch'eng I, and Hu An-kuo, suggests that by phrasing their appeal to authority in terms of absolute moral principles, to which even the ruler himself was clearly meant to be subject, they were attempting to limit, not justify, the arbitrary exercise of power by the ruler.

In order to understand fully the context in which these political ideas were expressed and the particularly strong sense of mission that Sung political thinkers (indeed, all neo-Confucians) brought to their work, one has to understand first the sweeping nature of the social, political, and economic changes that were occurring in the early Sung. Some of these were in consequence of developments that had been under way for some time, and some were of comparatively recent origin. Socially, the role of the old landed aristocracy had been diminishing since the T'ang dynasty, and by the early Sung it was no longer a significant force in national politics, leaving something of a vacuum that the Confucian literati moved in to fill. Politically, the power of the military in the Sung government had been restrained as a result of deliberate policies put into effect by the first two Sung emperors. In addition, by the early Sung printing had made possible the publication of the whole corpus of classical literature in relatively inexpensive editions, and these were in turn disseminated to a reading audience that was rapidly growing in size owing to the presence of new educational opportunities and the appearance of new urban centers. Emperors in the eleventh century staffed the majority of the higher-level and important positions in the government with members of the scholar-elite selected by means of rigorous competitive examinations that, in conjunction with the growth of printing and the wider availability of schools, gave rise to the expectation that the deserving talent of society would now have unprecedented opportunities of being sought out and recognized for their true worth. Commercial growth, the consequence of increases in agricultural productivity and the expansion of a nationwide market network, was bringing new levels of prosperity to the country after more than two hundred years of economic disruption. In addition, the Sung emperors were on the whole a humane lot. Following the example set by the Sung founder, T'ai-tsu, they refrained from abusing or executing their officials in the manner of many of their predecessors and successors. Not surprisingly, officials leaving for work in the morning who did not have to contemplate the prospect of returning home in a coffin were more likely to display initiative than those who knew that their very lives were always on the line.

These conditions and opportunities for participation in government by the scholar-elite coincided with a clearly defined military crisis in the Northern Sung. Externally, the country was menaced by two northern barbarian peoples, the Tangut Hsi-hsia in the northwest and the Khitan Liao in the northeast, who seriously challenged Sung military security. This obvious threat was complicated by the fear on the part of most neo-Confucian thinkers (and, of course, the emperors) in the Northern Sung that a strictly military response to the barbarians would facilitate the rise of the same sort of regional military commanders who had destroyed the T'ang not long before. The latter fear made them keenly aware of the need to have a strong centralized state headed by a vigorous emperor. Just as the Wars of the Roses in fifteenth-century England (which had drastically weakened the old English nobility, devastated the countryside, and converted a fractionalized Parliament into a more malleable object of manipulation by strong, centralizing rulers) were still a living memory in Shakespeare's England over a hundred years later, so did the anarchy of the T'ang and the fate of the subsequent Five Dynasties weigh heavily on the minds of the Sung neo-Confucians.

At the same time, however, they wanted to take every precaution possible to ensure that a centralized ruler would also be the willing vehicle of those moral principles that the neo-Confucians regarded as the main purpose of the political order. They were engaged in a delicate balancing act, as indeed are all thinkers who face this conflict between moral and political authority. Thomas Hobbes, for example, complained in his dedication to the *Leviathan* that for someone in his position, "in a way beset with those that contend, on one side, for too great liberty and, on the other side, for too much authority, 'tis hard to pass between the points of both unwounded."[2] Confronted by the chaos of the Civil War in England and the Thirty Years' War in Germany, Hobbes was one of the first to solve the moral problem of conflicting loyalties in the "modern" way, that is, by denying its existence (since no authority transcended the state), and so favored peace and order at any price, even despotism.

In China, it was in part the convergence of the new opportunities and serious challenges of the Sung period that induced the scholar-elite who were part of what came to be called the neo-Confucian movement to achieve so much. Scholars were drawn into the service of the state in such greater numbers than ever before, and with the prospect of such vastly increased authority, that it must have seemed to them as if the state would finally become the pliant instrument of their own moral purposes. The opportunities that were now spread out before them largely explain the sense of mission characteristic of the neo-Confucians. It was one of those rare moments in history when a particularly fortuitous constellation of circumstances and human talent acted on each other in such a way as to ignite a tremendous outburst of creative intellectual and aesthetic energy. The challenges were so great that only an intellectual effort of an equivalent magnitude would suffice to overcome them. But the challenges alone were not enough. Challenges, after all, had been present for some time, but without a particularly distinguished response. The critical difference was the prospect that the tools to resolve these problems now seemed to be at hand. The period of general optimism, however, did not last beyond the end of the eleventh century, when the obstacles to progress were more apparent. The disillusionment that followed was not, for various reasons, fully shaken off until the twentieth century.

In Sung political thought, this new burst of energy found expression most vividly in the form of commentaries on the *Ch'un-ch'iu.* In an effort to bring life and thought together, to integrate the practical and the theoretical, the first generation of *Ch'un-ch'iu* commentators, best represented by the pivotal figure of Sun Fu, took as their guiding principles the concepts of "revering the emperor and expelling the barbarians" *(tsun-wang jang-i)* on a practical level and ritual *(li)* on a metaphysical level. The association of these two ideas allowed them to support the necessity of obedience to centralized authority, on which the stability and unity of the state was thought to depend, while at the same time placing moral limits on the arbitrary exercise of power by the ruler. The argument, as one would expect, was analogical, based on examples drawn from the *Ch'un-ch'iu* that illustrated the catastrophic punishment that was visited by heaven on those who contravened the principles of *tsun-wang* and *li.* The moral responsibility of the various levels of the political community (rulers, feudal lords, and ministers) to bring earthly society into harmony with nature was paramount and overshadowed all other considerations.

The next generation of commentators on the *Ch'un-ch'iu,* of whom by far the most influential was Ch'eng I, based their system of thought on principle *(li)* rather than ritual, gathering their political arguments favoring obedience to the ruler into the broader framework of a rational metaphysics. This philosophical system synthesized cosmological and ontological speculation so persuasively that it was not dislodged from its position of eminence (although it was certainly attacked) until the twentieth century, when it gave way to Marxism. In this system, the hierarchical order of the universe was duplicated in the human order by virtue of a common participation in principle, specifically heavenly principle *(t'ien-li),* which enjoined obedience to those above and moral obligations to those below. The outward manifestation of this *li,* on both the macrocosmic and the microcosmic levels, was benevolence *(jen).* All this added a new dimension to the injunction of obedience, making it a necessary condition not only of bringing order to society but of perfecting human nature as well. It was thought that the only means of bringing the *li* of the human person to its highest expression (of fulfilling one's potential) was through devotion to the common good. But the common good required, as an indispensable ingredient, obedience to authority, without which unified action was impossible; therefore it followed that one fulfilled one's *li* through obedience.

But again, as mentioned above, it would be a mistake to conclude that the obedience owed to the ruler, as understood by the neo-Confucians, was unqualified. In order to show the significance of their reservations on the question of obedience, I have had recourse to the medieval European concept of natural law, which was more explicit with regard to the problem of divided loyalties but which nevertheless came to many of the same conclusions. Medieval natural law was based on a synthesis of Greek philosophy and orthodox Christian doctrine, the latter of which drew on scriptural authority to prescribe obedience to established political authority. Saint Paul's Epistle to the Romans (13:1–7) set the tone for much of later Christian attitudes toward the state: "Let every person be subject to the governing authorities. For there is no authority except from God, and those that exist have been instituted by God. Therefore he who resists the authorities resists what God has appointed, and those who resist will incur judgment."[3]

This statement appears to leave little room for ambiguity. Similarly, some of Thomas Aquinas' remarks seem on the surface very straightforward appeals to almost blanket obedience, as when he wrote that "in matters pertaining to salvation of the soul we should obey spiritual rather than temporal authority, but in those which pertain to the political good we should obey the temporal rather than the spiritual."[4] But there is another side to Aquinas and to natural law. In the medieval understanding of natural law, there was a deliberate ambiguity over the issue of obedience. As one observer has put it, "Within the doctrine of the Church, the right of active resistance and the duty of passive obedience contended one against the other with almost equal strength. And yet, in the last analysis, it must be recognized that this antagonism is necessary, permanent, and inevitable, because it is rooted in human nature."[5] That is, so long as one believes that the human personality develops itself naturally through social intercourse and through the exercise of moral judgment, then conflict is inevitable—the only way to remain morally pure is to remain alone. To act in society is to confront the messy business of conflicting loyalties. An awareness of that inescapable ambiguity is also present in the neo-Confucian tradition, which is one of the reasons why a comparison between the two traditions has the potential to yield insight.

No matter how much the Confucian body of classical thought may have emphasized obedience to authority, it has from very early times also advocated the right of the people to resist tyranny.[6] As we have noted above, this right to rebel was advanced not only by Mencius but also by such "authoritarian" Confucians as Hsün Tzu. Rebellion was held to be one of the means of punishing a tyrant, along with natural disasters and prodigies. In this sense, one might argue that natural disasters and prodigies represented the underlying (or efficient) cause of a ruler's downfall while rebellion represented the more immediate (or instrumental) cause, the rebellion itself being in large part a response to desperate circumstances brought about by famine, flood, drought, or disease (which were frequently, in fact, products of misrule). The reasoning, such as it was, was that only when the situation had reached an extreme state of disorder would a rebellion be likely to act as a constructive vehicle of the common good. In the absence of large-scale suffering, a rebellion organized by factions jostling for power at the top would most likely result in a civil war, which would be attended by far greater damage to the welfare of the average person than the conditions of misrule that prevailed before. For this reason, official Confucian historiography has approved of scholar-officials (such as Liu Chi [1311–1375], the exemplary early adviser to the first Ming emperor) who transferred their loyalties to a new ruler (i.e., a successful rebel) once the proliferation of popular revolts made it apparent that the mandate of heaven had been withdrawn from the present ruler.[7]

To what, then, can one attribute the persistent tendency, noted in chapter 1, to associate neo-Confucian views on authority with the later and indisputable growth of the institution of autocracy in China? To be sure, there is no doubt that many of the ideas of neo-Confucianism were manipulated by later emperors for their own narrow purposes. The book of *Mencius,* for example, raised by Chu Hsi to become one of the primary models of neo-Confucian studies, was censored by the first Ming emperor, who rose from humble origins and was himself only semiliterate in the great tradition, in order to remove passages that advocated rebellion against an unworthy ruler.[8] The Ch'ing emperor K'ang Hsi (r. 1662–1722) was also not averse to modifying the neo-Confucian "orthodoxy" to serve his own ends, as he did in his Sacred Edict.[9] One must not, however, punish the father for the crimes of the son. Just as one ought not attack Christianity for having spawned the Marxist-Leninist state (although it is impossible to conceive of Marxism apart from the context of Christian thought out of which it grew), one cannot blame the neo-Confucians for the hash made out of their thought by unscrupulous individuals who used certain parts of it as a political bludgeon against their enemies. The neo-Confucians may have unwittingly surrendered the instrument of their own future oppression into the hands of the state, but such oppression was justified only by emptying neo-Confucian political thought of much of its moral content, leaving little more than an empty shell. Indeed, some observers have argued for the existence of two "Confucianisms," one "imperial," representing the ideology of the court and modified to suit its interests, the other "philosophical," referring to that body of thought inspiring the loyalty of the educated scholar-elite.[10] Of course, officials were sometimes caught between the two, being required in the course of their official duties to manipulate the ideology in ways that vitiated the doctrines of philosophical Confucianism. But Wilhelm notes that "it is gratifying to note to what extent this pragmatic trap was avoided or circumvented by a number of philosophers whose intellectual integrity rendered them the responsible servants, and not infrequently the victims, of the cause of the human mind."[11] In the words of Joseph Levenson, the adoption by the state of Sung neo-Confucianism as orthodox "need not be taken to prove that monarchs at last had a perfect Confucian rationalization for their purposes, nor that the Confucian establishment had become a wholly-owned subsidiary. The imperially sanctioned neo-Confucian monopoly came about not because, in itself, the philosophy flattered the monarch, but because in itself (i.e., in intellectual terms, not political) it was impressive enough to be an orthodoxy."[12]

It seems far more likely that the most important ingredients in the rise of autocracy in China ought to be sought elsewhere, in many of the reasons so ably assembled by Mote.[13] The alien conquest dynasties that followed the Northern Sung (the Chin [1112–1234], the Yüan [1279–1368], and the Ch'ing [1644–1911]) fostered the growth of despotism by further centralizing the institutional structure of the government and by meting out occasionally harsh treatment to recalcitrant officials.[14] The Ming emperors, particularly the founder, Ming T'ai-tsu (1368–1398), were notably brutal in their treatment of officials. In addition, and perhaps most important, China lacked the pluralistic institutions of the West that might have exercised a check on the power of a centralized ruler in China. Chinese neo-Confucian intellectuals had no institutional source of power independent of the monarchy that they served and whose power they often wished to curb. They had only their own reinvigorated Confucian ideology, which, although it may have thwarted many of the abuses of the emperor's power, never grew the teeth it might have, had it been backed by autonomous social or political institutions. There was no church, through which in the West the moral values of natural law were embodied in a form that could command, if not always obedience, at least frequently a certain measure of respect and influence and that, by its claim over the conscience of all men (including that of the ruler), was a visible and tangible reminder that the power of the ruler lay only within the province of the temporal order.

The real root of our misapprehension about the contribution of neo-Confucianism to the growth of autocracy lies, at least in part, in the nature of the assumptions that we bring to the evidence. Obedience to authority and disobedience have been justified in the last few centuries on grounds that do not admit of metaphysical categories. Modern thinkers are reluctant to assert that there are absolute moral values independent of our individual perceptions of them (or independent of the state) and that there also exists an essence of human nature that can be agreed on by thinking men through reason. Even when natural law is appealed to, it is, as suggested above, a very different animal from its medieval ancestor. Deprived of its function as a vehicle of the common good, authority becomes instead a threat to individual freedom. Authority and freedom thus become antithetical rather than complementary. Freedom is understood primarily in its negative form, as an absence of restraint, as freedom *from* regulations or laws governing certain realms of behavior. The other dimension of freedom, the freedom *to* bring the potential of each human person to its fullest possible realization, is largely ignored, if only because there is no consensus in the modern world on what constitutes the "potential" of the human being (pleasure? survival? cultivation of reason? perfection of the soul?).

Such a view, which has penetrated to the very core of Western thought in the last few centuries, cannot have failed to influence the study of Chinese history both by Westerners and by Chinese historians. As Chow Tse-tsung has remarked of Chinese intellectuals in the May Fourth Movement, "In the main, the concept of freedom current among . . . Chinese intellectuals was derived from Rousseau's theory of the general will and from British utilitarianism. They talked of freedom in terms of human rights, and freedom of speech and of the press."[15] Hu Shih, for example, had such a starting point when he claimed that neo-Confucianism was responsible for China's "lack of political and intellectual freedom."[16] The result is that the modern historian often underestimates the degree to which moral beliefs may have once exercised a restraining influence on the ruler's power.[17] Nor is the modern historian likely to be receptive to the further notion that those whose advocacy of obedience to authority is rooted in a belief in universally valid moral principles may also have a profound sense of the limits of authority. It is easy to forget, for example, that Thomas More believed in obedience even as he disobeyed. It is difficult to imagine a modern intellectual following More's example and enjoining his listeners to obey the very same king who had ordered his imminent execution (although Hai Jui certainly would have understood).[18]

There is one last service that the concept of natural law can be called on to perform. We have noted how in both China and the West the understanding of obedience to authority according to natural law contained a fundamental ambiguity. Any particular action involving a moral choice had to be made on the basis of a prudent consideration of both absolute principles and the actual circumstances of the moment. No formula could possibly be devised that was capable of governing all situations. The great (some might say tragic) paradox is that, by abandoning the belief in moral absolutes within the context of which that moral dilemma of divided loyalties derived its meaning, both China and the West swept aside one of the most effective barriers to the rise of the totalitarian state. As the historian Christopher Morris put it,

> Natural Law and Natural Rights are not now fashionable concepts. . . . Strictly speaking, we cannot prove that Nature teaches any morals or gives men any rights; but the belief that she had done so was for many centuries a highly civilizing force; and no one has yet thought of a more satisfactory way of maintaining that a government ought not, for example, to make it a capital crime to be born with red hair. It may be significant that the modern government which most blatantly rejected all vestiges of the old idea was the government which made it a crime to have been born a Jew.[19]

Those intellectuals who have attacked traditional standards of authority, in both the West and China, were frequently seduced into believing a doctrine of Marxism-Leninism that in application has been more destructive of human freedom than they could possibly have imagined or desired. This was not necessarily inevitable—many did not fall into the trap, but those who did, naturally with the noblest of intentions, did so because they were searching for an easy way out of a moral dilemma that their ancestors understood more thoroughly than they did. For all their appreciation of the positive value of obedience to authority, the Sung neo-Confucian commentators on the *Ch'un-ch'iu* owed their ultimate loyalty to what they believed were universally valid moral principles, and in the practical application of those principles to political events (in the *Ch'un-ch'iu*) they demonstrated a deep understanding of the irreconcilable tension between what one can do in an imperfect world of conflicting interests and loyalties and what one ought to do.

In view of this predisposition of many modern Chinese thinkers to blame traditional neo-Confucianism for the growth of autocracy in China (and thus by extension for China's weakness in the face of Western military superiority), it seems ironic, at least on the face of it, that two of the most prominent reform movements in late nineteenth-century East Asia, one in Japan and the other in China, used many of the same ideas on the *Ch'un-ch'iu* and its commentaries as did the early Sung founders of neo-Confucianism. In Japan, the Tokugawa shogunate (1600–1868) was undermined, and the Meiji Restoration (1868–1912) brought about, in large part by adherents of the doctrine of *sonnō jōi,* that is, "revere the emperor and expel the barbarians," which is the Japanese pronunciation of the main theme of the Sung commentaries on the *Ch'un-ch'iu: tsun-wang jang-i.* At the same time, in China, the New Text reform movement of the nineteenth century (what Hellmut Wilhelm called the "latest and last offshoot from the trunk of Confucianism" and Fung Yu-lan characterized as "the first real break with Neo-Confucianism")[20] was inspired by a revival of interest, at first merely textual, in the *Ch'un-ch'iu* and its supporting commentaries. The ripples set in motion during the Sung thus lasted for a thousand years.

The Emperor in the Meiji Restoration (1868–1912)

Historians commonly believe that China influenced Japan in two waves. The first was during the Nara (710–794) and Heian (794–1167) periods, when the influence "flowed through the channels of Confucian political theory and practice, through the institutions and beliefs of organized Buddhism, and through the whole assemblage of Chinese cultural forms, such as the literature, art, and philosophy or the architecture, dress, and agricultural and transportation technology."[21] After that, Japan passed through a period of decentralized rule similar in many ways to the feudal period in Europe. By 1600, Japan's feudal states *(han)* came under the suzerainty of the Tokugawa shogunate, which located its administrative bureaucracy (the *bakufu*) in Edo and imposed a rule of what has been called "centralized feudalism" on all Japan. During the Tokugawa period, which lasted from 1600 to 1868, Japan experienced its second wave of influence from China, primarily in the form of Confucian theory and practice. In 1868, the Tokugawa shogunate was overthrown, inaugurating a period known as the Meiji Restoration, during which Japan underwent an unprecedented transformation of its basic institutions. During this transition (and lasting until 1945), the institution of the emperor functioned as a kind of gyroscope, helping stabilize Japanese society amid all the conflicting pressures and demands produced by decades of wrenching changes, and serving to keep the ship of state on a steady course of rapid modernization. That the emperor had so much authority, but no power, is one of the great paradoxes of modern history.[22]

It is most unlikely that modernization in Japan in the Meiji period would have proceeded as smoothly as it did had it not been for the stabilizing role of the institution of the emperor. John Whitney Hall has written that, "as an embodiment of Japan's sense of national identity, as the bridge linking traditional sources of legitimacy to the new state authority, as the father figure which justified his subjects' self-discipline and sacrifice, the monarch became both a rallying point for his people and a means of concentrating authority behind the emerging national leadership."[23] What is most interesting for our purposes is that the movement that rallied around the emperor and became the driving force of the modernizing process in Japan used as its slogan the phrase that was first employed by Sun Fu in the early Sung: "revere the emperor and expel the barbarian" *(sonnō jōi)*. Given the importance of the term for the Meiji Restoration and the subsequent modernization of Japan, it is surprising that there seems to be no awareness among Japanese historians of the provenance of this term. I have been unable to find, in any of the secondary literature on modern Japanese history in English, any acknowledgment of the origin of this term in the Sung commentaries on the *Ch'un-ch'iu.* Indeed, one Japanese scholar on the subject, Bitō Masahide of Tokyo University, has even claimed that "the expression *sonnō jōi* was never used by the Chinese."[24]

On reflection, it is not surprising that the Japanese should have found parallels between the late Tokugawa and the early Sung. Both faced a common problem of how to centralize institutions of government after a period of decentralized rule in order to strengthen the state against a powerful military threat from outsiders. Both the reforming Japanese and the Northern Sung neo-Confucians believed in discarding the commentarial tradition and returning directly to the classics themselves for inspiration. Both sought to unify life and thought, to carry theory into practice.[25] Given those similarities, it seems natural that both would try to use the authority of the emperor, by invoking the doctrine of *tsun-wang,* to justify increasing the practical power of the bureaucracy. That the Japanese succeeded and the Chinese did not is owed most probably to the greater institutional pluralism of Japan than China. Throughout Japan's feudal period there existed an autonomous class of militarily powerful landowners (from which the leaders of the Meiji period came). China had no equivalent institution whose base of power was not subject to state control.

The doctrine of *sonnō jōi,* as it came to be interpreted in Japan, had its roots in the revival of interest in Japan of Chinese neo-Confucian thought *(Shushigaku),* based on Chu Hsi's synthesis, which took place during the beginning of the Tokugawa period. Chu Hsi had been known in Japan before the Tokugawa, of course. The scholar Kitabatake Chikafusa (1293–1354), author of a major work on the institution of the emperor, had even been inspired in his views on loyalty to the emperor by Chu Hsi (one of the most popular of Chu Hsi's works in Japan was the *T'ung-chien kang-mu,* which was modeled on the *Ch'un-ch'iu).*[26] But before the Tokugawa there had been no systematic study of neo-Confucianism. The Tokugawa revival owed much to the activities of several generations of the Hayashi family, beginning with Hayashi Razan (1583–1657) in his capacity as adviser to the early shoguns.[27] Hoshina Masayuki (1611–1672), a regent to the fourth shogun, in turn sponsored the work of Yamazaki Ansai (1618–1682), who combined an enthusiasm for Chu Hsi with a veneration of Shinto beliefs (and therefore of the emperor) and contributed to the rise of a new school of Shintoism.[28] Another thinker of this period, Arai Hakuseki (1657–1725), is of interest because of his preoccupation with the problem of the split in authority between the emperor and the shogun. He recommended bridging the split by arguing that the emperor "had delegated the substance of his authority to the shogun."[29] He failed to accomplish his designs but in the process established the terms of the argument that would later be turned against the shogun and employed in favor of increasing the authority of the emperor. He also expressed a common tendency in Japanese neo-Confucianism to stress loyalty more than filial piety (which the Chinese placed at a much higher level). In any case, by the end of the eighteenth century, the vigor of the *Shushigaku* school began to diminish, at which point it became the official teaching of the shogunate (as a result of the Kansei Reforms in 1787–1793) and thereby exerted a powerful influence even on those doctrines that developed as a reaction to it.

One of the earliest of those reactions to Chinese neo-Confucianism was the doctrine of "Ancient Learning" *(Kogaku)*. The most important thinkers in this school were Yamaga Sokō (1622–1685), Itō Jinsai (1627–1705), and Ogyū Sorai (1666–1728), who shared a desire to bypass the last two thousand years of Chinese philosophy and draw inspiration directly from the Confucian classics themselves. The influence of *Shushigaku* is apparent since the classics that were recommended were, in the case of Sokō, the same Four Books recommended by Chu Hsi. Sokō is generally acknowledged to be the first thinker to incorporate Confucian virtues into the samurai ethic, which culminated in the doctrine of *bushidō*. This doctrine, fortified by the later addition of *sonnō jōi*, provided much of the inspiration for the samurai who eventually overthrew the Tokugawa and established the Meiji Restoration. Ogyū Sorai is also credited, at least by Maruyama Masao, as having demolished the intellectual credibility of the *Shushigaku* school and set Japan off in the direction of undermining rational philosophy in favor of more subjective and emotional doctrines.[30]

One of those newer doctrines was the school of National Learning, *Kokugaku*. The most important representative of this school was Motoori Norinaga (1730–1801), a prodigious scholar whose driving ambition was to seek for the identity of the Japanese people in the ancient classics of the Japanese (not the Chinese) tradition. His work contributed as well to the revival of Shinto and was continued by Hirata Atsutane (1776–1843). Atsutane became a champion of what was later to be called "Restoration Shinto" *(Fukko Shintō)*, whose followers helped bring down the shogunate and which then became the basis for the state Shinto that lasted in Japan until 1945.

All these various strains came together in what became known as the Mito school. In the domain of Mito, north of Edo, a Tokugawa prince (a grandson of the Tokugawa founder, Ieyasu) by the name of Mitsukuni (1628–1700) sponsored a school of thought that ultimately provided the ideological focal point for the movement that overthrew the Tokugawa and established the Meiji Restoration in 1868. This school originated in a project to compile a history of Japan, the *Dai Nihon-*

shi (which was not completed in final form–in 397 volumes–until 1906 and whose writing was modeled on the *Ch'un-ch'iu*).[31] With the aid of the Chinese Ming loyalist scholar Chu Shun-shui (Shu Shunsui, who lived from 1600 to 1682), the project attracted a number of important scholars. But, by the end of the eighteenth century, a new spirit was introduced by Fujita Yūkoku (1774–1826), who provided the catalyst for the "late Mito school" and who set in motion the forces that toppled the Tokugawa *bakufu* in 1868.[32] Under the wing of the daimyo of the Mito domain, Tokugawa Nariaki (1800–1860), a number of prominent thinkers and organizers gathered. One of the most important was Yūkoku's son Fujita Tōko, who first used the term *sonnō jōi* explicitly in the 1840s in a political manifesto entitled the *Kōdōkanki jutsugi*.[33] Another figure was a student of Fujita Yūkoku's, Aizawa Seishisai (1782–1863), who published a work in 1825 called the *Shinron* (New proposals). This book became the first important expression of a new ideology known as *kokutai* (national polity).[34] Combining Shinto beliefs in the divine origin of the royal family and the Japanese people with the Confucian virtues of loyalty and filial piety, Aizawa exhorted his readers to respond to the threat of the West by drawing strength from traditional Japanese moral beliefs surrounding the institution of the emperor. Gradually, this doctrine of *sonnō jōi* evolved from an ignorant rejection of everything Western to a more balanced understanding of the value of Western learning, under the influence of Sakuma Shozan (1811–1864) and his student Yoshida Shoin (1830–1859). Sakuma himself was the first to champion the slogan "Eastern ethics and Western science" *(tōyō dōtoku, seiyū geijutsu)*.[35] The impact of the doctrine of *sonnō jōi* began to diminish after August 1864, when the British bombardment of Shimonoseki coastal defense batteries demonstrated that "expelling the barbarians" was not going to be an easy matter. Thereafter, the doctrine of "enriching the country and strengthening the military" *(fukoku-kyōhei)* came into the ascendant.[36]

Scholarly opinions vary on the significance of the Mito movement of *sonnō jōi* for nineteenth-century Japanese history. Nationalistic Japanese historians have tended to magnify the impact of the movement on the Meiji Restoration. More recently, Japanese historians like Tōyama Shigeki have noted the paradox between a *sonnō jōi* doctrine originally designed to shore up the feudal system and a *sonnō jōi* political movement designed to tear it down.[37] Others, like Ueyama Shunpei, have even suggested that the opposition inspired by the movement "gave expression to a bourgeois democratic revolution in Japan."[38] H. D. Harootunian takes a middle position, acknowledging its revolutionary outcome but arguing that its real significance lay in its role in politicizing what had been a shapeless school of ethical thought. Bridging the gap between thought and action then became a precedent and inspiration for the active involvement of a whole generation of samurai *shishi* (men of spirit) who rejected the actual doctrines of the Mito school. The Northern Sung doctrine of *tsun-wang jang-i* thus became, mutatis mutandis, a doctrine of political opposition. In nineteenth-century Japan, a doctrine advocating obedience became revolutionary by calling on everyone to obey someone who had no power whatsoever.[39]

There are, naturally, many differences between the Japanese experience and the Chinese experience. In Japan, the emperor had reigned but not ruled for centuries, while in China the two functions were united.[40] There were other differences between the Chinese and the Japanese institutions of the emperor. In Japan, the emperor was racially and culturally Japanese, while in China during the Ch'ing the emperor was not Han Chinese. The Japanese monarchy has been unique, in fact, in basing its claims to legitimacy almost entirely on heredity.[41] The list could continue, but my object is not to establish a parallel so much as to show that the theory of *tsun-wang* was used, not only as a program of moral reform in Northern Sung China, but also as an inspiration for political reform in modern Japan. Indeed, the culmination of the movement was to establish a "modern," constitutional government. To be sure, Meiji "democracy" left a great deal to be desired, but no one would deny that it laid the groundwork for further development of democratic institutions in prewar and postwar Japan.[42] One is entitled to question, in other words, the received wisdom that neo-Confucian views on loyalty to the emperor contributed inevitably to the growth of despotism in China since the same doctrine, in another set of circumstances—namely, Japan—was used to promote the modern transition to constitutional government.[43]

Indeed, the same outcome—constitutional government—was also promoted by late Ch'ing reformers in China, using many of the same texts that Japanese (and Northern Sung) reformers had used.

The New Text School in the Ch'ing

Intellectual trends in the Ch'ing were a consequence of both circumstance and ideas. The non-Chinese origin of the ruling Manchus, and their appropriation of Ch'eng-Chu Confucianism (which came to be known as "Sung learning") as the orthodox interpretation of all the Confucian classics, caused many literati to look elsewhere for inspiration. Following the lead of Huang Tsung-hsi, Ku Yen-wu, and Wang Fu-chih in the seventeenth century, they (like their Northern Sung counterparts) called for a return to the text of the classics themselves. Searching for ways to bridge the gap between life and thought, they turned their attention to the application of ideas to practical problems. Because the texts they relied on were from the Han dynasty, their efforts came to be known as "Han learning." By the middle of the dynasty, their efforts began to focus on sophisticated methods of textual criticism, which were refined over time and adopted by such a wide number of scholars that a new movement came into being known as the "School of Empirical Research" *(k'ao-cheng)*. The most important thinker of this group was Tai Chen (1724–1777), and their research included linguistics, phonology, philology, mathematics, geography, astronomy, and archaeology.

With the passage of time, however, scholars of this school succumbed to the temptation to pursue textual research as an end in itself and to forget that the original intention was to make those methods serve practical ends. The idealistic and reforming impulse then had to cut a new channel through the countryside, and it did so in the form of the "New Text school" that arose in the middle of the eighteenth century. This movement began as a relatively innocuous project in textual research. Scholars in the School of Empirical Research had already begun to turn their main guns on targets that had been relatively neglected during the previous few centuries. One of those was the *Ch'un-ch'iu,* and specifically the *Kung-yang* commentary. The first major Ch'ing scholar to take it up as an object of textual criticism was Chuang Ts'un-yü (1719–1788), who was "the first great scholar of the Ch'ing period to stress the importance of the Kung-yang commentary for study of the *Spring and Autumn Annals,* and paved the way for the revival of the *Chin-wen* or 'modern text' school of historical criticism."[44]

As we saw in chapter 3, the *Kung-yang* commentary had yielded pride of place by the end of the Han dynasty to the *Tso-chuan,* championed by the Old Text school, and had not recovered its former position since then. We have also seen, however, that it had undergone a major comeback in the Sung, although it never again became as important as the *Tso-chuan.* Many modern scholars of the period, incidentally, seem to have been unaware of the importance of the *Kung-yang* in the early stages of the Sung revival of Confucianism. Liang Ch'i-ch'ao, for example, claimed that after the Han the *Kung-yang* "became a lost subject for almost two thousand years," and Fung Yu-lan asserted that the *Ch'un-ch'iu* and the *Kung-yang* had been "largely neglected" since the Han.[45] Such a characterization is misleading. In fact, when Chuang focused on elucidating the "great principles hidden in esoteric language" *(wei-yen ta-yi)* of the text,[46] he was merely renewing an interest in the *Kung-yang* that dated from Sun Fu and others in the Northern Sung. The *Kung-yang* commentary was particularly attractive to late Ch'ing intellectuals since it appeared to support the New Text contention that Confucius was not just a teacher but a charismatic leader and reformer, an "uncrowned king" *(su-wang)* who advocated institutional changes as well as moral renewal. Chuang's interest, however, was prompted by the corruption at the court associated with the rise of the Ch'ien-lung emperor's favorite, Ho-shen, toward the end of the eighteenth century.[47] Since the *Kung-yang* commentary railed against the usurpations of power common in the Ch'un-ch'iu period, it represented a convenient weapon, a kind of political sword disguised as a scholarly brush. In Chuang's words,

> A state cannot [survive] without its exalted status and mandate [to rule from heaven]. Without [the mandate], the ruler is a usurper. According to the meaning articulated by Master Kung-yang, there were eight cases in which those who took power were all usurpers. Ho Hsiu recorded it in his commen-

tary. Yes! Yes! The position of ruler is what licentious men use to gain the upper hand. Therefore, the *Annals,* with regard to a time when secret dealings determine life and death, tried mightily to prevent such [usurpations of power].[48]

Having spent most of his career as an active official, Chuang himself did not leave a voluminous scholarly legacy.[49] His views, however, were continued by his grandson Liu Feng-lu (1776–1829), who advocated Ho Hsiu's ideas concerning the " 'Unfolding of the Three Epochs,' 'Going through the Three Periods of Unity,' 'Relegating the Chou Dynasty and Entrusting the Kingship to Lu,' and 'Receiving the Mandate to Reform Institutions.' "[50] Liu Feng-lu was also the first to suggest that Liu Hsin had rearranged the *Tso-chuan* in the Han in order to make it appear as if it had been composed as a commentary on the *Ch'un-ch'iu.* According to Fang Chao-ying,

> Liu Feng-lu stressed the study of the *Annals* because it was the only work that could conceivably have been written by Confucius himself. He favored the *Kung-yang* commentary above either of the others because it seemed to take him closer to the time of Confucius and because it embodied certain recondite concepts that could be elaborated into a social and political philosophy consonant with the needs of a changing social order. In the hands of his followers his aims became political rather than historical. Such an approach is known to modern Chinese scholars as *t'o-ku kai-chih,* the practice of "finding in antiquity the sanction for present-day changes." This accommodation of ancient thought to modern ideals was in vogue until the close of the dynasty.[51]

Liu's influence was considerable. According to Benjamin Elman, Liu "transformed *Kung-yang* Confucianism from an idiosyncratic theoretical position into a legitimate form of Han Learning . . . and opened the door for full recognition of the scope of New Text Confucianism *(chin-wen hsüeh).*"[52] He passed on his ideas to two students, Wei Yüan (1794–1856) and Kung Tzu-chen (1792–1841), who widened their scope into a nationally influential school of interpretation. Wei was the author of the *Hai-kuo t'u-chih* (Illustrated gazetteer of the maritime countries), published in 1844, a huge compendium of information on foreign countries based on materials assembled by Commissioner Lin Tse-hsü. It represented the first major response of

Chinese intellectuals to the challenge of the West and focused primarily on the need to beef up maritime defenses. In the preface, Wei made his famous comment that the work was compiled "for the purpose of using barbarians to attack barbarians, using barbarians to negotiate with barbarians, and learning the superior techniques of the barbarians to control the barbarians."[53] The last phrase of that remark became the rallying cry of the Self-Strengthening Movement during the last half of the nineteenth century. Kung Tzu-chen's influence was based not on a successful career in administration (he held only minor offices, owing partly to poor handwriting) but on his writings, which often drew on the *Kung-yang* to "satirize current political events and inveigh against despotism."[54] Both K'ang Yu-wei and Liang Ch'i-ch'ao were directly inspired by Kung's writings.

The Modern Text school in the Ch'ing culminated in the thought of K'ang Yu-wei (1856–1927) and Liang Ch'i-ch'ao (1873–1929), the most influential intellectuals of the last two decades of the Ch'ing dynasty. They were the leaders of a group that might best be called syncretists, "seeking to identify truth whether it was to be found in China or the West (or Japan, where several of them began to learn about the West, and some of whose thinkers were themselves wrestling with the problem of what form Westernization should take in their country), and to combine the best of both intellectual worlds."[55] K'ang went much farther than any of his predecessors and asserted that the *Tso-chuan,* among other texts, was not only tampered with by Liu Hsin in the Han but actually forged by him for reasons of political expediency. K'ang's purpose was to reinterpret the Confucian classics in such a way that Confucius could be represented as a reforming angel who advocated sweeping institutional changes in order to restore the wealth and prosperity of the state. According to Liang Ch'i-ch'ao, K'ang "decided that the *Spring and Autumn Annals* had been Confucius' creation for the purposes of institutional reforms, and that written words were nothing but symbols, like a secret telegraphic code and the notes of musical scores, which cannot be understood without oral instructions."[56]

The extent to which the attitudes and approaches of the Sung *Ch'un-ch'iu* scholars come to life again in K'ang Yu-wei (who apparently saw no connection) is illustrated by Hsiao's evaluation of K'ang's thought:

K'ang lived in an age when drastic social and political changes dictated a thorough reexamination of the Confucian tradition and an earnest endeavor to adapt the empire intellectually and institutionally to the new conditions. His interpretations of the classics constituted the most serious attempt to date to make this adaptation. They were often forced and arbitrary because Confucianism did not anticipate the problems of modern times. In order to bridge the gap K'ang found it necessary to depart, often radically, from the accepted interpretations of the classics.[57]

K'ang's student Liang Ch'i-ch'ao became "the foremost intellectual leader of the first two decades of twentieth-century China."[58] Liang was one of the most powerful writers in modern China, and his ideas on constitutional government and popular sovereignty did much to prepare the ground for the Revolution of 1911 and the May Fourth Movement that followed. He read widely in Western philosophy and literature (in translation) and traveled to both Europe and the United States on several occasions. He was, in many ways, the father of liberalism in modern China and inspired a new generation of thinkers, among the most prominent of which was Hu Shih, to place a special value on the dignity of the human individual.[59]

It is remarkable how closely many of the attitudes of K'ang Yu-wei and Liang Ch'i-ch'ao parallel those of Sun Fu in the Northern Sung. In both the early Sung and the late Ch'ing, it was a sense of crisis and a profound sense of responsibility that impelled Chinese intellectuals like K'ang and Liang to try to unify life and thought, to synthesize the world outside with the world inside (in Mencian terms).[60] In Hsiao's words, K'ang sought to weave "a synthetic philosophical fabric out of Confucian warp and Western woof."[61] As leader of the Hundred-Day Reform in 1898, K'ang had come very close to implementing many of his ideals in practice and had been stopped only by the last-minute intervention of the Empress Dowager Tz'u-hsi. Both men, in fact, failed to accomplish the task they had set for themselves and for China in their lifetime.

On the other hand, perhaps they were not as far off the mark as many later Chinese intellectuals believed. Both K'ang and Liang, and the Sung thinkers whom we have considered in this work, placed great importance in the institution of the emperor. Their reasons for doing so were often different (hav-

ing to do with the different circumstances of life at the time),
but they realized that the emperor represented a force for
unity at a time when unity was threatened. In the time of the
Sung, that unity had been enforced by an emperor who centralized political institutions in his own hands but who admin-
istered all-under-heaven through a bureaucracy now in the
hands of a Confucian elite, an elite who hoped that the emperor would reign while they ruled. In the late Ch'ing, K'ang
and Liang looked to the emperor not as a ruler but as a constitutional monarch, who represented in his person a symbol of
national unity but who would take no active role in governance.
K'ang and Liang's views, as it happened, were rejected by
younger intellectuals infatuated with more fashionable republican views imported (with Liang's help) from the West, and
toward the end of their lives the two ceased to exert much
influence on the intellectual life of their contemporaries. Indeed, both came to be looked on by many as reactionaries. If
now, however, we can see some benefits to a constitutional
monarch in East Asia that may not have been as apparent to
previous generations, it is partly because of the contribution
that the institution of the emperor made to the modernization
of Japan.[62] In any case, the neo-Confucian legacy of the Northern Sung was clearly present in the modernization of both
Japan and China and employed to advocate a limited, constitutional monarchy, not blind obedience to the ruler.

Relevance for the Future in China

Modern intellectuals in China have generally been unwilling to
see the many parallels between their own ideas and those of the
early Sung. One can only suppose that they considered themselves such mortal enemies of the neo-Confucian tradition that
they assumed that they had nothing in common with the origi-
nators of that tradition. In this regard, it is tempting to compare the reactions of French intellectuals to their monarch just
prior to the French Revolution, and those of Russian intellectuals to the autocracy of the tsar, with the reactions of Chinese
intellectuals just prior to their own republican revolution in the
twentieth century. In all three cases, the intellectuals were in
complete revolt against the privileges enjoyed by a ruling class

that was no longer capable of assuming the responsibilities of governance but that barred the door to participation in government by other segments of the educated population. The hatred of those privileges, combined with the intellectuals' sense of impotence in influencing the course of events around them, made them so obsessed with equality that they were quite willing to sacrifice their liberties in order to achieve it. All these revolutions then produced, in the course of time, despotisms that were far more damaging to freedom than the governments they had originally set out to overthrow. As Tocqueville remarked, prophetically for China, although he intended it as a description of the French Revolution:

> In tracing the course of the Revolution I shall draw attention to the events, mistakes, misjudgments which led . . . Frenchmen to abandon their original ideal and, turning their backs on freedom, to acquiesce in an equality of servitude under the master of all Europe [i.e., Napoleon]. I shall show how a government, both stronger and more autocratic than the one which the Revolution had overthrown, centralized once more the entire administration, made itself all-powerful, suppressed our dearly bought liberties, and replaced them by a mere pretense of freedom; how the so-called "sovereignty of the people" came to be based on the votes of an electorate that was neither given adequate information nor an opportunity of getting together and deciding on one policy rather than another; and how the much vaunted "free vote" in matters of taxation came to signify no more than the meaningless assent of assemblies tamed to servility and silence. Thus the nation was deprived both of the means of self-government and of the chief guarantee of its rights, that is to say the freedom of speech, thought, and literature which ranked among the most valuable and noblest achievements of the Revolution—though the then government professed to be acting under its auspices and invoked its august name.[63]

But, whatever the cause of the misunderstanding by modern Chinese intellectuals of neo-Confucian views on obedience, the result has been that they have oversimplified and greatly underestimated the significance of neo-Confucian political thought. The time has come to put those prejudices aside. The great task that lies ahead for Chinese intellectuals is to rediscover the classical roots of Chinese civilization and let their nourishment revitalize the ideas and institutions of modern China. Perhaps one way to begin is to do what the early Sung neo-Confucians did: discard the accumulated commentaries of the centuries and go back to the classics.[64] Chinese intellectuals might do worse than to pick up the task where K'ang Yu-wei and Liang Ch'i-ch'ao left off. In both cases, they advocated neither a mindless imitation of the Chinese past and rejection of the West, nor an equally mindless denial of the Chinese past and acceptance of the most intellectually fashionable Western ideas such as liberalism or socialism, but a new synthesis composed of what is both best and practically possible from both traditions.[65]

The task ahead for the next generation of Chinese intellectuals is a formidable one—nothing less than reconciling the Chinese heritage with the influences emanating from the West. To put it another way, China must find a way to be both fully modern and fully Chinese. In the past, the Confucian heritage has been an astonishingly flexible and rich source of inspiration. The last major reassessment was in the Sung dynasty in response to a wide range of challenges and opportunities, which included the intellectual and spiritual contributions of Buddhism and Taoism, as well as a new confidence among the literati that they could bridge the gap between life and thought.

A new reevaluation of the Confucian heritage similar in magnitude but entirely different in content to the neo-Confucian revival in the Sung is now called for. It is well to remember that early neo-Confucian thinkers like Chou Tun-yi, Shao Yung, and Chang Tsai were so well versed in Buddhist and Taoist categories of thinking that they were able to integrate them fully into a new, but Confucian, view of the world. In like manner, a new generation of Chinese thinkers must now appropriate and digest the basic categories of thinking of Western civilization as well as Chinese civilization, by making these categories their own, and then reformulating them in a new way. They must seek to do in the realm of thought what painters like Hsü Pei-hung have done in the realm of art—absorb the Western views, immerse themselves in the Western mind—and then return to draw on the deep well of the Chinese tradition to create something new that represents a synthesis of both.[66] This is an ambitious undertaking, to be sure, requiring intellectuals less inclined than their predecessors to accept uncritically the most current Western ideas and in the process abandon their own cultural traditions.[67]

The task may take several generations to complete. It will have to begin with a consideration of how Chinese civilization may have been predisposed to a more centralized model of institutional development from the very origins of civilization itself, as K. C. Chang has proposed.[68] It will then trace how Confucian ideology, and various accidental factors (such as the control of China by various conquest dynasties), accelerated the growth of autocratic power in China and then speculate on possible currents within the Confucian (and Taoist) heritage that might provide a foundation for a new Confucian ethic embodying the aspirations of the Chinese people for greater political freedom and social responsibility, but within the framework of the Chinese heritage. Democracy in China, after all, must grow out of Chinese soil if it is to be successful.[69] The tragic mistake of the Chinese intellectuals who followed K'ang Yu-wei and Liang Ch'i-ch'ao was to adopt the extreme position either of repudiating the Confucian heritage altogether or of trying to breathe life into a form of Confucianism that had in effect already become a corpse. The real task is not to bury one or the other but to reconcile them.

I began this study by claiming that authority is the right by which power is exercised and that all cooperative action requires authority.[70] In China, the final source of authority, even before Confucius, was believed to reside in nature, or heaven. This belief enabled later Confucian officials to hold rulers accountable to a higher moral authority. Exactly how heaven manifested its wishes remained a point on which later Chinese thinkers often disagreed. Taoists claimed (two thousand years before Adam Smith) that spontaneity and not guidance by the state was most likely to approximate the natural way. Legalists, with a supremely pessimistic assessment of the natural endowments of the human personality, believed that the common good was served only when the ruler set numerous limits, through the mechanism of law, to the scope of human action.

Confucians tried a more middle ground between the Taoist

children of light and the Legalist children of darkness. In general, they took human nature to be good, but susceptible to corruption. Education, particularly moral education, was necessary in order to develop the potential for good and avoid the potential for evil. Since the development of one's potential was thus in some way related to the degree of one's education, and since not everybody could afford an education, or for that matter was inclined to seek one even if he could, the Confucians were placed in the position of advocating rule by an educated elite.

Unfortunately for that elite, rulers customarily gained or lost power by force, not moral suasion. If they were so inclined, they recognized the value of moral laws in governing a state and thus retained the services of Confucian officials. But many were not so inclined. Under those rulers, Confucian officials were often unemployed. Without any institutional autonomy, they appealed to the only force greater than the ruler—nature. Their solution to the problem of what to do with a bad ruler was thus to hope that they could kick him upstairs and turn him into a symbol while they actually ran the government. Of course, they were never able actually to say that in so many words (hence the value of encoding their message in the form of commentaries on the *Ch'un-ch'iu*). They advocated, in effect, a *wu-wei* ruler, presiding over a state governed by officials trained in Confucian values and dedicated to the common interest of increasing the prosperity of the people and the power of the state. Their dream was realized, paradoxically, in Meiji Japan, but the Japanese got there via feudal institutions based on military force, not moral suasion.

Idealistic intellectuals in China in the twentieth century face a situation in some ways similar to the predicament of the Sung Confucians. They have no institutional base of support and a government that has all the power. When they invoke a higher authority, as they did in the May Fourth Movement by appealing to science and democracy (and then to Marxism-Leninism) or in Tiananmen Square in June 1989 by appealing to democracy and human rights, that authority originated in the West (or derived its legitimacy from having originated in the West). Those in power were then able to claim that by suppressing such movements they were defending China from outside influences.

Tom Metzger has argued that modern Chinese intellectuals have continued to manifest traditional Chinese assumptions even as they attack them using terminology derived from Western categories of thinking. Their crucial assumption, he believes, is one of optimism regarding human nature, which, when combined with the Western strain of optimistic thought exemplified by the Enlightenment (and introduced into China in the form of either Marxism or liberalism), produces a vision of the future in which human conflict will one day cease.[71] The outcome of such an assumption is very different from the Western notion of democracy as it evolved in nineteenth-century Britain and America, which assumes a state of perpetual contention between colliding interests (based on the belief that the interests of the butcher and the interests of the cow can never be fully reconciled). From the perspective of the Sung neo-Confucians studied here, I would add to Metzger's argument another ingredient.

All the Chinese thinkers whom I have reviewed in the Sung operated on the assumption that the appropriate metaphor for order is harmony. If followed properly, nature's laws, manifested either by Sun Fu's ritual or by Ch'eng I's principle, would issue forth in a political community in which all parts fit together perfectly. Furthermore, nature's laws are complicated and can be fully understood only by those trained in their ways, that is, an elite. The notion that the unwashed masses, contending against each other in a perpetual struggle of conflicting interests, would be capable of self-government is so utterly foreign to the Chinese tradition that it does not even enter the equation.[72]

If this metaphor for order—of harmony, not balance—does indeed still dominate the Chinese way of thinking, then the form that democracy will take in places like Taiwan (and, one hopes someday, China itself) may be different from what we have come to expect in the West. It will likely have more affiliations with the European tradition focusing on seeing the common good *(kung)* emerging not so much from the clash of individual wants *(ssu)* as from a willingness to see those wants in the larger context of the human need to be part of a community. The human personality is a complicated and mysterious thing. Liberal democracy rooted in a belief in the autonomy of the individual is one expression of a fundamental truth about the nature of the human personality. But so is a democracy rooted in an equally fundamental truth that the full potential of the human personality can be realized only in the context of a community. These goods may—and do—come into conflict, but that does not diminish their validity or the value of political systems based on an emphasis on one more than the other.[73]

There is no reason to believe that the West has managed to achieve a perfect balance between the needs of the individual and the needs of the community. (Indeed, there is plenty of evidence to the contrary.)[74] China may even be able to make its own contribution to democratic theory and practice (or stimulate the West to return to its own roots for inspiration) by defining human nature as fundamentally social, as fulfilling its potential through contributing to the common good, cultivating its reason and virtue instead of surrendering to individual appetites, stressing responsibility as well as rights, cooperation as well as competition, reciprocal relationships as well as individual assertion. Whatever the case, it seems undeniable that attitudes toward authority that reach back to the Sung dynasty, and beyond, will turn out to have momentous consequences for the present and future of China. It is well to remember, once again, that the whole concept of human rights in the West is based on the assumption that there exist universal moral laws that transcend the positive laws of any particular sovereign state. Human rights, in short, grew out of a tradition of natural law that shared many important features with Confucian universalism.

The events of history, meanwhile, rush on. In the last few years, two trends seem to have emerged that will have a bearing on how these intellectual assumptions are carried out in practice. First, the miraculous growth of the postwar economies in East Asia has created a wide spectrum of pluralistic institutions, a necessary but admittedly not sufficient condition for real democracy and freedom. Second, a middle class has arisen that has demanded, and in some cases received (in Taiwan and Korea), democratic concessions from the government. Confucianism has played an undeniable role in fostering that economic transformation in East Asia.[75] One can only hope that these practical developments will offer a new sense of confidence to Chinese intellectuals who want so desperately to get off the benches and rejoin the great game of politics as players and not spectators. This is not the place for a detailed treatment of these developments or for predictions of how the Chinese experience can be integrated into the international terms of discourse on democracy and human rights. Suffice it to say that, when such a task is undertaken, it must take into account the rich heritage of the Sung neo-Confucians. They are not outdated and irrelevant ancestors of contemporary heroes of democracy like Wei Jingsheng. They are his brothers. (And they are ours.)

I have hanging in my office a pair of scrolls with a poem in K'ang Yu-wei's own calligraphy, given to my parents in China by one of their students in the early 1930s. The poem goes something like this: "Now to ride the winds of heaven on a phoenix and now to plunge into the azure sea on the back of a mighty whale." The Northern Sung thinkers had that kind of spirit. What China needs now is another generation with the courage of the early Sung thinkers (and K'ang) who dared to rise above the narrow horizons of time and place and ride the winds of heaven.

Abbreviations

Abbreviations Used in the Notes and the Bibliography

AHR	*American Historical Review*
CCC	*Ch'un-ch'iu chuan,* by Liu Ch'ang
CCCC	*Ch'un-ch'iu ching-chieh,* by Sun Chüeh
CCFL	*Ch'un-ch'iu fan-lu,* by Tung Chung-shu
CCHC	*Tsung Kung-yang-hsüeh lun Ch'un-ch'iu ti hsing-chih,* by Juan Chih-sheng
CCTWFW	*Ch'un-ch'iu tsun-wang fa-wei,* by Sun Fu
CHY	"Sung-ju Ch'un-ch'iu tsun-wang yao-yi ti fa-wei yü ch'i cheng-chih ssu-hsiang," by Ch'en Ch'ing-hsin
CYK	*Ching-i k'ao,* compiled by Chu I-tsun
ECCP	*Eminent Chinese of the Ch'ing Period*
FEQ	*Far Eastern Quarterly*
HJAS	*Harvard Journal of Asiatic Studies*
IESS	*International Encyclopedia of the Social Sciences*
JAOS	*Journal of the American Oriental Society*
JAS	*Journal of Asian Studies*
JHI	*Journal of the History of Ideas*
LSCY	*Ch'un-ch'iu chi-yi,* compiled by Li Ming-fu
PEW	*Philosophy East and West*
SKTY	*Ssu-k'u ch'üan-shu tsung-mu t'i-yao*
SMFHC	*Sun Ming-fu hsiao-chi,* by Sun Fu

Notes

Chapter 1: Introduction

1. "On the Nature of Political Obligation," *Journal of the Royal Institute of Philosophy* 43 (October 1968): 321.

2. Isaiah Berlin, "Does Political Theory Still Exist?" in *Concepts and Categories* (New York: Penguin, 1981), p. 148.

3. Michael Oakeshott prefers to list three responses, but his third is really a combination of the first two and represents a modern development (see his introduction to the Basil Blackwell edition of *Leviathan* [Oxford, 1960], p. liv).

4. See *IESS,* s.v. *authority.*

5. Amitai Etzioni, e.g., defines *authority* as "legitimate power" (*Complex Organizations,* p. 14). It is clear from Etzioni's discussion of the term, in which he describes authority (normative, remunerative, and coercive) in terms strictly "of the kind of power employed" (p. 15), that he is interested primarily in those aspects of authority that can be measured empirically. This is further implied by his remark in the introduction that "sociology was born out of the intellectual search for a secular and empirical explanation of the social order" (p. xv). For an interesting discussion of this issue in the context of the early T'ang, see Wechsler, *Offerings of Jade and Silk,* esp. pp. 9–36.

6. See Peter Winch's discussion ("Authority," pp. 107–108) of Max Weber's three categories of authority, in which he argues that Weber's categories are not conceptually distinct at all and that the effort to see them as such is misleading.

7. Arendt, "What Is Authority?" pp. 92–93.

8. See also Friedrich, *Tradition and Authority:* "Philosophically, the

anarchist argument rests upon an assumed 'goodness of human nature,' and of nature in general; hence also the equality of all men. Authority, even if understood as the capacity for reasoned elaboration, rests upon the contrary assumption that men are unequal in this respect, and that 'goodness' cannot be specified, except in terms of values which imply this capacity for reasoning. Authority and liberty are, therefore, not antithetical, but complementary. Only a measure of order which authority makes possible will enable men to enjoy a degree of liberty. There can be no authority without liberty, as there can be no liberty without authority, and to juxtapose them is to falsify both" (p. 121).

9. Arendt, "What Is Authority?" p. 97. Arendt goes on to say, prophetically, "Modern spokesmen of authority, who, even in the short intervals when public opinion provides a favorable climate for neo-conservatism, remain well aware that theirs is an almost lost cause, are of course eager to point to this distinction between tyranny and authority. Where the liberal writer sees an essentially assured progress in the direction of freedom, which is only temporarily interrupted by some dark forces of the past, the conservative sees a process of doom which started with the dwindling of authority, so that freedom, after it lost the restricting limitations which protected its boundaries, became helpless, defenseless, and bound to be destroyed. (It is hardly fair to say that only liberal political thought is primarily interested in freedom; there is hardly a school of political thought in our history which is not centered around the idea of freedom, much as the concept of liberty may vary with different writers and in different political circumstances. The only exception of any consequence to this statement seems to me to be the political philosophy of Thomas Hobbes, who, of course, was anything but a conservative.)"

10. Dennis Wrong, *Power: Its Forms, Bases, and Uses* (New York: Harper & Row, 1979), p. 2. The first three chapters of *Power* deal explicitly with this issue.

11. Wrong adds two more: authority by coercion and by inducement, by means of which he makes a distinction between coercion (punishment) and inducement (reward), on the one hand, which he sees as falling within the province of a relationship based strictly on power, and the threat of punishment or the promise of reward, on the other, which he sees as falling more within the province of authority— a police officer's "authority" does not have to be backed up by actual shooting in order to compel obedience to his command, e.g. I do not agree with Wrong, simply because I do not think that such a distinction—although a real one—justifies including the threat of coercion or the promise of reward when defining the term *authority* (see ibid., pp. 35–49).

12. Winch, "Authority," p. 102.

13. See Romeyn Taylor's "Chinese Hierarchy in Comparative Perspective," which begins with the following question: "How are we to understand the history of a nonmodern civilization without refracting and distorting what we see through the prism of the ostensibly individualistic and egalitarian modern culture in which most of us live and which we tend to take as normative?" (p. 490). Taylor is influenced by Louis Dumont's study of Indian caste, *Homo Hierarchicus,* which according to Taylor argues that "the structuring principle in the historical development of Indian social hierarchy—that is, of caste— proves to be the encompassment of politics and economy by religion. Thus, hierarchical relationships in India are to be understood in religious rather than in economic terms" (p. 492). In applying Dumont's paradigm to China, Taylor concludes that the hierarchical views of the Chinese are similarly rooted in a religious understanding: "Chinese society in its entirety came to be hierarchically organized in an empire, and this empire-society was understood by its members to be universal (*tianxia,* 'all under heaven'). No autonomous political domain, no body politic, no state was acknowledged to exist in contradistinction to society. But the social whole itself was encompassed by the pantheon of the official religion, and this in turn was encompassed by the cosmos. It was the task of the official religion to integrate these three domains, all of which were hierarchical in form, nested one within another to constitute a hierarchy of hierarchies. They were understood to be the products of a continuous cosmogonic process of differentiation and interaction that proceeded from the transcendent One and were therefore ultimately consubstantial and identical" (p. 493).

14. Ibid., p. 495.

15. Kwang-chih Chang, *The Archaeology of Ancient China,* 4th ed. (New Haven, Conn.: Yale University Press, 1986), pp. 415–422.

16. As Romeyn Taylor put it, "The formal hierarchy of social groups is intelligible when its encompassment by pantheon and cosmos is borne in mind. The highest in rank were responsible for maintaining the social order in a state of submission to the cosmic harmony. The son of heaven, with his agents, mediated between humankind and the pantheon and governed the world. The civil officials, unlike their military counterparts, had a double loyalty to their emperor and to their master, Confucius. They were at once the emperor's servants and the autonomous custodians of the Way" ("Chinese Hierarchy in Comparative Perspective," p. 498).

17. See Chow, *The May Fourth Movement,* esp. pp. 300–313.

18. Bo Yang, *Ch'ou-lou ti chung-kuo jen* (Taipei: Lin Pai, 1985), pp. 36–37. The translation is taken from Barmé and Minford, eds.,

Seeds of Fire, p. 171. See also Lu Hsün, "Diary of a Madman," in *Selected Stories of Lu Hsün* (New York: W. W. Norton, 1977), pp. 7–18.

19. For a discussion of the program, see Edward Gunn, "The Rhetoric of *River Elegy:* From Cultural Criticism to Social Act," in *Chinese Democracy and the Crisis of 1989: Chinese and American Reflections* (Albany: State University of New York Press, 1993), pp. 247–261.

20. Zhengyuan Fu, *Autocratic Tradition and Chinese Politics,* pp. 58–59.

21. Wright's remarks are taken from the "comments" section in Ho Ping-ti and Tang Tsou, *China in Crisis,* vol. 1, *China's Heritage and the Communist Political System* (Chicago: University of Chicago Press, 1968), p. 39.

22. Nathan, *Chinese Democracy,* p. 114.

23. George Yu, e.g., has written that "the Confucian concept of loyalty began with the ideal that the emperor as Son of Heaven represented the final source of authority, and by implication made correct decisions. To differ with the emperor's wishes and policies was tantamount to disagreeing with the will of Heaven. Thus the concept of loyalty became in practice that of loyalty to the emperor's will" (*Party Politics in Republican China* [Berkeley: University of California Press, 1966], p. 2). For a discussion of Max Weber's views on this issue, see Thomas Metzger's *Escape from Predicament.* Metzger notes that Confucianism, in Weber's words, "reduced tension with the world to an absolute minimum. . . . Completely absent in the Confucian ethic was any tension . . . between ethical demand and human shortcoming" (p. 4). He also notes that S. N. Eisenstadt has concluded that Confucian ideology "did not focus on a moral order differentiated from the political status quo" (p. 4).

24. *The Analects,* trans. Lau, 13:18.

25. See Lei Tsung-hai, "Rise of the Emperor System."

26. See Creel, *Origins of Statecraft,* pp. 81–100.

27. Legge, trans., *The Shoo King,* p. 292.

28. Legge, trans., *Mencius,* pp. 392, 296.

29. *Works of Hsüntze,* trans. Homer Dubs, p. 125. Hsün Tzu also said, "Heaven does not beget the people for the sake of the ruler; Heaven institutes the ruler for the sake of the people" (see *Hsün Tzu,* 27, "Ta Lüeh," quoted in Hsiao, "Legalism and Autocracy in Traditional China," p. 114).

30. Hsiao, *Chinese Political Thought,* p. 602.

31. See Hsiao, *Cheng-chih ssu-hsiang,* p. 432 (405), on Wang T'ung, and p. 434 (406), on Han Yü. (The page numbers given first are to the 1982 edition. This edition is much easier to read than the previous one, which came out in several reprints, each one more difficult to read than its predecessor. For those who have the older edition (1945–1946), page numbers to that edition appear in parentheses.)

32. Ibid., p. 451 (423).

33. See Chan, "Neo-Confucian Concept *Li*," esp. pp. 137–142.

34. For a partial list of some of those men, see Hartwell, "Demographic, Political, and Social Transformations of China," p. 406. Hartwell refers to this group collectively as the "founding elite."

35. *Tzu* was Ming-fu. He was from P'ing-yang in Chin-chou in present-day Shansi province. *Tzu* was Cheng-shu. He was also known as I ch'uan hsien-sheng and was from Lo-yang in present-day Honan province. *Tzu* was K'ang-hou, *hao* was Wu-yi, and he was posthumously known as Wen-ting. He was from Ch'ung-an in Chien-ning chün (modern-day Chien-yang in Fukien province).

36. Quoted in Treadgold, *The West in Russia and China*, vol. 1, *Russia*, p. 423.

37. The translation is W. W. Jackson's, from Dante's *Convivio* (Oxford: Clarendon Press, 1909), quoted in Hazard Adam's anthology *Critical Theory since Plato* (New York: Harcourt, Brace, Jovanovich, 1992), p. 121.

38. *SKTY* 1:539.

39. Two additional primary sources, other than those mentioned above, have been particularly valuable in collecting the comments of prominent scholars on the *Ch'un-ch'iu* during the period covered by this study. One is the *Ch'un-ch'iu chi-yi* compiled by the Southern Sung scholar Li Ming-fu. The work consists of fifty *chüan* preceded by an introduction *(kang-ling)* of three *chüan*, with a preface by Li dated 1220. It is a compilation of comments on the *Ch'un-ch'iu* by Chou Tun-yi (1017–1073), Ch'eng Hao (1032–1085), Ch'eng I (1033–1107), Fan Tsu-yü (1041–1098), Hsieh Liang-tso (1050–1103), Yang Shih (1053–1135), Hou Chung-liang (fl. 1100), Yin T'un (1071–1142), Liu Hsüan (1045–1087), Hsieh Shih, Hu An-kuo (1074–1138), Lü Tsu-ch'ien (1137–1181), Hu Hung (1105–1155), Li T'ung (1088–1158), Chu Hsi (1130–1200), and Chang Shih (1133–1180). The other is the *Ching-i k'ao*, compiled by the Ch'ing scholar Chu I-tsun (1629–1709), a copiously annotated bibliography of works dealing with the classics in three hundred *chüan* (of which *chüan* 168–210 are concerned with the *Ch'un-ch'iu*) from the Han (202 B.C.–A.D. 220) to the end of the K'ang-hsi reign (1661–1722) in the Ch'ing (included in Ssu-yu Teng and Knight Biggerstaff, *An Annotated Bibliography of Selected Chinese Reference Works*, 3rd ed. (Cambridge, Mass.: Harvard University Press, 1971), pp. 41–42). It also contains prefaces of works that have been lost. There are no studies in English that focus specifically on *Ch'un-ch'iu* studies in the Northern Sung. In his early work on neo-Confucianism, de Bary dealt in passing with some of the important issues and figures of the period, as has James T. C. Liu in his monographic studies on Fan Chung-yen (989–1052), Wang An-shih (1021–1086), and Ou-yang Hsiu (1007–1072) (see de Bary, "Reappraisal,"

and "Common Tendencies"). There is, of course, a long and distinguished tradition of scholarship in Western languages on the *Ch'un-
ch'iu* and its three commentaries, including the work of such pioneers
as Henri Maspero, Bernard Karlgren, and Göran Malmqvist. These
works, however, concern themselves with textual questions and are of
little assistance in dealing with questions of political theory during the
Sung dynasty. Outside these few safe havens of scholarship the waters
are all uncharted. The best coverage of the subject in Japanese is in
Morohashi Tetsuji's work on Sung neo-Confucianism, published originally as his dissertation in the late 1930s ("Jūgaku no mokuteki to
Sō-ju no katsudō" [pp. 199–279 deal with the *Ch'un-ch'iu*]). There is
also an article published in 1943 by Sanaka Sō dealing with the rise of
a critical attitude toward the classics in the Sung, which covers in part
the work of Sun Fu ("Sōgaku ni okeru iwayuru hihan-teki kenkyū no
tanchō ni tsuite"). Fumoto Yasutaka's book on the development of
Confucianism in the Northern Sung also deals in part with *Ch'un-ch'iu*
scholarship *(Hoku-sō ni okeru jugaku no tenkai,* esp. pp. 61–79). These
works, however, do not depart substantially from the mainstream of
traditional Chinese historical interpretation and are therefore of
limited value for my purposes. Major secondary literature in Chinese
on the role of the *Ch'un-ch'iu* in Northern Sung China is confined
principally to two articles written by Chinese scholars in Hong Kong,
Ch'en Ch'ing-hsin ("Sung-ju Ch'un-ch'iu yao-yi ti fa-wei yü ch'i cheng-
chih ssu-hsiang") and Mou Jun-sun ("Liang Sung Ch'un-ch'iu hsüeh
chih chu-liu"). Juan Chih-sheng published his dissertation on the
Kung-yang tradition, "Ts'ung Kung-yang-hsüeh lun Ch'un-ch'iu ti
hsing-chih," and this has been very helpful. For background on the
classical tradition, P'i Hsi-jui's (1850–1908) *Ching-hsüeh li-shih,* written
in the nineteenth century and published in the twentieth in an annotated edition by Chou Yü-t'ung, remains unsurpassed.

Chapter 2: The Background of Neo-Confucianism

1. See Miyakawa Hisayuki, "Outline of the Naitō Hypothesis,"
pp. 537, 545. The validity of Naitō's argument depends greatly on
his definition of *modernity,* a topic too complex to be considered here.
For our purposes, it serves to underscore the importance of the Sung
as a major transition in Chinese history. Among other developments,
the breakup of the older social order made possible more channels
of social mobility, reminiscent in some ways of the new opportunities for men of merit that appeared during the late Ch'un-ch'iu and
early Chan-kuo periods. Then, as in the late T'ang, the Five Dynasties
period, and the Sung, society was becoming much more open. Sound-
ing a cautionary note, James T. C. Liu has written that "neither did the
'early modern' Sung period generate something more modern than

itself, nor did any 'late modern' age ever appear. And to call it a 'renaissance' hardly explains how the Sung established itself as an orthodox model in many ways for almost a thousand years" (see "A Note on Classifying Sung Confucians," p. 2). Liu prefers to call all Confucian scholars who were not members of the Ch'eng-Chu school "neo-traditional" Confucians (see also his "The Neo-Traditional Period in Chinese History").

2. See de Bary's introduction to *Principle and Practicality,* ed. de Bary and Bloom (pp. 4–12), where he treats the complexity of such terms as *secularism* as they apply both to the Renaissance and to China. In both contexts, to say that there was a greater turning to the affairs of this world is not to say that those affairs were devoid of religious content or significance.

3. Thomas Metzger calls the confidence of the early Sung neo-Confucians the "radical optimism" of the eleventh century (*Escape from Predicament,* p. 78).

4. Whether the *Ch'un-ch'iu* should be referred to as *history* or *classic* is a problem, as there is evidence for both interpretations. The subject matter is history, so it should be considered history. On the other hand, most Chinese commentators have believed that Confucius imbedded in the text certain judgments of praise and blame regarding these historical events and that the value of the text lies in these judgments. This interpretation would suggest placing the text in the category of a classic. Traditionally, in fact, it has been included as one of the "Five Classics." In this study, I will refer to it as a classic, but the reader should remember that there is more than one opinion on this matter.

5. For the standard treatment of the history between the fall of the T'ang and the rise of the Sung, see Wang Gungwu, *The Structure of Power in North China during the Five Dynasties.* The similarities, in terms of the existence of many states contending with each other for control of China, between the Ch'un-ch'iu period in ancient China and the more immediate Five Dynasties period might have made the *Ch'un-ch'iu* seem more than distantly relevant to Chinese politics to eleventh-century scholars.

6. The terms *tsun-wang* and *jang-i,* incidentally, first appear in Ssu-ma Ch'ien's (145?–90? B.C.) *Shih-chi,* but separately, not together.

7. In Wang Gungwu's words, the Shan-yüan treaty began a period of peace "that lasted almost one hundred and twenty years. Liao's relations with the Sung were the nearest thing to equality in Chinese history until modern times" ("The Rhetoric of a Lesser Empire," p. 55). As will become evident below, the Sung commentators on the *Ch'un-ch'iu* were less than enthusiastic about this policy of using diplomacy with "barbarians" to compensate for China's weakness. They reflected

a long-standing tradition. As Tao Jing-shen puts it, "The traditional attitude toward the alien peoples was based largely on the *Ch'un-ch'iu*" ("Barbarians or Northerners," p. 66). Tao's article contains a very interesting discussion of the Sung attitudes toward "barbarians" and points out that Sung officials made a distinction between other northern tribes and the Khitan, who had become almost "civilized" by having adopted so many Chinese institutions and were therefore no longer to be considered "barbarians."

8. This is a variation of George Hatch's formulation (see his "The Thought of Su Hsün," esp. the introduction). Wing-tsit Chan's umbrella is even bigger. He speaks of the "all-inclusive character of Neo-Confucianism," which "embraces all essential phases of life—philosophy, ethics, religion, government, literature, mental discipline, etc." ("Integrative Force," p. 317). The Sung thinker Liu Yi (1017–1086) divided Confucianism (the Way) into three parts—substance *(t'i)*, function *(yung)*, and literary expression *(wen)*—which correspond roughly to metaphysics (the foundation of moral philosophy and moral cultivation), politics, and aesthetics (see de Bary, Chan, and Watson, eds., *Sources of Chinese Tradition*, 1:384).

9. See Tillman, "A New Direction in Confucian Scholarship"; and the introduction to Tillman's *Confucian Discourse*.

10. James T. C. Liu, e.g., wants to restrict the definition to the Ch'eng-Chu school: "The term Neo-Confucianism was originally used in Western literature to designate the Chu Hsi school of thought. Since the middle of the present century, it has also been loosely applied to other Sung Confucians, in the broad sense that they were different from those of earlier periods. This has led to some confusion and needs to be clarified. Recent scholarship prefers to revert to the original, narrow usage. Neo-Confucianism refers exclusively to the Chu Hsi school or Li-hsueh, the School of Principles, and no one else" (*China Turning Inward*, p. 43).

11. Tillman, *Confucian Discourse*, pp. 2–3.

12. Ch'ien Mu, *Cheng-chih te-shih*, p. 64. See also Hucker's discussion of Sung government in the introduction to *Dictionary of Official Titles*.

13. Much of this paragraph is based on Worthy, "Founding of Sung China," pp. 180–195, 264–294.

14. See Labadie, "Rulers and Soldiers." Labadie questions the conventional wisdom that the Sung military was weak, arguing that it was, on the contrary, remarkably effective: "The Northern Sung basically solved the military problems that it faced at the beginning of the dynasty. The Khitan and Hsi-hsia were kept at bay through a combination of military and political methods. There were no significant internal rebellions. The military were kept under control and did not

threaten the security of the throne. In other words, the Sung was able to maintain an armed force effective enough to ward off foreign threats yet fully under the control of the civil government. This was accomplished by effective management that combined institutional mechanisms and personal relationships, drawing the military into the government apparatus" (p. 221).

15. Worthy, "Founding of Sung China," pp. 213–214.

16. Kracke, *Civil Service*, p. 59.

17. Lo, *Civil Service of Sung China*, p. 121. For comparative purposes, there were 3,123,731 employees of the federal government in the United States in 1989 (U.S. Bureau of the Census, *Statistical Abstracts of the United States, 1991* [Washington, D.C., 1991], p. 111).

18. Winston Lo notes that the personnel of the Byzantine bureaucracy "were drawn from a narrow segment of the population with traditions of scholarship and government service. Thus the vast majority of the people were excluded from it for lack of social standing, connections, or the wherewithal for purchasing entry positions. The Byzantine bureaucracy was therefore essentially a self-perpetuating closed system with few organic links to society at large. As such it could do little by way of disseminating the values and symbols of the Great Tradition or promoting support for the empire. The consequence was an unbridgeable gap between the people and the state. This gap explains why, for instance, a thousand years into the Hellenistic era, the people of Syria, Palestine, and Egypt still had little regard for Byzantium or for the Greco-Roman heritage that Byzantium stood for. This apathy facilitated the Arab conquest in the seventh century and led to the permanent loss of these provinces" (*Civil Service of Sung China*, p. 21).

19. Chaffee, *The Thorny Gates of Learning*, p. 142.

20. Bol, "The Sung Examination System and the *Shih*," p. 155. Bol also stresses the value of the examination system to integrating the educated elite of the country: "Local elites who chose to be *shih* found themselves reading the same books, practicing on the same questions, learning the same methods of composition, knowing about the same great aspirations, and (as the spread of neo-Confucian academies illustrates) choosing between the same alternatives" (p. 167).

21. Specifically, according to Chaffee, 57 percent of the civil service in 1046 held degrees, 45 percent in 1119, 31 percent in 1191, and 27 percent in 1213 (*The Thorny Gates of Learning*, p. 27).

22. Bol, "The Sung Examination System and the *Shih*," p. 152.

23. Chaffee, *The Thorny Gates of Learning*, p. 27. Even though the total number of officials had increased, the percentage drop in degree holders still resulted in a decline in absolute numbers of suc-

cessful candidates who came into the bureaucracy through the exams from 7,207 in 1046 to 5,256 in 1213 (ibid.).

24. Ch'ien Mu, *Cheng-chih te-shih,* pp. 63–72; and Worthy, "Founding of Sung China," pp. 245–253.

25. On these changes, see Kracke, *Civil Service,* pp. 40–41, 43–44, 36, respectively.

26. Kracke, "K'ai-feng," pp. 71–73.

27. Indeed, the world historian William McNeill has argued that the Commercial Revolution that began the long process of the modernization of Europe in the twelfth century was in part a consequence of the remarkable prosperity of the Chinese economy during the Sung. In *The Pursuit of Power* (Chicago: University of Chicago Press, 1982), he argues that "China's rapid evolution towards market-regulated behavior in the centuries on either side of the year 1000 tipped a critical balance in world history. I believe that China's example set humankind off on a thousand-year exploration of what could be accomplished by relying on prices and personal or small-group (the partnership or company) perception of private advantage as a way of orchestrating behavior on a mass scale" (p. 25). McNeill argues that the vast increase in the production of spices in Southeast Asia stimulated by the expanding market in China attracted the attention of Muslim traders, who then began to import spices into Europe in much larger quantities than ever before. See also Philip Curtin, *Cross-Cultural Trade in World History* (Cambridge: Cambridge University Press, 1984), particularly chap. 6.

28. Ho, "An Estimate of the Total Population," p. 50.

29. Chao, *Man and Land in Chinese History,* p. 35. Chao further notes that the population growth of the Northern Sung was a significant development in Chinese history: "The crucial turning point [in population growth] finally occurred when, after steady growth for 150 years during the Northern Sung, the population surpassed previous peaks by a sizable margin so that major wars and natural disasters became relatively less destructive. The only reason China survived the onslaught of the Mongols in the thirteenth century was . . . that the Mongol armies were too small and the Chinese population too large" (p. 42).

30. Ma, *Commercial Development,* p. 13.

31. Ho, "Early-Ripening Rice," pp. 200–218.

32. Ma, *Commercial Development,* p. 14. Kang Chao notes that, after the population growth of the Sung, the demand for labor-saving devices fell and with it the invention of new technology. Up to the Sung, "there had been a flow of inventions of new farm implements, including the improved plow that required less draft power, the share-plow that could turn over the sod to form a furrow, and the deep-

tooth harrow. All of these devices were labor saving by nature. This stream of inventions had run its course by the end of the twelfth century." After the Sung, "the technological development of farm tools in China literally stopped" (*Man and Land in Chinese History,* pp. 224, 225). This is one reason why China never went on to produce an Industrial Revolution analogous to what happened in England in the eighteenth century, in spite of the fact that all the necessary ingredients appeared to be present. There was simply no incentive (p. 227).

33. According to Shiba Yoshinobu, by the time of the Sung, "the Chinese had made great advances in the construction of seagoing junks. The ships were built with iron nails and waterproofed with a special oil. Their equipment included watertight bulkheads, buoyancy chambers, floating anchors, axial rudders in place of steering oars, scoops for taking samples off the sea floor, and small rockets propelled by gunpowder. The Chinese learned many of their techniques of navigation and shipbuilding from the Arabs, and in their use of iron nails, watertight bulkheads, pinewood planks, and floating anchors surpassed their teachers. Their ships were, in fact, more seaworthy than those of the Arabs. It is not surprising, therefore, that from the tenth century on, foreign merchants chose, when possible, to travel on Chinese ships" ("Sung Foreign Trade," p. 104).

34. Shiba Yoshinobu, "Urbanization," pp. 14, 30.

35. For more detailed treatment, see Shiba Yoshinobu, "Commercialization of Farm Products in the Sung Period."

36. Ma, *Commercial Development,* pp. 82–91; and Shiba Yoshinobu, "Urbanization," p. 42.

37. In this regard, the Sung example was not followed by later dynasties. The Sung policy of exploiting commercial activity as a major source of tax revenue was not repeated again in Chinese history until the nineteenth century, when the provinces needed money to pay for military expenses in connection with the Taiping rebellion. This appears to be at odds with the European experience, where the income financing the rise of the modern state was based on revenue from the commercial sector. In China, the state derived the bulk of its revenue from the extractive industries such as agriculture and salt.

38. According to Shiba Yoshinobu, "In the early Northern Sung, government revenue from the maritime trade amounted to 300,000 to 500,000 strings of cash, accounting for 2 or 3 percent of the total revenue" ("Sung Foreign Trade," p. 106). For a more detailed list of items traded with Southeast Asia, see ibid., p. 107.

39. Hartwell, "Northern Sung Monetary System," p. 285. Payments of silver to the Liao were offset by the increasing output of Chinese silver mines.

40. Hartwell, "International Commerce and Monetary Policy in Sung China," p. 2.

41. Hartwell, "Northern Sung Monetary System," p. 288.

42. Hartwell, "Financial Expertise," pp. 309–310.

43. Elvin, *Pattern of the Chinese Past*, p. 13.

44. Winston Lo notes that, "in the management of these monopolies, the bureaucracy showed considerable ingenuity. To maximize revenue from the wine monopoly, for instance, the state actually operated taverns featuring singing girls (who were registered as official courtesans)" (*Civil Service of Sung China*, p. 12).

45. Worthy, "Southern Sung Salt Administration," pp. 104, 110.

46. Hartwell, "Cycle of Economic Change," pp. 102–159.

47. By contrast, pig iron production in seventeenth-century England amounted to only twenty to forty-three thousand tons (Lo, *Civil Service of Sung China*, p. 11).

48. Shiba Yoshinobu, *Commerce and Society*, pp. 4–40.

49. Chao, *Man and Land in Chinese History*, pp. 43, 50–55. Chao refers to Lin-an in the Southern Sung as "the most magnificent city in Chinese history" (p. 50). For a fascinating and detailed description of the city, consult Jacques Gernet, *Daily Life in China on the Eve of the Mongol Invasion, 1250–1276* (Stanford, Calif.: Stanford University Press, 1962). Chao also notes that no other city in China after the Sung reached a population of even one million until after the middle of the nineteenth century. Shanghai—the largest city in modern China—did not reach 2.5 million until after 1925 (p. 56).

50. Kang Chao estimates that in 1220 about 21 percent of the population in China lived in cities, in sharp contrast to the estimated 7.7 percent of the population of urban dwellers in the late nineteenth century in China (*Man and Land in Chinese History*, p. 60). Chao believes "the most crucial factor underlying this pattern of development [in the Sung] to be the gradual increase in the output per unit of agricultural labor inputs. With an enhanced rate of surplus grain, the rural sector could support a larger and larger urban sector" (p. 61).

51. Ma, *Commercial Development*, pp. 161–162.

52. See the map in ibid., p. 64.

53. Chao, *Man and Land in Chinese History*, p. 49.

54. According to Kang Chao, "land fragmentation was a result of tremendous population pressure and shortage of farmland, which became pronounced after the eleventh century" (ibid., p. 95).

55. See ibid., esp. pp. 173, 192.

56. Ma, *Commercial Development*, p. 19. Mark Elvin deals with this in chap. 6 of *Pattern of the Chinese Past*. The arguments are dealt with in Myers, "Transformation and Continuity," esp. pp. 271–273; and Golas, "Rural China in the Song."

57. Ma, *Commercial Development,* p. 23.

58. According to Peter Golas, "The remarkable fact that the Song is the only period in China before modern times when receipts from land taxes dipped below fifty percent of total central government receipts suggests very strongly that, as compared with other dynasties, Song agricultural taxation on the whole promoted agricultural productivity" ("Rural China in the Song," p. 311).

59. Kracke, *Civil Service,* p. 17. Some scholars have suggested a different picture. Albert Feuerwerker, e.g., has calculated that the revenue of the Sung government amounted to 13 percent of national income, compared with 5–7 percent for the Ming and 3–7.5 percent for the Ch'ing. Peter Golas goes much higher, estimating that the revenue of the Sung central government may have amounted to about 24 percent of national income in 1080 (see Golas, "The Sung Economy"). While it is still possible to spend more than one makes, no matter how much the latter figure may be, such research does suggest that the economy in general, and the government's revenues in particular, were significantly higher in the Sung dynasty than they were at any other time in Chinese history or in any other premodern society in the world. Much of this research remains speculative owing to a paucity of reliable data.

60. Ma, *Commercial Development,* p. 11.

61. What was bad for the farmer was often good for literature, however. The Fang La rebellion was the inspiration for one of the greatest novels in Chinese history, the *Shui-hu chuan* (see Kao Yu-kung, "A Study of the Fang La Rebellion," *HJAS* 24 [1963]: 17–63).

62. Kracke, *Civil Service,* pp. 11–18.

63. According to John Labadie, "The total number of soldiers increased from 370,000 in 960 to 660,000 in 995. In 1017, twelve years after the Treaty of Shan-yüan which ended the fighting between Sung and Liao, the armies had swelled to 900,000. The war with the Hsi-Hsia in 1038 brought an increase in troop strength to 1,250,000" ("Rulers and Soldiers," p. 47). By contrast, the Roman army during Hadrian's reign (117–138) amounted to only about 350,000 men, although the total population of the empire was comparable to that of the Northern Sung (Lo, *Civil Service of Sung China,* p. 7).

64. Wong, "Government Expenditures," p. 60.

65. Even though the Sung managed to spend more than it earned, it was still much better off than the Ming. According to Winston Lo, "The aggregate nonagricultural revenue of the Sung government was nine times larger than that of the Ming and the per capita revenue still larger" (*Civil Service of Sung China,* p. 9).

66. For a detailed treatment of one such family, see David Johnson, "The Last Years of a Great Clan: The Li Family of Chao-chun in the Late T'ang and Early Sung," *HJAS* 37 (1977): 51–59.

67. Wong, "Government Expenditures," p. 64.

68. Kato Shigeshi, "Associations of Merchants," pp. 66–67.

69. Kracke, "Sung Society," pp. 484–485. In her study *Change and Continuity in Chinese Local History*, Harriet Zurndorfer notes the blurring of the distinctions between merchants and officials during the Sung: "There is also evidence that some members of the same families, successfully participating in the examination system, were also becoming professional merchants" (p. 41). These families then financed educational institutions with profits earned from commercial activity (pp. 41–42).

70. Richard Davis notes that the first two emperors of the Sung deliberately used military officials to staff the civilian agencies in order to prevent the rise to power of any remnants of the T'ang aristocracy. According to Davis, "Contrary to popular myth, the founders of Sung did not abruptly replace military with civilian officials. . . . Nishikawa and others also note that centralization of political and military authority, which is often identified with the Sung, actually has its roots in the Five Dynasties" (*Court and Family in Sung China*, p. 8). See Nishikawa Masao, "Kahoku godai ōchō no bunshin kanryō," *Tōyō bunka kenkyūjo kiyō* 27 (March 1962): 211–261. For a discussion of how the examination quota system arose and how it could be manipulated, see Lee, "Social Significance of the Quota System."

71. Davis, *Court and Family in Sung China;* Lee, *Government Education and the Examinations in Sung China;* Umehara Kaoru, *Sōdai Kanryō seido kenkyū* (Kyoto: Dōhō, 1985); Hymes, *Statesmen and Gentlemen;* Chaffee, *The Thorny Gates of Learning.* See also Patricia Ebrey's superb review article on these books, "The Dynamics of Elite Domination."

72. Ho, *Ladder of Success,* p. 260. Kracke's conclusions can be found in "Family vs. Merit" and also in his "Region, Family, and Individual in the Chinese Examination System," in *Chinese Thought and Institutions,* ed. John King Fairbank (Chicago: University of Chicago Press, 1957), pp. 251–268.

73. Hartwell's arguments are in "Transformations of China," Hymes's in *Statesmen and Gentlemen.*

74. In Hartwell's words, "The social transformation of the Chinese bureaucratic elite at the end of the eleventh and beginning of the twelfth century was far more than simply a demographic transition. It marked the disappearance of the professional elite as a cohesive status group made up of families who specialized in government service and the coming to the fore of a multitude of local gentry lineages who encouraged a division of labor among their progeny with government service as only one possible career choice" (ibid., p. 416). Hilary Beattie, whose work focuses on T'ung-ch'eng county in Anhwei during the Ming and the Ch'ing, has written that "the history of lineage

organizations in T'ung-ch'eng thus confirms Fei Hsiao-t'ung's view that they were deliberately used by the elite to perpetuate themselves and their privileges. It also confirms the suspicion voiced earlier, that the reason why interest in kinship organization began to revive so strongly in the Sung dynasty, following the demise of the aristocracy with its automatic claims to political power on both local and national levels, was precisely because the new bureaucracy had to try to find ways to shore up its social position and power in the long term, and insure against the hazards of the competitive examination system" (*Land and Lineage in China,* p. 128).

75. See Hartwell, "Transformations of China," esp. p. 404. In addition, Hartwell believes that Ho's figures are "meaningless" (p. 418). However, in a review of Hymes' study (*JAS* 48 [May 1989]: 361–363), Mark Elvin states that it is incorrect for Hymes to dismiss Kracke's (and presumably Ho P'ing-ti's) findings as "simply useless."

76. Specifically, "Kin groups of the Sung tended to rise from obscurity to political prominence and back to obscurity, completing an entire cycle, within ten generations or less. In this respect, mobility within the Sung civil service bears striking similarity to that of Ming and Ch'ing times, while differing markedly from the earlier period" (Davis, *Court and Family in Sung China,* p. 10).

77. Ebrey, "The Dynamics of Elite Domination," p. 518. In her study "Kinship, Marriage, and Status in Song China," Linda Walton also stresses the importance to a family's status of local kinship and marriage ties. Her conclusions would appear to support the Hartwell and Hymes position. For further discussion of some of the major issues in kinship from a variety of perspectives, see Ebrey and Watson, eds., *Kinship Organization in Late Imperial China,* which contains papers from a conference on family and kinship in Chinese history held in Asilomar, California, in 1983.

78. For more on this, see de Bary and Chaffee, eds., *Neo-Confucian Education.* Although the product of a conference focusing on Chu Hsi's ideas on education, much of the material is relevant to the Northern Sung as well.

79. For a fascinating discussion of the conflicts between immigrant Han Chinese and native peoples in southern Sichuan—the new frontier—during the Sung, see von Glahn, *Country of Streams and Grottoes.*

80. Kracke, "Sung Society," pp. 479–480.

81. Liu Wu-chi, *Chinese Literature,* pp. 151, 154; Ch'en Shou-yi, *Chinese Literature,* pp. 466–467. The translation "transformation texts" is Victor Mair's. For a complete account of the origin and development of this literary genre, see his *T'ang Transformation Texts.*

82. Prusek, "Chinese Popular Novel," pp. 107–109.

83. Common people were exposed to history as well as fiction (the distinction between the two being sometimes blurred). Narrations of the histories of the Five Dynasties, e.g., were very popular (see ibid., p. 640).

84. Ginzburg, *The Cheese and the Worms,* p. xii.

85. A useful example of the meeting of Confucian theory and practice is Patricia Ebrey's translation (with a long and interesting introduction) of the Southern Sung official Yüan Ts'ai's manual on how to run a household, entitled *Family and Property in Sung China: Yüan Ts'ai's Precepts for Social Life* (Princeton, N.J.: Princeton University Press, 1984). His text offers a corrective to any tendency to exaggerate the impact of Confucian doctrine when it runs counter to common sense. In "Neo-Confucianism and the Chinese *Shih-ta-fu,*" Ebrey discusses at some length the degree to which everyday thinking often departed from a strict construction of neo-Confucian philosophy. For an account of a more orthodox neo-Confucian approach to practical problems, see her translation (with annotations and an introduction) of Chu Hsi's advice on how to carry out practical rituals, *Chu Hsi's "Family Rituals."*

86. According to Thomas Lee, "There are five important features in Sung education: the rise in the importance of the civil service examinations; the opening up of a large number of local schools and the government's willingness to invest in these institutions; the rise of Neo-Confucianism and its eventual victory in the struggle to define Chinese educational ideals; the rise of academies *(shu-yüan);* and finally, the widespread use of printing presses and their influence on mass education" (*Government Education and the Examinations in Sung China,* p. 20).

87. Ibid., p. 23. Chu Hsi also took a great interest in supporting local schools when he was an official, writing in one proclamation that "in recent years the scholarly tradition [in this prefecture] has declined, with the school supporting a mere thirty students. . . . Now I entreat the village elders to select young men who are dedicated to learning and send them to the school. They will be given assistance and be eligible to attend lectures and participate in classes. Meanwhile, the prefecture will take various steps to provide more support for schooling. And the prefect himself, when official duties permit, will visit the school regularly and discuss the meaning of the Classics with the school officials and in a variety of ways guide and encourage them" (*Learning to Be a Sage,* trans., Gardner, pp. 27–28).

88. See ibid., p. 29. See also Liu Po-chi, *Sung-tai cheng-chiao shih,* 2:826–837; and Chaffee, "The Revival of the White Deer Grotto Academy." *Neo-Confucian Education,* ed. de Bary and Chaffee, contains a number of valuable studies on this subject.

89. Lee, "Education in Northern Sung China," pp. 13–14.

90. Ch'en Shou-yi, *Chinese Literature,* pp. 352–353. See also Goodrich, "Development of Printing in China."

91. According to Thomas Carter, "The printing of the classics was one of the forces that restored Confucian literature and teaching to the place of national and popular regard that it had held before the advent of Buddhism, and a classical Renaissance followed that can be compared only to the Renaissance that came in Europe after the rediscovery of its classical literature and that there, too, was aided by the invention of printing" *(The Invention of Printing in China,* p. 83; see also Twitchett, *Printing and Publishing in Medieval China).*

92. Chan, "Integrative Force," p. 328.

93. Ching, *Wang Yang-ming,* p. 268. On *li,* see also Ch'en, *Buddhism in China,* pp. 316–319.

94. Chan, "Neo-Confucian Concept *Li,*" pp. 129–132. Of course, the philosophical context of the Sung was different. See also Wing-tsit Chan's introduction to Ariane Rump's translation of Wang Pi's commentary on the *Lao Tzu,* where he says that "Wang practically anticipated all that the Sung Neo-Confucianists had to say about principle" (p. xii).

95. For a much fuller explication of this aspect of neo-Confucianism, in China as well as throughout East Asia, see de Bary's *Neo-Confucian Orthodoxy,* and *The Message of the Mind in Neo-Confucianism.*

96. According to Ann Birdwhistell, "In Shao's thought, this classic [the *Ch'un-ch'iu*] was second in importance only to the *Yi-ching*" *(Transition to Neo-Confucianism,* p. 38). Birdwhistell also notes that "among Shao's contemporaries there was little recognition of the role and influence of the *Ch'un-ch'iu* in Shao's philosophy" (p. 204). Shao believed that history passed through a cyclic pattern of birth, growth, maturity, and death corresponding to the four seasons. The classics, moreover, each focused on one of those seasons. The *I-ching* represented spring and dealt with the three sages Fu Hsi, Yao, and Shun; the *Shu-ching* represented summer and dealt with the two emperors Yü and T'ang; the *Shih-ching* represented fall and dealt with the three kings Wen, Wu, and the duke of Chou; the *Ch'un-ch'iu* represented winter and dealt with the five hegemons Duke Huan of Ch'i, Duke Mu of Ch'in, Duke Hsiang of Sung, Duke Wen of Chin, and King Chuang of Ch'u. According to Shao's interpretation, "In the first stage, the rulers use *tao,* and in the following stages, they respectively use virtue *(te),* accomplishments *(kung),* and force *(li).* Each ruler uses a method that reflects the people's capabilities and needs at that stage in history. Like the Buddhists, Shao saw a decline in the level of morality across the people in the four stages. That is, at first the people spontaneously or naturally behaved in a moral way. Then they needed an ethical

code to help them behave morally, a development represented by the ruler's valuing the virtue of yielding. In the third stage, the people were even less moral and so needed government, an idea that implied *cheng*, rectification or correctness. By the fourth stage, morality had declined so much that rulers had to adopt the method of struggle. Small struggles were conducted with words and large ones with troops" (ibid., p. 155). In Shao's view, the rise of the Ch'in represented the end of the first cycle of Chinese history. The Han was the beginning of a new cycle, and Shao Yung believed that the Sung was also the beginning of a new stage in history. For a more detailed treatment of Shao's views on how history revealed the cosmic principles of change, see ibid., pp. 144–161.

97. As Ira Kasoff put it, "For Chang *ch'i* is not just vapor or breath. In its different states, it constitutes everything in the universe. In its most rarefied state it is without form. It also comprises the air we breathe, all living beings, and all inanimate objects" (*The Thought of Chang Tsai*, p. 37).

98. Ibid., pp. 40–43.

99. According to Wing-tsit Chan, Chu Hsi "synthesized Confucius' concept of *jen* (humanity), Mencius' doctrines of humanity and righteousness, the idea of the investigation of things in the *Great Learning*, the teaching of sincerity in the *Doctrine of the Mean*, the *yin yang* (passive and active cosmic forces) and the Five Agents (Water, Fire, Wood, Metal, Earth) doctrines of Han times (206 B.C.–A.D. 220), and practically all the important ideas of the Neo-Confucianists of early Sung. . . . His most radical innovation was to select and group the *Analects*, the *Book of Mencius*, the *Great Learning*, and the *Doctrine of the Mean* (both of which are chapters of the *Book of Rites*), as the Four Books" (*Sourcebook*, p. 589).

100. Chin Chung-shu, "Ku-wen yün-tung," p. 98.

101. For a discussion of Han Yü's intellectual drive to unify thought and action, see Hartman, *Han Yü and the T'ang Search for Unity*. A dissenting view, which interprets Han Yü more as a creature of his own time and less as a progenitor of Sung neo-Confucianism, is expressed by David McMullen in "Han Yü: An Alternative Picture."

102. De Bary, "Reappraisal," p. 84.

103. And the greatest contribution of the *ku-wen* movement was the changing of the examinations in 1057, under the supervision of Ou-yang Hsiu, to the clear and practical *ku-wen* style (Egan, *The Literary Works of Ou-yang Hsiu*, p. 26). Egan speaks further of Ou-yang's "desire generally in the arts to avoid preoccupation with external forms or technical brilliance and to concentrate instead upon the meaning that lies beneath those forms" (p. 200).

104. Yoshikawa, *Sung Poetry*, p. 42.

105. See Chang, *The Evolution of Chinese Tz'u Poetry*.

106. Yoshikawa, *Sung Poetry,* pp. 24–28, 43–44.

107. Liu Wu-chi, *Chinese Literature,* p. 133.

108. Chaves, *Mei Yao-ch'en,* p. 163.

109. Bush, *Chinese Literati,* pp. 22, 29, 25. See also James F. Cahill, "Confucian Elements in the Theory of Painting," pp. 115–140.

110. See the studies of Sung statecraft in *Ordering the World,* ed. Hymes and Schirokauer, the result of a conference held in Scottsdale, Arizona, in 1986.

111. Liu, "Early Sung Reformer," pp. 105, 111.

112. See the discussion in Hsiao, *Cheng-chih ssu-hsiang,* pp. 479–493 (449–461).

113. Ibid., p. 492 (460).

114. Liu, *Ou-yang Hsiu,* p. 100.

Chapter 3: Background of the Ch'un-ch'iu *Commentaries*

1. I am using John Henderson's translation, from *Scripture, Canon, and Commentary,* p. 14. The quotation is from the *Chu-tzu ta-chüan chi,* in the *T'u-shu chi-ch'eng* 55:871.

2. See the "Yi-wen chih" chapter of the *Sung-shih,* pp. 5056–5066. It notes (p. 5066) that there were 240 works listed, in 2,799 *chüan.* Ch'en Fang-ming has noted that the next most numerous of the Sung commentaries were those regarding the *I-ching* ("Sung-tai cheng-t'ung-lun," p. 421).

3. One might wish that more Chinese political thinkers had collected their thoughts into discrete essays focused on one topic (as Hsün Tzu did). Instead, they usually expressed their most important ideas in the form of commentaries on earlier works. Nor were they alone. Most premodern societies used commentaries as the standard vehicle of expression. See Henderson's *Scripture, Canon, and Commentary,* esp. chap. 3.

4. Legge, "Prolegomena," *Chinese Classics,* vol. 5, pp. 11–12.

5. Juan Chih-sheng, "Ts'ung Kung-yang-hsüeh," pp. 31–36.

6. Maspero, *China in Antiquity,* pp. 361, 363–364.

7. Ibid., p. 482, n. 21. Burton Watson notes that the Japanese scholar Kamata Tadashi puts it at 320 B.C., while the Chinese scholar Yang Po-chün claims that it was written somewhere between 403 and 389 B.C. (see Watson, *Tso Chuan,* p. xiv).

8. *SKTY* 1:515.

9. Maspero, *China in Antiquity,* pp. 355 and 477, n. 83.

10. P'i Hsi-jui, *Ching-hsüeh,* pp. 103–107.

11. Pan Ku, *Former Han,* 2:271.

12. There are approximately 41,500 characters in the *Ku-liang* and approximately 44,000 in the *Kung-yang,* as opposed to about 180,000 in the *Tso-chuan* (see Ch'i Ssu-ho, "Professor Hung," p. 52).

13. Maspero, *China in Antiquity,* p. 355. Watson is of the same

mind, citing Japanese authorities who base their conclusions on astronomical information contained within the *Ku-liang* (*Ssu-ma Ch'ien*, p. 77).

14. See the Ch'ing scholar Chi T'ang-yen's remarks, quoted in Wang Hsi-yüan, "Liu-shih nien lai," p. 431.

15. Dubs, *Former Han*, pp. 271–274.

16. Maspero, *China in Antiquity*, pp. 355 and 478, n. 83. Wang Hsi-yüan quotes from Chang T'ai-yen in support of this position ("Liu-shih nien lai," p. 437). See also Wang's discussion of Liu Shih-p'ei's views (pp. 450–451).

17. See Juan Chih-sheng, "Ts'ung kung-yang-hsüeh," pp. 37–45. See also Schneider, *Ku Chieh-kang*, esp. pp. 52–84, 188–217. William Hung's ideas on the *Ch'un-ch'iu* are enunciated in his preface to the *Harvard-Yenching Institute Sinological Index Series*, suppl. no. 11 (combined concordances to the *Ch'un-ch'iu*, *Kung-yang*, *Ku-liang*, and *Tso-chuan*) (Peiping, 1937; Taipei: Ch'eng-wen Press, 1966, photocopy), pp. i–cvi. See also Ch'i Ssu-ho, "Professor Hung." This article inspired a short note by Helmut Wilhelm, "Confucius and the *Ch'un-ch'iu*," *Yenching Journal of Social Science* 2 (1939): pp. 297–300. Wilhelm is not willing to turn his back on the *Kung-yang* tradition and follow Hung's line of argument.

18. Legge, *Mencius*, pp. 281–283.

19. Watson, *Ssu-ma Ch'ien*, pp. 88–89. Watson argues that, in this context, "theoretical judgment" is a more accurate translation of *k'ung-yen* than "empty words."

20. Juan Chih-sheng, "Ts'ung Kung-yang-hsüeh," p. 42.

21. *CCFL* 5:3.22, quoted in Fung, *History of Chinese Philosophy*, 2:75. This view lasted throughout Chinese history. In the Ch'ing, the scholar Liu Feng-lu (1776–1829) wrote that the *Ch'un-ch'iu* was the key to all the other classics: "One who does not understand the *Annals* cannot discuss the Five Classics" (quoted in Henderson, *Scripture, Canon, and Commentary*, p. 16).

22. Lee, "Education in Northern Sung China," p. 137.

23. *CHY*, p. 282.

24. Tain, "Tung Chung-shu," pp. 280–282. For a brief account of Tung's life and thought and the context in which he lived, see Michael Loewe, "Imperial Sovereignty: Dong Zhongshu's Contribution and His Predecessors," in *Foundations and Limits of State Power in China*, ed. S. R. Schram (London: School of Oriental and African Studies, 1987), pp. 33–57.

25. The quotation is from the *CCFL* 81:17.1, as quoted in Fung, *History of Chinese Philosophy*, 2:57.

26. Tain, "Tung Chung-shu," pp. 6–7.

27. *CCFL* 35:17.12, quoted in Fung, *History of Chinese Philosophy*, 2:46.

28. *CCFL* 44:11.9, quoted in ibid., p. 47; and *CCFL* 18:6.5a–6a, quoted in de Bary, Tsunoda, and Keene, *Sources,* pp. 174–175.

29. *Huai-nan tzu* 9:1a, 6b–7a, quoted in ibid., p. 174. The *Huai-nan tzu* was an anthology produced in the Han dynasty by Liu An and may have been submitted to the Han emperor Wu-ti by 140 B.C. Roger Ames has translated book 9 (out of a total of twenty) in *The Art of Rulership.* Ames regards the work as a synthesis of Legalism, Taoism, and Confucianism, "which expressed the Taoist conviction in the primacy of natural realization and the Confucian commitment to the primacy of the people's welfare" (p. xvi).

30. *CCFL* 30:8.13b–14b, quoted in de Bary, Tsunoda, and Keene, *Sources,* p. 187.

31. See the long discussion of this in Tain, "Tung Chung-shu," pp. 268–280. See also Hsiao, *Chinese Political Thought,* pp. 485–486. One of the most interesting examples of a Confucian official acting in the name of moral authority was the case of Ho Kuang. Ho was a trusted official under the Han emperor Wu-ti who was given the responsibility of acting as regent for the young Emperor Chao after the death of Wu-ti. Chao ruled from 86 to 74 B.C. and then died without a male heir. After his death, several high officials met and decided to name a grandson of the Emperor Wu by the name of Liu Ho, king of Ch'ang-i, to the throne. But after he came to the throne he acted in a manner so contrary to the norms of Confucian behavior that after a very short time Ho Kuang had him replaced with a great-grandson who became the Emperor Hsüan (see Ho Kuang's biography in the *Han Shu,* translated by Burton Watson in *Courtier and Commoner in Ancient China* [New York: Columbia University Press, 1974], pp. 121–138).

32. Hsiao, *Chinese Political Thought,* p. 513.

33. Hsiao, *Chinese Political Thought,* p. 504.

34. Dull, "Historical Introduction to the Apocryphal Texts," pp. 26–42.

35. Tain, "Tung Chung-shu," pp. 285–288.

36. Liu Te-han, "Ch'un-ch'iu Kung-yang chuan," pp. 39–40.

37. Hsiao, *Chinese Political Thought,* pp. 524, 526.

38. The three ages are disorder *(chü-luan),* ascending peace *(sheng-p'ing),* and universal peace *(t'ai-p'ing).* For a translation of Ho's comments on the three ages, see Hsiao, *Chinese Political Thought,* p. 530; and Fung, *History of Chinese Philosophy,* 2:83–84. Fung's age of disorder reads *shuai-luan.* See also Hsiao, *Modern China,* pp. 77–78.

39. *SKTY* 1:515.

40. Compare, e.g., the *Chin-wen* phrase "borrow from the past in order to reform institutions" *(t'o-ku kai-chih)* with Hu Yüan's admonition that a scholar of the classics has a threefold task: understanding substance *(t'i),* putting it into practice *(yung),* and clarifying it in writing *(wen).* The Northern Sung also followed the *Chin-wen* argument

that Confucius' principles were carefully hidden *(wei-yen ta-yi)*. For a discussion of the relation between classical interpretation and practical politics in the Han, see Liu Te-han, "Ch'un-ch'iu Kung-yang chuan."

41. Chou Yü-t'ung, *Ching Chin-Ku-wen hsüeh,* pp. 12–27; and P'i Hsi-jui, *Ching-hsüeh,* pp. 82–97.

42. Although these scholars were primarily interested in textual criticism, some, especially Cheng Hsüan, Fu Ch'ien, and Chia K'uei, were not averse to drawing on the *Kung-yang* and the *Ku-liang* traditions to fortify their arguments (P'i Hsi-jui, *Ching-hsüeh,* pp. 161 and 20, n. 6).

43. Ibid., pp. 10–13, 172. Also discussed in Juan Chih-sheng, "Ts'ung Kung-yang-hsüeh," pp. 37–38.

44. P'i Hsi-jui, *Ching-hsüeh,* pp. 172 and 177–178, nn. 19–20.

45. Hsiao, *Chinese Political Thought,* pp. 602–606.

46. Ibid., p. 606.

47. Quoted in ibid., pp. 613, 614, 612.

48. Quoted in ibid., pp. 653, 654 (the latter quote is from the *Pao-p'u Tzu, Wai-p'ien, chüan* 7, "Liang kuei").

49. P'i Hsi-jui, *Ching-hsüeh,* pp. 218 and 220, n. 6.

50. There is a short and valuable description of this period in Pulleyblank, "Neo-Confucianism in T'ang Intellectual Life," esp. pp. 88–89.

51. Quoted in *CYK* 176:4b.

52. Tan Chu's *Ch'un-ch'iu chi-chuan* (one *chüan*) and *Ch'un-ch'iu li-t'ung* (also one *chüan*) are preserved in the *Yü-han shan-fang chi-yi shu,* published in 1883 in Ch'angsha and compiled by Ma Kuo-han (1794–1857).

53. His *Ch'un-ch'iu ch'an-wei tsuan-lei yi-t'ung* (one *chüan*) can also be found in the *Yü-han shan-fang chi-yi shu.*

54. P'i Hsi-jui, *Ching-hsüeh,* p. 231, n. 2; and *CYK* 176:7a–7b.

55. *CYK* 176:6a, 8a.

56. The first was published in the *Ssu-k'u ch'üan-shu* in ten *chüan.* A *Fu chiao-k'an chi* in one *chüan* is preserved in the *Ts'ung-shu chi-ch'eng ch'u-pien.* The second was also published in the *Ssu-k'u ch'üan-shu* in three *chüan.* The last was published in the *Ssu-k'u ch'üan-shu* in ten *chüan.*

57. Mou Jun-sun, "Liang Sung Ch'un-ch'iu," p. 103.

58. *CYK* 178:1a–11a; and also the *Ch'ien-yüan tsung-chi,* by the late Ch'ing bibliophile Lu Hsin-yüan (1834–1894).

59. *CYK* 178:4b.

60. *CYK* 178:2b.

61. One example is his statement that "clarifying the principle of revering the Son of Heaven with regard to things that are above, and

the principle of condemning the feudal lords with regard to things that are below, is the way to rectify the kingly way" (*CYK* 178:3a–3b).

62. P'i Hsi-jui, *Ching-hsüeh,* p. 237.

63. *SKTY* 1:575.

64. De Bary, Tsunoda, and Keene, *Sources,* p. 524. It is here that there appears the much-quoted passage: "Heaven is my father and earth is my mother, and even such a small creature as I finds an intimate place in their midst. Therefore that which extends throughout the universe I regard as my body and that which directs the universe I consider as my nature. All people are my brothers and sisters, and all things are my companions."

65. Lewis, *The Discarded Image,* p. 12.

66. P'i Hsi-jui, *Ching-hsüeh,* p. 272.

67. *Tzu* Yi-chih, *hao* An-ting. The *Sung-shih* says that he is from Hai-ling in T'ai-chou (now T'ai-hsien in Kiangsu province), but the *Sung-Yüan hsüeh-an* says that he is from Ju-kao, also in T'ai-chou.

68. De Bary, "Reappraisal," pp. 88–91.

69. Quoted in de Bary, Tsunoda, and Keene, *Sources,* p. 439, from the first chapter of the *Sung-Yüan hsüeh-an,* which begins with a consideration of Hu Yüan.

70. *Sung-shih* 432:12837–12838.

71. The *Hung-fan k'ou-yi* was copied into the *Ssu-k'u ch'üan-shu* and is also published in the *Ts'ung-shu chi-ch'eng* (see Michael Nylan, *The Shifting Center: The Original "Great Plan" and Later Readings* [Nettetal: Steyler Verlag, 1992], pp. 63-102). The *Chou-yi k'ou-yi* was also included in the *Ssu-k'u ch'üan-shu.* The lost *Ch'un-ch'iu k'ou-yi* is listed in the *Sung-shih* (202:5058).

72. *Tzu* Yüan-fu, *hao* Kung-shih. He was from Hsin-yü in Lin-chiang (present-day Kiangsi province).

73. His *Ch'un-ch'iu chuan* (fifteen *chüan*), *Ch'un-ch'iu ch'üan-heng* (seventeen *chüan*), and *Ch'un-ch'iu yi-lin* (two *chüan*) are all in the *T'ung-chih t'ang ching-chieh* collection. His *Ch'un-ch'iu chuan shuo-li* is in both the *Ssu-k'u ch'üan-shu* (as are the above three as well) and the *Ts'ung-shu chi-ch'eng ch'u-pien.*

74. See the discussion of Liu's works in *SKTY* 1:528–530. Liu Ch'ang does not escape censure by the Ch'ing editors, however, who accuse him of cutting out words or sentences from the passages he sometimes quotes, thus deliberately distorting the meaning of the original. In one case, he is supposed to have altered a quotation from the *Tso-chuan,* changing the phrase "take pity on him, and spare him if he sneaks out of the country" to "spare him if he is willing to fight against rebels" (*SKTY* 1:529). Could Liu have wanted to emphasize the danger of rebellion against central authority by praising those who supported the ruler and suppressed rebels?

75. *SKTY* 1:528.

76. *Ch'un-ch'iu Liu-shih chuan, T'ung-chih t'ang ching-chieh* ed., 19:10865, Yin-kung, 1.

77. Ibid., p. 10866, Yin-kung 2.

78. The Ch'ing scholars who compiled the *SKTY* report that he was referred to as a *T'ai-ch'ang po-shih* (erudite of the Court of Imperial Sacrifices), but elsewhere that he was a Han-lin academician, which would have been a higher ranking than an erudite, during the T'ien-hsi period (1017–1021) of the reign of the Chen-tsung emperor. According to the *SKTY* editors, Wang Ying-lin mentions that Wang had written his commentaries by the time of the middle of the Chih-he period (1054–1055). According to the *Ching-i k'ao* (p. 179:7a), he wrote a *Ch'un-ch'iu t'ung-yi* in twelve *chüan* and a *Ch'un-ch'iu ming-li yin-kua* in one *chüan,* both of which have been lost. His most influential surviving piece is a collection of essays known by the title *Ch'un-ch'iu huang-kang lun* (On imperial authority in the *Spring and Autumn Annals*) (the translation of the title is that of Jack Langlois ["Law, Statecraft, and the *Spring and Autumn Annals,*" p. 124]). This work is in the *T'ung-chih t'ang ching-chieh* collection. The *SKTY* editors note that Wang's style is easy to read, and I must agree with them. His writing is a welcome relief from Liu Ch'ang's tortuous prose.

79. *SKTY* 1:527.

80. *Ch'un-ch'iu huang-kang lun,* p. 10835.

81. Ibid., p. 10857.

82. *Tzu* Hsin-lao. He was from Kao-yu (in present-day Kiangsu province). His *Ch'un-ch'iu ching-chieh* is in the *Ssu-k'u ch'üan-shu* in thirteen *chüan* and the *T'ung-chih t'ang ching-chieh* in fifteen *chüan.*

83. *Sung-shih* 344:10926–10927.

84. *SKTY* 1:530–531. See also Sun's foreword in the *CYK* (181: 1a–3a).

85. *Tzu* Cheng-shu, known as I-ch'uan hsien-sheng, from Lo-yang (in present-day Honan).

86. According to the *CYK* (183:3a), Hsieh wrote two works on the *Ch'un-ch'iu,* the *Ch'un-ch'iu yi* in twenty-four *chüan* and the *Ch'un-ch'iu tsung-yi* in three *chüan,* both of which are no longer extant. *Tzu* was Ch'ih-cheng, from Chin-t'ang (in present-day Szechuan province).

87. *Tzu* Chih-fu, also called Ho-nan hsien-sheng, from Ch'ang-shan (in present-day Chekiang province).

88. Liu Hsüan wrote a work called simply *Ch'un-ch'iu,* which has been lost (*CYK* 184:1a).

89. Ts'ai Yung-ch'un, "The Philosophy of Ch'eng I," pp. 49–50.

90. *Tzu* Yen-chih, or Po-chih, *hao* Hsi-ch'ou chü-shih, from Fu-ling (in present-day Szechuan province).

91. *Tzu* Shao-yün, *hao* Hsiao-weng and Shih-lin, from Wu-hsien (in present-day Kiangsu province).

92. *Tzu* Chü-jen, *hao* Tung-lai hsien-sheng, from Pien-liang (in present-day Kaifeng in Honan province).

93. *SKTY* 1:533–535.

94. *SKTY* 1:536–538.

95. *SKTY* 1:538.

Chapter 4: Sun Fu's Views on Obedience to Authority

1. For example, Ssu-ma Kuang disagreed with Mencius' rejection of the hegemon (see Hsiao, *Cheng-chih ssu-hsiang,* pp. 515–516 [482–483]).

2. *CCFL* 5:12.

3. For Li Kou and a more general discussion of centralization, see Hsiao, *Cheng-chih ssu-hsiang,* pp. 479–487 (449–456). For some further background, consult also Hsieh, *The Life and Thought of Li Kou.* Julia Ching discusses Chang Tsai briefly in "Neo-Confucian Utopian Theories," p. 44.

4. *Tzu* Ming-fu, from P'ing-yang in Chin-chou in present-day Shansi.

5. The *Ch'un-ch'iu tsun-wang fa-wei* is referred to in an essay dated summer 1040 by Shih Chieh (1005–1045), Sun's student (see "T'ai-shan shu-yüan chi," in *Shih Tzu-lai chi,* pp. 63–64). The *Sun Ming-fu hsiao-chi* is available in the *Ssu-k'u ch'üan-shu chen-pien pa-chi,* vol. 148. Sun also wrote a work on the *I-ching,* which has not survived, entitled *I-shuo,* in sixty-four *pien* (see Shih Chieh, "T'ai-shan shu-yüan chi," p. 64).

6. Chu Hsi said that Sun's contribution was awe inspiring. Although Chu also claimed that Sun was not learned in the classics of the sages, Chu believed that Sun still captured their intentions in his commentary (see *Chu-tzu yü-lei, chüan* 83).

7. See Mou Jun-sun, "Liang Sung," p. 104. The epitaph is quoted on p. 109.

8. "Hsin-tao t'ang chi," *SMFHC,* p. 35a.

9. Shih, "Metaphysical Tendencies," p. 320. On Mencius as a bridge, see p. 104.

10. *SMFHC,* pp. 11a–12a.

11. *SMFHC,* pp. 11b–12a.

12. *SMFHC,* p. 4a. In another context, Sun Fu said that one should study the *I-ching* to ascertain Confucius' mind and the *Ch'un-ch'iu* to find out how to put it into practice (see Shih Chieh, "T'ai-shan shu-yüan chi," p. 64).

13. Knechtges, "Yang Shyong," 1:77 and 127, n. 123. For a discussion of the influence of Yang Hsiung on Shao Yung, see also Birdwhistell, *Transition to Neo-Confucianism,* esp. pp. 141–144.

14. See the *Ts'ung-shu chi-ch'eng ch'u-pien* ed., 697:1–6, 36–37.

15. *SMFHC,* pp. 19a–22a.

16. Hsiao, *Chinese Political Thought,* pp. 549–550.

17. *SMFHC,* p. 21a.

18. *CCTWFW,* 10828, Ai-kung 14.

19. See Mou Jun-sun, "Liang Sung," pp. 105–106, in which he quotes from Sun's commentary, *CCTWFW,* 10727, Yin-kung 1, and 10728, Yin-kung 2. In fact, Sun did have words of praise, which are noted occasionally as they appear later in the chapter. In 699 b.c., e.g., when the same date is repeated twice, Sun says that this was intended to connote praise, without, however, explaining why. The *Kung-yang* does not say anything, and the *Ku-liang* (Malmqvist, "Studies," p. 107) merely states, "The text repeats the day in order to make decisive the significance of the dating." The *Tso-chuan* also does not have any commentary on this point.

20. Liu Yen (1048–1102) criticized him for introducing purely personal ideas, inappropriate to a commentary (*CHY,* p. 287). Ch'ang Chih (1019–1077) called him a latter-day Shang Yang for focusing on trivial questions. Yeh Meng-te said that he did not get to the heart of the classic, that his understanding of *li* (ritual) was superficial (Mou Jun-sun, "Liang Sung," p. 110).

21. Legge, trans., *Confucian Analects,* p. 310. The translation is Legge's. See *CCTWFW,* 10729, Yin-kung 2. Actually, Sun does not quote the last sentence.

22. For further details, see Legge, trans., *Ch'un Ts'ew,* p. 208.

23. *CCTWFW,* 10772, Hsi-kung 28, as quoted in *CHY,* p. 308.

24. Thucydides, *The Peloponnesian War,* trans. Rex Warner (New York: Penguin, 1954), 2:40. To be sure, the Greek understanding of politics was tied in with certain specific institutions of self-government associated with the *polis.* Nevertheless, Pericles would have agreed with Mencius' warning about the corrosive effects of unrestrained self-interest on political order: "If your Majesty say, 'What is to be done to profit my kingdom?' the great officers will say, 'What is to be done to profit our families?' and the inferior officers and the common people will say, 'What is to be done to profit our persons?' Superiors and inferiors will try to snatch this profit the one from the other, and the kingdom will be endangered. In the kingdom of ten thousand chariots, the murderer of his sovereign shall be the chief of a family of a thousand chariots. In a kingdom of a thousand chariots, the murderer of his prince shall be the chief of a family of a hundred chariots. To have a thousand in ten thousand, and a hundred in a thousand, cannot be said not to be a large allotment, but if righteousness be put last, and profit be put

first, they will not be satisfied without snatching all" (Legge, trans., *Mencius,* p. 126).

25. *CCTWFW,* 10800, Hsiang-kung 11. Legge discusses this in greater detail (*Mencius,* p. 452).

26. *CCTWFW,* 10810, Chao-kung 5.

27. *CCTWFW,* 10727, Yin-kung 1.

28. The only reason given for the praise is that "he [Chu] gradually advanced" (see Malmqvist, "Studies," p. 70). When the commentaries are as enigmatic as the text, the possibilities of interpretation are multiplied many times.

29. *CCTWFW,* 10728, Yin-kung 3.

30. As quoted in *CHY,* pp. 325–326, from his *Ch'un-ch'iu chuan,* Yin-kung 1.

31. *CCTWFW,* 10728, Yin-kung 1.

32. Legge, trans., *Li Chi,* 1:214.

33. On altering the pattern of succession, see *CCTWFW,* 10779, Wen-kung 14. On officials not appointed by the king, see, e.g., *CCTWFW,* 10728, Yin-kung 2, and 10737, Huan-kung 2. Regarding hereditary right, in the *CCTWFW,* 10730, Yin-kung 3, Sun claims that hereditary offices were partly responsible for the decline of the Hsia and Shang dynasties and appear again in the Chou when it begins to decline. See also *CCTWFW,* 10785, Hsüan-kung 10, in which Sun follows the *Kung-yang* in criticizing hereditary offices.

34. For the former, see *CCTWFW,* 10757, Chuang-kung 31, for the latter, *CCTWFW,* 10783, Hsüan-kung 1.

35. See *CCTWFW,* 10737, Huan-kung 1; 10791, Ch'eng-kung 8; 10802, Hsiang-kung 19; and 10827, Ai-kung 8.

36. *CCTWFW,* 10729, Yin-kung 3.

37. *CCTWFW,* 10737, Huan-kung 1.

38. *CCTWFW,* 10767, Hsi-kung 15.

39. *CCTWFW,* 10767, Hsi-kung 16. See Legge, trans., *The Ch'un Ts'ew,* pp. 170–171.

40. *CCTWFW,* 10778, Wen-kung 9, and 10737, Hsüan-kung 16.

41. *CCTWFW,* 10730–31, Yin-kung 4.

42. *CCTWFW,* 10753, Chuang-kung 22. Even the son of the Chou king did not escape blame for engineering the murder of one of the feudal lords (*CCTWFW,* 10787, Hsüan-kung 15). See also Legge, trans., *The Ch'un Ts'ew,* p. 329.

43. On sons and heirs, see *CCTWFW,* 10804, Hsiang-kung 26, and 10783, Hsi-kung 5. On regicide, see *CCTWFW,* 10806, Hsiang-kung 30. On sacrifice, see *CCTWFW,* 10812, Chao-kung 11.

44. *CCTWFW,* 10787, Hsüan-kung 15. With regard to this passage, see Legge, trans., *The Ch'un Ts'ew,* p. 329, which explains that this was

an extra tax on the produce of a crop. There is not total agreement on the meaning of this passage, but for our purposes it is how Sun took it that is important. See also *CCTWFW,* 10827, Ai-kung 12; and Legge, trans., *The Ch'un Ts'ew,* p. 828.

45. *CCTWFW,* 10727, Yin-kung 1.

46. *CCTWFW,* 10727, Yin-kung 1. The exact nature of the violation is not agreed on, but that there was something wrong was believed by all the commentators.

47. *CCTWFW,* 10739–10740, Huan-kung 5.

48. *CCTWFW,* 10769, Hsi-kung 24, and 10792, Ch'eng-kung 12.

49. *CCTWFW,* 10764, Hsi-kung 5.

50. On the Chou king Chuang, see *CCTWFW,* 10747, Chuang-kung 1. On doing away with heirs, see *CCTWFW,* 10763, Hsi-kung 5. On murdering brothers, see *CCTWFW,* 10806, Hsiang-kung 30.

51. Sun Chüeh as quoted in *CHY,* p. 321.

52. Sun Chüeh as quoted in *CHY,* p. 275.

53. Ch'en Ch'ing-hsin as quoted in *CHY,* p. 323.

54. *LSCY, chüan* 19, as quoted in *CHY,* p. 321.

55. *LSCY, chüan* 1, 3, as quoted in *CHY,* pp. 321, 324.

56. *CCTWFW,* 10798, Hsiang-kung 3. Sun mentions the meeting at Chi-tse (in present-day Hopei) several times later as marking the beginning of the officials' usurpation of power. See, e.g., *CCTWFW,* 10801, Hsiang-kung 16.

57. Hsü, *Ancient China,* pp. 78–82.

58. On killing the son of a ruler, see *CCTWFW,* 10756, Chuang-kung 27, and 10784, Hsüan-kung 5. On holding meetings, see *CCTWFW,* 10765, Hsi-kung 9.

59. *CCTWFW,* 10801, Hsiang-kung 16. Now, according to Sun, power is fully in the hands of the officials. This meeting took place in 556 B.C., at Chü-liang (in present-day Honan), which belonged to Chin.

60. *CCTWFW,* 10804–10805, Hsiang-kung 27. Again in the same year, the ministers met by themselves in Sung. See also *CCTWFW,* 10809, Chao-kung 4.

61. *CCTWFW,* 10812–10813, Chao-kung 13.

62. On not obeying orders, see *CCTWFW,* 10784, Hsüan-kung 8, and 10788, Hsüan-kung 18. On offering refuge, see *CCTWFW,* 10803, Hsiang-kung 21, and 10803, Hsiang-kung 23.

63. *CCTWFW,* 10794, Ch'eng-kung 17.

64. Legge, trans., *The Ch'un Ts'ew,* p. 405.

65. On robbers committing murder, see *CCTWFW,* 10800, Hsiang-kung 10. On the marquis' brother, see *CCTWFW,* 10814, Chao-kung 20.

66. *CCTWFW,* 10750, Chuang-kung 10. See also Legge, trans., *The*

Ch'un Ts'ew, p. 86. This is the first mention in the *Ch'un-ch'iu* itself of the state of Ch'u.

67. *CCTWFW,* 10762–10763, Hsi-kung 4. See also Malmqvist, "Studies," pp. 162–163; and Mou Jun-sun, "Liang Sung," pp. 106–107.

68. *CCTWFW,* 10765, Hsi-kung 9. See also Mou Jun-sun, "Liang Sung," p. 107; and Malmqvist, "Studies," p. 163.

69. *CCTWFW,* 10771, Hsi-kung 28.

70. Sun's views on this subject were not shared by all his fellow *Ch'un-ch'iu* enthusiasts in the Northern Sung. For example, although he came close, Ou-yang Hsiu did not take such a strong position: "With regard to relations between China and the barbarians from ancient times, when China was in possession of the *tao,* the barbarians did not necessarily submit, and when China was not in possession of the *tao,* they did not necessarily stay away" (*Hsin Wu-tai shih* 72:885).

71. *CCTWFW,* 10789, Ch'eng-kung 1.

72. *CCTWFW,* 10820, Ting-kung 4. See also Malmqvist, "Studies," p. 212. Hsiao also draws on the same example from the *Kung-yang* to make the same point (see *Chinese Political Thought,* 1:24–25, n. 55).

73. *CCTWFW,* 10811, Chao-kung 11. From its first appearance in the text in 583 B.C., Wu is blamed for usurping the title *viscount* (see *CCTWFW,* 10791, Ch'eng-kung 7).

74. Hu Ch'ang-chih, "Lü Tzu-ch'ien ti shih-hsüeh," *Shu-mu chi-k'an* 10 (1976): 125–126.

75. Confucius, *The Analects of Confucius* (New York: Macmillan, 1939), pp. 94–95.

76. On the occupation of P'eng-ch'eng, see *CCTWFW,* 10797, Hsiang-kung 1. On the destruction of Ch'en and Ts'ai, see *CCTWFW,* 10813, Chao-kung 13.

77. *CCTWFW,* 10828, Ai-kung 13. One must guard against the tendency to see this interpretation as an attempt to hide one's head in the sand—the barbarian threat will go away if one just pretends that it doesn't exist. Sun's purpose was not to explain the barbarians away but to challenge the legitimacy of their power whenever it did not conform to standards of *li.*

78. Quoted in de Bary, Tsunoda, and Keene, *Sources,* p. 506.

79. Legge, trans., *Confucian Analects,* p. 208. In his commentary, Legge notes that *li* refers, not only to "mere conventionalities, but the ordinations of man's moral and intelligent nature in the line of what is proper."

80. Ibid., p. 220.

81. Legge, trans., *Ch'un Ts'ew,* p. 33.

82. Watson, *The Tso Chuan,* p. xxiii. See also the more detailed discussion of *li* in the *Tso Chuan* in Watson, *Early Chinese Literature,* pp. 40–66.

83. Knoblock, *Xunzi*, 1:47.

84. Watson, *Hsün Tzu*, p. 94. See also the record of a statement by the great prime minister of the state of Cheng, Tzu-ch'an, in the *Tso-chuan* (Legge, trans., *The Ch'un Ts'ew*, p. 708): "Ceremonies [are founded in] the regular procedure of Heaven, the right phenomena of earth, and the actions of men."

85. See Legge, trans., *Li Chi*, 1:386–388, 388–89.

86. See also Hos. 10:13–14: "You have ploughed iniquity, you have reaped injustice, you have eaten the fruit of lies. Because you have trusted in your chariots and in the multitude of your warriors, therefore the tumult of war shall arise among your people, and all your fortresses shall be destroyed."

87. *LSCY, Kang-ling shang*, p. 18b.

88. See, e.g., Ch'ien Mu, *Kuo-shih ta-kang*, pp. 394–401. The fact that this work was written when China was at war of course added to Ch'ien Mu's sense of urgency.

89. Jack Lindsay, *The Normans and Their World* (London: Hart-Davis, MacGibbon, 1973), p. 128.

90. Ibid., pp. 282–283.

91. Painter and Tierney, *Western Europe in the Middle Ages*, p. 168.

Chapter 5: The Views of Ch'eng I and Hu An-kuo

1. The passage is clearly demarcated. See *Ch'eng-shih ching-shuo* 5:30b (*Ssu-k'u ch'üan-shu* ed.) and *I-ch'uan ching-shuo* 4:16a (*Ssu-pu pei-yao* ed.).

2. *Ch'un-ch'iu chi-yi, kang-ling* 1, pp. 1b–2a. Mencius' ambivalence on the importance of obedience to the ruler is well known. It is worth noting that Ch'eng I drew heavily on Mencius and once remarked that both the *Ch'un-ch'iu* and the *I-ching* should be read in the context of the *Mencius* (from the *Ch'eng-tzu i-shu* in the *T'u-shu chi-ch'eng* 56:1849, as quoted in Henderson, *Scripture, Canon, and Commentary*, p. 19).

3. See *Ch'un-ch'iu chi-yi, kang ling* 1, p. 8a. Louis XIV, presumably, would not have found fault with that analogy.

4. It appears in the *Li-chi* in the chapter on music: "It belongs to the nature of man, as from Heaven, to be still at his birth. His activity shows itself as he is acted on by external things, and develops the desires incident to his nature. Things come to him more and more, and his knowledge is increased. Then arise the manifestations of liking and disliking. When these are not regulated by anything within, and growing knowledge leads more astray without, he cannot come back to himself, and his Heavenly principle is extinguished . . . , that is, he stifles the voice of Heavenly principle within, and gives the utmost indulgence to the desires by which men may be possessed.

On this we have the rebellious heart, with licentious and violent disorder.... Such is the great disorder that ensues" (Legge, trans., *Li Chi,* 2:96–97).

5. Ch'ien Mu, *Sung Ming li-hsüeh kai-shu,* p. 71.

6. Ching, "Confucian Way," p. 385.

7. Ch'ien Mu, "Wang Pi," p. 135.

8. Chiu Hansheng, "Zhu Xi's Doctrine of Principle," in *Chu Hsi and Neo-Confucianism,* ed. Wing-tsit Chan (Honolulu: University of Hawai'i Press, 1986), p. 116.

9. Ching, "Confucian Way," p. 376.

10. *Yü-lei,* chap. 41, sec. 22 (p. 1671), quoted in Wing-tsit Chan, *Chu Hsi: New Studies,* p. 200.

11. *Ch'eng-shih ching-shuo,* pp. 18b, 25a.

12. *Ch'un-ch'iu chi-yi, kang-ling* 2, p. 1a.

13. *CYK* 183:6b.

14. *Ch'eng-shih ching-shuo* 5:12b.

15. *CYK* 182:4b–5a. This preface is not included in the *Ssu-k'u ch'üan-shu* edition, but it is in the *Ssu-pu pei-yao* edition.

16. *Ch'eng-shih ching-shuo,* p. 25b. See also Hsieh Shih's comment (*Ch'un-ch'iu chi-yi, kang-ling* 1, p. 7b): "The *Ch'un-ch'iu* clarifies the disasters of heaven and earth and gives form to the changes of the *yin* and the *yang;* the *tao* of harmony can be found in just this aspect."

17. Ch'eng I could also praise, whereas Sun only condemned. In 709, when representatives from two states meet without making a covenant, Ch'eng I notes that by not agreeing to a covenant the parties are "drawing close to principle and therefore (the *Ch'un-ch'iu*) is praising them" (*Ch'eng-shih ching-shuo,* p. 24a).

18. *Ch'eng-shih ching-shuo,* p. 5b. In fact, he uses *yi* several times (as on pp. 16a and 24b—in the latter passage, both the *Tso-chuan* and Sun Fu use the term *contrary to ritual* [*fei-li*]).

19. The first is as on p. 126 of the *Ch'eng-shih ching-shuo,* the second as on p. 21a, the third as on pp. 13a, 27b, and 29a.

20. Adapted from Legge, trans., *The Ch'un Ts'ew,* p. 3. Duke Hui was the father of the present ruler, Duke Yin, who was ruling in place of his younger brother, the future Duke Huan. The younger brother had the stronger claim to the throne because the status of his mother, Chung-tzu, was held to be higher than that of Duke Yin's mother. He later made good his claim by murdering his brother Duke Yin and becoming Duke Huan.

21. *Ch'eng-shih ching-shuo,* pp. 3b–4a.

22. See esp. the following passage: "The calculation of the passage of events is the function of experts whose duty it is to perform divination. When three of them divine, follow the words of two of them. If you have any doubt about important matters, consult with your own

conscience, consult with your ministers and officers, consult with the common people, and consult the tortoise shells and stalks. If you, the tortoise shells, the stalks, the ministers and officers, and the common people all agree, this is called a great concord. There will be welfare to your own person and prosperity to your descendants. The result will be auspicious. If you, the tortoise shells, and the stalks agree but the ministers and officers and the common people oppose, the result will be auspicious. If the ministers and officers, the tortoise shells, and the stalks agree but you and the common people oppose, the result will be auspicious. If the common people, the tortoise shells, and the stalks agree but you and the ministers and the officers oppose, the result will be auspicious. If you and the tortoise shells agree but the stalks, ministers and officers, and the common people oppose, internal operations will be auspicious but external operations will be unlucky. If both the tortoise shells and stalks oppose the views of men, inactivity will be auspicious but active operations will be unlucky" (Chan, *Sourcebook*, p. 10).

23. Legge, trans., *The Shoo King*, pp. 331, 333.

24. Wing-tsit Chan has written that this adherence to the mean *(chung)* became a central principle in neo-Confucianism, arising from the neo-Confucian impulse to discover unity in opposites, to unify life and thought. Hu Yüan was at the forefront of this movement (see Chan, "Integrative Force," pp. 334–335).

25. Ch'eng I quoted in Hsiao, *Cheng-chih ssu-hsiang*, p. 533 (498).

26. Ch'eng I tended to be direct in his criticism of others, which probably did not endear him to those whose conduct he felt called on to correct. He is said, e.g., to have incurred the dislike of the emperor Che-tsung when, as his tutor, he reprimanded the young emperor for breaking off a willow branch in the springtime. Ch'eng I scolded him for failing to carry out his special responsibility to cultivate life in the season of the year in which new life is being born (Ch'ien Mu, *Sung-Ming li-hsüeh kai-shu*, p. 86). The number of enemies he made, of whom the most prominent was Su Shih, suggests that the emperor was not the only one put off by Ch'eng's commitment to moral righteousness (see Fung, *History of Chinese Philosophy*, 2:499).

27. See Freeman, "Lo-yang and the Opposition to Wang An-shih," esp. chap. 5.

28. See Fung, *History of Chinese Philosophy*, 2:500–508.

29. Hu was from Ch'ung-an (present-day Chong'an) in Chien-ning *chün*, in the northwestern portion of Fukien province. His *tzu* was K'ang-hou, *hao* was Wu-yi, and he was posthumously known as Wen-ting. When he passed his *chin-shih* exam in 1097, he was placed fourth (and subsequently raised to third by the emperor) and his policy recommendations on the exam criticized for failing to attack the repeal of Wang An-shih's reforms in the Yüan-yu era (1086–1093).

30. The title of the *Ssu-pu ts'ung-k'an hsü-pien* edition in the bibliography is *Ch'un-ch'iu Hu-shih chuan.* Hereafter it will be referred to by the title as it was originally published: *Ch'un-ch'iu chuan.*

31. *Tzu* was Po-yüan, *hao* Yüeh-fu, from Wu-hsien in Su-chou (modern-day Kiangsu province). Chu taught and wrote and did not accept public office until the middle of the Yüan-yu period (1086–1093), when he was appointed correcting editor of the Imperial Library *(mi-shu sheng cheng-tzu).* He was the author of a work entitled *Ch'un-ch'iu t'ung-chih* in twenty *chüan,* which is no longer extant.

32. See his biography in Herbert Franke, ed., *Sung Biographies* (Wiesbaden: Franz Steiner Verlag, 1976).

33. Mou Jun-sun, "Liang Sung," p. 113.

34. This does not mean that Hu An-kuo had no criticism of Sun Fu. He thought, e.g., that Sun was much too harsh in his judgments (ibid., p. 116; and *CYK* 179:4a).

35. P'i Hsi-jui, *Ching-hsüeh li-shih,* p. 272.

36. *SKTY* 1:539. The *SKTY* notes that Chu Hsi himself was ambivalent about Hu An-kuo's commentary. On the positive side, Chu Hsi claimed that Hu's commentary "clarifies the principles of heaven and rectifies the minds of people" (*Ching-i k'ao* 199.3a [vol. 6], quoted in Henderson, *Scripture, Canon, and Commentary,* p. 55). More critically, Chu Hsi remarked that "the commentary has some far-fetched interpretations but the theories nevertheless manage to create a spirit of openness and synthesis" (*SKTY* 1:539). He also said, even less generously, that Hu An-kuo's "learning is all right for government, but he has not arrived at the Way" (from the *Yü-lei,* chap. 104, sec. 37 [p. 4164], as quoted in Chan, *Chu Hsi: New Studies,* p. 18). Chu Hsi also had a deeper philosophical disagreement with Hu An-kuo, which came out in a conflict between Chu Hsi and Hu An-kuo's son Hu Hung (1106–1161). Hu Hung's position, which he inherited from his father, was that heavenly principle and human desires were the same in substance but different in function. Chu Hsi rejected this identification on the grounds that something evil (human desires) could not originate in something good (heavenly principle). For the details of this philosophical difference, see Schirokauer, "Chu Hsi and Hu Hung." For a sympathetic treatment of the Hu position, see Mou Tsung-san, *Hsin-t'i yü hsing-t'i* (Taipei: Cheng-chung, 1968–1969). Mou argues that the Hu school of neo-Confucianism was insufficiently defended from Chu Hsi's attacks and deserves more attention by modern scholars (see also Tu Wei-ming's review article in *JAS* [30 (May 1971): pp. 642–647]).

37. *Ch'un-ch'iu chi-yi,* pp. 18a–18b.

38. This stress on the primacy of moral values begins in the home. In his commentary, Hu An-kuo argues that the relationship between a man and his wife is in fact the root, the core of the five relationships,

followed by that between a father and his son, and then and only then by the relationship between a ruler and his subjects (*Ch'un-ch'iu chuan*, Yin-kung 2, the ninth month). He repeats the same message in the passage dealing with the twelfth month.

39. See the preface to the *Ch'un-ch'iu chuan*, p. 2b.

40. *Ch'un-ch'iu chuan*, preface, p. 2b.

41. *Ch'un-ch'iu chuan*, Yin-kung 3, the second month.

42. *Ch'un-ch'iu chuan*, Yin-kung 7, summer.

43. *Ching-hsüeh li-shih*, p. 272.

44. This appeal to Mencius serves to underline once again Hu's preoccupation with moral cultivation. The term *hao-jan chih-ch'i* is translated by Legge as "vast, flowing passion-nature" (*Mencius*, p. 189) and by D. C. Lau as "flood-like *ch'i*" (*Mencius*, p. 77). Legge's introduction to the passage is useful (p. 185, n. 2): "Man's nature is composite [according to Mencius's view]; he possesses moral and intellectual powers (comprehended by Mencius under the term *hsin*, 'heart,' 'mind,' interchanged with *chih*, 'the will') and active powers (summed up under the term *ch'i*, and embracing generally the emotions, desires, appetites). The moral and intellectual powers ought to be supreme and govern, but there is a close connexion between them and the others which give effect to them. The active powers must not be stunted, for then the whole character will be feeble. But on the other hand, they must not be allowed to take the lead. They must get their tone from the mind, and the way to develop them in all their completeness is to do good."

45. Lau, trans., *Mencius*, p. 77. *Ch'un-ch'iu chuan*, Ch'eng-kung 16, summer.

46. Lau, trans., *Mencius*, p. 134. The passage in which the quote appears is Hsi-kung 30, autumn.

47. *Ch'un-ch'iu chuan*, Yin-kung 1, the ninth month.

48. *Ch'un-ch'iu chuan*, Yin-kung 3, summer. In a closely following passage, Hu alludes to another violation of *li*: "Whenever the term *yü* is used, it signifies that the *li* governing how rulers see each other has not been observed" (Yin-kung 4, summer).

49. *Ch'un-ch'iu chuan*, Yin-kung 1, summer, the fifth month.

50. The term originates in the *Li yün* chapter of the *Li-chi*. For a translation of the passage in which it appears, see de Bary, Tsunoda, and Keene, *Sources*, 1:176. De Bary translates the term as follows: "the world was shared by all alike." Legge translates it as "a public and common spirit ruled all under the sky" (*Li Chi*, p. 364). The term became very popular in the twentieth century, having been one of Sun Yat-sen's favorites, and was emblazoned on public buildings all over China.

51. For example, *Ch'un-ch'iu chuan*, Yin-kung 3, winter, twelfth month; and again on Yin-kung 8, spring, seventh month.

52. *Ch'un-ch'iu chuan,* Hsiang-kung 11, spring.

53. *Ch'un-ch'iu chuan,* Huan-kung 5, summer.

54. Factionalism, incidentally, can also be seen as a natural outcome of the moralistic (or prophetic) stance of the neo-Confucians themselves, who believed that they had repossessed the truth and were not about to compromise it (see de Bary, *Neo-Confucian Orthodoxy,* pp. 9–13).

55. *Ch'un-ch'iu chuan,* Yin-kung 1, winter, the twelfth month.

56. *Ch'un-ch'iu chuan,* Yin-kung 3, summer. See also Huan-kung 5, where the same opinion is expressed.

57. *Ching-hsüeh li-shih,* p. 272. It might be added that, since P'i himself was a New Text scholar, he was usually sympathetic to Hu's positions.

58. The quotation is from Hsiao, *Chinese Political Thought,* p. 24, n. 52, and comes from the passage on a meeting at Chung-li in the fifteenth year (not the sixteenth, as noted by Hsiao) of Duke Ch'eng (576 B.C.). What prompts this remark is that it is the first instance in the *Ch'un-ch'iu* of a meeting with the state of Wu, according to the *Tso-chuan.*

59. *Ch'un-ch'iu chuan,* Yin-kung 9, spring. Without carrying the analogy too far, in one way at least Hu's views on the preeminence of moral factors (and of course Sun Fu's and Ch'eng I's as well) can be compared with Thucydides' belief that the blame for the military defeat of the Athenians at the hands of the Spartans in the Peloponnesian War (431–404 B.C.) lay with the Athenians themselves. According to that great historian—the Greek Ssu-ma Ch'ien—a corruption in the moral life of the Athenians led them to put their own personal interests *(ssu)* above those of the community *(kung),* and "in the end it was only because they had destroyed themselves by their own internal strife that finally they were forced to surrender" (*The History of the Peloponnesian War,* trans. Rex Warner [New York: Penguin, 1954], p. 164). Having wandered, in other words, from a true understanding of *t'ien-li,* they became slaves to their *jen-yü.*

60. *Ch'un-ch'iu chuan,* Yin-kung 11, summer.

61. *Ch'un-ch'iu chuan,* Yin-kung 11, winter.

62. *Ch'un-ch'iu chuan,* Yin-kung 17, summer.

63. Quoted in Hsiao, *Chinese Political Thought,* pp. 24–25, n. 55, where the quotation is mistakenly attributed to the *Kung-yang* commentary. See Legge, trans., *The Ch'un Ts'ew,* 5, pt. 1:81; and Malmqvist, "Studies," p. 218.

64. Hsiao, *Chinese Political Thought,* p. 25. The *Ku-liang* follows suit, saying, "Why does the Text here use the term *pai* ('defeat') without having used the term *chan* ('to battle')? In order to treat Ch'in as a barbarian state" (adapted from Malmqvist, "Studies," p. 170).

65. This strategy for civilizing the barbarians, incidentally, calls to mind the strategy used by the Christian church in converting Europe after the fall of the Roman Empire. The first generation was generally written off, or, more precisely, was held to a lower standard of understanding of the basic tenets of Christian doctrine, in the expectation that through education future generations would gradually be led to a mature understanding of the faith (hence the critical role of monasteries in the missionary effort).

66. *Ch'un-ch'iu chuan,* Yin-kung 9, spring, the third month.

67. The full quotation is as follows: "'Suppose a subject of Your Majesty's, having entrusted his wife and children to the care of a friend, were to go on a trip to Ch'u, only to find, upon his return, that his friend had allowed his wife and children to suffer cold and hunger, then what should he do about it?' 'Break with his friend.' 'If the Marshal of the Guards was unable to keep his guards in order, then what should be done about it?' 'Remove him from office.' 'If the whole realm within the four borders was ill-governed, then what should be done about it?' The King turned to his attendants and changed the subject" (*Mencius,* trans. Lau, pp. 66–67). Mencius made his point even more explicit when he claimed that the term *regicide* did not apply to assassinating a bad ruler since a bad ruler was not a ruler (ibid., p. 68).

68. Hsiao, *Chinese Political Thought,* p. 121.

Chapter 6: Statecraft and Natural Law in the West and China

1. For a fascinating discussion of the dangers—and the value—of comparing philosophical concepts across cultural boundaries, see Yearley, *Mencius and Aquinas,* in which Yearley speaks about locating "similarities within differences and differences within similarities" (p. 3). He also writes that "my whole enterprise rests on the belief that we must acquire the intellectual virtues needed for comparing ideals of religious flourishings if we are to meet successfully the challenges that our diverse society presents" (pp. 3–4).

2. In the words of George Sabine, "The divine right of kings . . . was essentially a popular theory. It never received, and indeed was incapable of receiving, a philosophical formulation" (*A History of Political Theory,* p. 365).

3. In English, the term *statecraft* is of comparatively recent provenance. The *Oxford English Dictionary* lists the first appearance in 1642 and defines it as "the art of conducting state affairs; statesmanship. Sometimes with sinister implication: crafty or overreaching statesmanship." Often the term carries with it, at least in the West, strong connotations of international relations and presupposes the existence of such a thing as a state, which in the West is of comparatively

recent vintage, at least in its recognizably modern form. A study by Alexander George and Gordon Craig entitled *Force and Statecraft: Diplomatic Problems of Our Time* (New York: Oxford University Press, 1983), e.g., takes as its point of departure the rise of the modern state in Europe, which the authors, along with most historians, see as reaching its present configuration during the Thirty Years' War from 1618 to 1648 (pp. 4–5).

4. Aristotle, *Politics,* trans. Benjamin Jowett (New York: Random House, 1941), p. 1127 (par. 1252a). Aristotle also wrote, in the same work (pp. 1187–1189 [pars. 1280–1281a]), that "a state exists for the sake of a good life, and not for the sake of life only: if life only were the object, slaves and brute animals might form a state, but they cannot, for they have no share in happiness or in a life of free choice. Nor does a state exist for the sake of alliance and security from injustice, nor yet for the sake of exchange and mutual intercourse. . . . Virtue must be the care of a state which is truly so called, and not merely enjoys the name: for without this end the community becomes a mere alliance which differs only in place from alliances of which the members live apart; and law is only a convention . . . and has not real power to make the citizens good and just. . . . It is clear then that a state is not a mere society, having a common place, established for the prevention of mutual crime and for the sake of exchange. These are conditions without which a state cannot exist; but all of them together do not constitute a state, which is a community of families and aggregations of families in well-being, for the sake of a perfect and self-sufficing life. . . . The end of the state is the good life, and these are the means towards it. . . . Our conclusion, then, is that political society exists for the sake of noble actions, and not of mere companionship." Plato wrote in the *Laws* that "laws generally should look to one thing only; and this, as we admitted, was rightly said to be virtue" (*Works of Plato,* trans. Benjamin Jowett [New York: Random House, 1937], p. 697 [par. 963]).

5. I confine myself to Plato and Aristotle since there were other Greeks in the classical period, such as the Sophists, who held different views on many of these questions.

6. *Works of Plato,* trans. Jowett, 1:522 (par. 464), 579 (par. 519).

7. I have relied principally on d'Entrèves' *Natural Law* and Simon's *The Tradition of Natural Law.* Sabine's *History of Political Theory* and Sibley's *Political Ideas and Ideologies* have also been very helpful. See also Turner's "Sage Kings and Laws in the Chinese and Greek Traditions," in Ropp, *Heritage of China,* pp. 86–111.

8. *Ethics* 5.7. "There are two sorts of political justice, one natural and the other legal. The natural is that which has the same validity everywhere and does not depend upon acceptance; the legal is that

which in the first place can take one form or another indifferently, but which, once laid down, is decisive" (*The Ethics of Aristotle*, trans. J. A. K. Thomson [New York: Penguin, 1976]).

9. Simon, *The Tradition of Natural Law*, p. 30.

10. Hooker, *Of the Laws of Ecclesiastical Polity*, 1:187–188.

11. Sibley, *Political Ideas*, p. 133.

12. From Cicero's *De Republica*, 3.22.33, quoted in d'Entrèves, *Natural Law*, p. 25.

13. Sabine, *Political Theory*, p. 169.

14. Quoted in d'Entrèves, *Natural Law*, p. 39.

15. Quoted in ibid., p. 37.

16. Sibley, *Political Ideas*, pp. 216–217.

17. D'Entrèves, *Natural Law*, p. 38.

18. Sibley, *Political Ideas*, p. 243.

19. Ibid., pp. 243–245.

20. Aquinas, *Summa theologica*, 1a 2ae.95.2, quoted in d'Entrèves, *Natural Law*, p. 46.

21. Sibley, *Political Ideas*, pp. 244–245. See also d'Entrèves, *Natural Law*, p. 46. Even here, however, Aquinas is ambivalent, for he also argues that "a tyrannical government is not just, because it is directed, not to the common good, but to the private good of the ruler. . . . Consequently there is no sedition in disturbing a government of this kind, unless indeed the tyrant's rule be disturbed so inordinately that his subjects suffer greater harm from the consequent disturbance than from the tyrant's government. Indeed it is the tyrant rather that is guilty of sedition, since he encourages discord and sedition among his subjects, that he may lord over them more securely" (*Summa theologica*, 2 2.42.2).

22. By far the most famous passage dealing with the consequences of upsetting the hierarchical order occurs in a speech by Ulysses in *Troilus and Cressida*, when he exhorts the Athenians to look for the cause of their impotence against the Trojans in their own moral degeneration, not in mere inferiority of arms (1.3.85–137). Note also the conversation in *Macbeth* between the old man and Ross that opens act 2, scene 4. The ideas could almost have been taken out of a *Ch'un-ch'iu* commentary in the Sung dynasty noting the disasters and prodigies that would follow on the actions of an evil ruler and arguing that the nation's strength or weakness against its enemies lay primarily not in force of arms but in moral cultivation. Ulysses' speech reads as follows:

> The heavens themselves, the planets and this centre
> Observe degree, priority and place,
> Insisture, course, proportion, season, form,
> Office and custom, in all line of order;

In noble eminence enthroned and sphered
Amidst the other; whose medicinable eye
Corrects the ill aspects of planets evil,
And posts, like the commandment of a king,
Sans check to good and bad: but when the planets
In evil mixture to disorder wander,
What plagues and what portents! what mutiny!
What raging of the sea! shaking of earth!
Commotion in the winds! frights, changes, horrors,
Divert and crack, rend and deracinate
The unity and married calm of states
Quite from their fixture! O, when degree is shaked,
Which is the ladder to all high designs,
The enterprise is sick! How could communities,
Degrees in schools and brotherhoods in cities,
Peaceful commerce from dividable shores,
The primogeniture and due of birth,
Prerogative of age, crowns, sceptres, laurels,
But by degree stand in authentic place?
Take but degree away, untune that string,
And, hark, what discord follows! each thing meets
In mere oppugnancy: the bounded waters
Should lift their bosoms higher than the shores
And make a sop of all this solid globe:
Strength should be lord of imbecility,
And the rude son should strike his father dead:
Force should be right; or rather, right and wrong,
Between whose endless jar justice resides,
Should lose their names, and so should justice too.
Then everything includes itself in power,
Power into will, will into appetite;
And appetite, an universal wolf,
So doubly seconded with will and power,
Must make perforce an universal prey,
And last eat up himself. Great Agamemnon,
This chaos, when degree is suffocate,
Follows the choking.
And this neglection of degree it is
That by a pace goes backward, with a purpose
It hath to climb. The general's disdain'd
By him one step below, he by the next,
That next by him beneath; so every step,
Exampled by the first pace that is sick
Of his superior, grows to an envious fever

Of pale and bloodless emulation:
And 'tis this fever that keeps Troy on foot,
Not in her sinews. To end a tale of length,
Troy in our weakness stands, not in her strength.

23. Daly, *Cosmic Harmony,* p. 11. See Daly's book generally on prevailing beliefs.

24. *Ch'eng-shih ching-shuo,* p. 8a.

25. Reese, *The Cease of Majesty,* p. 110.

26. D'Entrèves, *Natural Law,* p. 55.

27. In the words of Leo Spitzer (*Classical and Christian Ideas of World Harmony* [Baltimore, 1963]), "The world-embracing metaphysical cupola that once enfolded mankind disappeared, and man is left to rattle around in an infinite universe" (quoted in Daly, *Cosmic Harmony,* p. 34).

28. D'Entrèves, *Natural Law,* p. 59.

29. Hu, "The Natural Law in the Chinese Tradition," esp. pp. 119–120. Hu draws, however, strictly modern liberal conclusions from it: "In short, the most significant historical role of the concepts of Natural Law and Natural Rights has been that of a fighting weapon in Man's struggle against the tyranny of unlimited power and authority" (p. 122).

30. Ibid., p. 147.

31. Ibid. Chao P'u was no intellectual, which makes his answer all the more interesting.

32. Ibid., p. 152.

33. Latourette, *The Chinese,* p. 535. In the 1934 second edition of this text (2:44), the *li* referred to was "ritual," not "principle." It is from this edition that Hu Shih quoted the above passage approvingly ("The Natural Law in the Chinese Tradition," pp. 142–143). In the third edition, the *li* for "ritual" is replaced by the *li* for "principle," with no change in the surrounding text. The confusion is understandable if one believes that the two words have overlapping meanings when they refer to natural law.

34. Hummel, "Case against Force," p. 338.

35. Creel, *Confucius,* pp. 268, 164. See also Mungello, *Leibniz and Confucianism,* p. 16.

36. Needham, *Science and Civilisation,* 2:544. Needham's understanding of natural law is distinctly modern—one might even say anthropological. He regards it as "the sum of the folkways whose ethical sanctions had risen into consciousness" (ibid.). In fact, Needham's failure to understand fully the history of natural law in the West causes him to attribute a continuity to the ideas of natural law that they did not possess. When he says that "we may find it equally reasonable to relate the rise of the concept of laws of Nature at the Renaissance to

the appearance of royal absolutism at the end of feudalism and the beginning of capitalism" (p. 543), he apparently does not realize that the content of the natural law used to justify absolutism was very different from what had preceded it, nor did it "rise" at the Renaissance. Derk Bodde appears to agree with Needham's definition of *natural law* as being restricted to the human realm, while "laws of nature" have to do with the physical world. Although Bodde is more concerned with the latter than the former, he does appear to accept Needham's views on the existence of natural law in China (see Bodde's "Authority and Law in Ancient China" and "Chinese 'Laws of Nature,'" both reprinted in *Essays on Chinese Civilization,* ed. Charles Le Blanc and Dorothy Borei [Princeton, N.J.: Princeton University Press, 1981], pp. 161–170, 299–315, respectively).

37. In fact, when he discusses Hsün Tzu's use of the term *ritual (li),* Donald Munro writes that it is one of "the Chinese equivalents for natural law" (*Images of Human Nature,* p. 31).

38. Kracke, *Civil Service,* pp. 18–19.

39. Hartwell, "Historical Analogism," pp. 696–697. For a detailed history of this institution, see Kwon, "The Imperial Lecture of Sung China." Kwon notes that the imperial seminar was "an apparatus of indoctrination by means of which Confucian ideologists exerted some measure of moral influence on their ruler. It was an attempt to direct the exercise of imperial authority according to a set of Confucian principles of government. Briefly, this was an effort to regulate the imperial power through moral suasion" (p. 103).

40. De Bary, *Neo-Confucian Learning of the Mind-and-Heart.* See also Ching, "Neo-Confucian Utopian Theories," esp. pp. 45–47.

41. See Liu, "The Sung Emperors and the Ming-T'ang." Derk Bodde quotes from a memorial submitted to Wang Mang in A.D. 6: "You have established the Pi Yung and set up the Ming T'ang to propagate the laws of Heaven *(t'ien-fa)* and to spread the influence of the sages." He then goes on to explain that "the Ming T'ang or Cosmic Hall was a building consisting of rooms corresponding to the months of the year and oriented around a central axis so as to face the compass points corresponding to the months. At monthly intervals, within the appropriate room, the emperor, following the prescriptions laid down in the *Yüeh ling (Monthly Ordinances)* and clad in colors appropriate to the particular season, allegedly performed the ceremonies designed to accord with the cosmic conditions of that month" ("Chinese 'Laws of Nature,'" in *Essays on Chinese Civilization,* p. 311).

42. The construction of a special temple for the *ming-t'ang* ceremony was begun under Hui-tsung (1101–1125). It was delayed because of the appearance of a comet, considered to be a bad omen (Liu, "The Sung Emperors and the Ming-T'ang," p. 54).

43. Ibid., pp. 52–53.

44. Kern, *Kingship and Law,* p. 138.

45. Without such confidence, one might argue, they never would have dared to take such a fresh look at the classical tradition and dispense with the textual baggage that had accumulated over the past several centuries. According to Daniel Gardner, this "new, Neo-Confucian approach to the canon was no doubt conditioned by the epistemological assumption that underlay Neo-Confucian philosophical reflection—namely, that the mind was endowed with the ability to be instructed in and discern the truth. This belief was by no means entirely new in the Sung. . . . But it was only in the Northern Sung that the belief in the mind's capacity for apprehension of the truth came to be generally accepted. . . . This epistemological assumption must have imbued Neo-Confucian thinkers with a new and great self-confidence, a faith that, with the effort, the proper spirit, and the appropriate curriculum, they could come to apprehend the message embedded in the canonical texts" (see "Modes of Thinking," pp. 580–581).

Chapter 7: Implications for Modern China and Japan

1. Legge, trans., *Analects,* pp. 138–139.

2. Thomas Hobbes, *Leviathan* (Indianapolis: Bobbs-Merrill, 1958), p. 1.

3. It should be remembered that the Roman rule of which Paul spoke, however conducive its transportation and legal system were to the spread of Christianity, was also responsible for sporadic and sometimes savage persecution of Christians until the fourth century. See also 1 Pet. 2:13–17: "Be subject for the Lord's sake to every human institution, whether it be to the emperor as supreme, or to governors as sent by him to punish those who do wrong and to praise those who do right. For it is God's will that by doing right you should put to silence the ignorance of foolish men. Live as free men, yet without using your freedom as a pretext for evil; but live as servants of God. Honor all men. Love the brotherhood. Fear God. Honor the emperor."

4. Aquinas, *Commentary on the Sentences of Peter Lombard,* 2.D.44, question 2, article 3, quoted in Sibley, *Political Ideas and Ideologies,* p. 248.

5. Stern, *Kingship and Law,* p. 143.

6. Some examples have already been given above. See also the discussion of the hexagram for revolution, *ko,* in the *I-ching* (Wilhelm, trans., pp. 182–192, 635–640).

7. Chan Hok-lam, "Liu Chi," p. 159.

8. See Liu, "How Did a Neo-Confucian School Become the State

Orthodoxy?" According to Ching ("Truth and Ideology," p. 371), "the evolution of Confucian teachings in China revealed a pattern that may be described as the interplay of truth and ideology. By 'truth' is understood here that interpretation of reality suggested by the great philosophical minds with the help of the Classical texts. By 'ideology' is meant here the institutionalization of 'truth' by the state authority selecting and manipulating the commentaries on the Classics, through the educational and examination system, in such a manner as to present a certain interpretation of man, society, and the world which contributes to the consolidation of that same authority. The historical process by which truth becomes institutionalized can first be discerned in the case of Confucianism around the first century B.C. during the Han dynasty (202 B.C.–A.D. 220). It was later repeated in the T'ang (618–906) and Sung (960–1279) dynasties, which witnessed another attempt by the state to reconstruct a Confucian ideology. In this case, however, the new ideology failed to take hold of men's minds, largely because of the challenges posed by Taoist and Buddhist philosophies. But the movement of reinterpretation of Confucianism became important with the emergence of several independent thinkers who sought to go beyond ideology and recover the lost truth, until, in its turn, the new synthesis which they created became established as state doctrine in the Yüan dynasty (1260–1368)."

9. Huang, *Autocracy at Work,* p. 188.

10. Wilhelm, "Chinese Confucianism," p. 287. The term *imperial Confucianism* appears to have originated with James Legge.

11. Ibid., p. 284.

12. Levenson, *Confucian China and Its Modern Fate,* 2:66.

13. See Mote, "The Growth of Chinese Despotism."

14. See Tao Jing-shen, "The Influence of Jürchen Rule on Chinese Political Institutions," esp. p. 130.

15. Chow, *The May Fourth Movement,* p. 295.

16. *IESS,* s.v. *Confucianism.*

17. For a discussion of both the possibilities and the limitations of a powerful official with integrity, see Ray Huang's chapter on the Ming official Hai Jui (1513–1587) in *1587, Year of No Significance,* pp. 130–155. When he sent his famous memorial to the court, directly and bluntly criticizing the behavior of the emperor, Hai said good-bye to his family, ordered that a coffin be prepared for him, and awaited the outcome. Although the emperor's first impulse was to arrest such an outspoken official, he changed his mind after he learned of Hai's willingness to sacrifice his life for his principles (although Hai was later imprisoned and may have been spared execution only by the death of the emperor himself).

18. More's last words on the scaffold were to the effect that he

died "the King's good servant but God's first" (see Chambers, *Thomas More*, p. 349). In speaking of John Houghton, prior of the London Charterhouse, a Carthusian monastery that refused to recognize the right of Henry VIII to act as head of the church in England, and who along with several other monks was executed a few days before Thomas More, Chambers wrote that "he was hanged, cut down, and disemboweled while still alive; as his entrails were torn out, he was heard to say gently 'Oh most merciful Jesus, have pity on me in this hour!' The other monks had to watch his tortures, and, as each awaited his turn, also those of their fellows. Whilst waiting, they urged the crowd to obey the King in all that was not against the honour of God and the Church" (p. 326). Those were the days when monks were monks.

19. Morris, *Political Thought in England,* pp. 141–142.

20. Wilhelm, "Chinese Confucianism," p. 307; Fung, *Chinese Philosophy,* 2:673. Was Fung not aware of the importance of the *Ch'un-ch'iu* in the rise of neo-Confucianism?

21. John Whitney Hall, "The Historical Dimension," in *Twelve Doors to Japan* (New York: McGraw-Hill, 1965), p. 138.

22. Machiavelli would have understood. Three hundred fifty years before the Meiji Restoration, he wrote that, "if one desires or intends to reform the government of a city so that the reform will be acceptable and will be able to maintain itself to everyone's satisfaction, he should retain at least a shadow of ancient customs so that it will not seem to the people that they have changed institutions, whereas in actual fact the new institutions may be completely different from those of the past; for the majority of men delude themselves with what seems to be rather than with what actually is; indeed, they are more often moved by things that seem to be rather than by things that are. . . . Since new things disturb the minds of men, you should strive to see that these disturbing changes retain as much of the ancient regime as possible" (*Discourses,* chap. 25, as quoted in *The Portable Machiavelli,* trans. Peter Bondanella and Mark Musa [New York: Penguin, 1979], p. 231).

23. Hall, "Monarch for Modern Japan," p. 14.

24. *Kodansha Encyclopedia of Japan,* s.v. *sonnō jōi* (Tokyo: Kodansha, 1983). David Earl notes that the terms *sonnō* and *jōi* appear in different places in Ssu-ma Ch'ien's preface to the *Shih Chi* but assumes that it was the Tokugawa Japanese who brought them together for the first time (*Emperor and Nation in Japan,* p. 105).

25. As H. D. Harootunian has said with regard to the Japanese context, "It is my view that Mito writers, in trying to come to grips with what they perceived as serious domestic moral failure, began a process of politicization that ended with and in the Meiji achieve-

ment. By politicizing the elements of an ethical tradition into a theory of action, they offered subsequent writers and activists not so much a workable theory as a method by which to deal with changing political reality" (*Toward Restoration: The Growth of Political Consciousness in Tokugawa Japan* [Berkeley: University of California Press, 1970], pp. xxxi–xxxii).

26. Ibid., p. 14.

27. For a more detailed treatment of this early period, see Herman Ooms, "Neo-Confucianism and the Formation of Early Tokugawa Ideology," in *Confucianism and Tokugawa Culture,* ed. Peter Nosco (Princeton, N.J.: Princeton University Press, 1984), pp. 27–61.

28. Yamazaki's ideas remained influential long after his death. One of his students, Asami Keisai (1652–1712), wrote a work known as the *Seiken Igen* that greatly influenced members of the *sonnō jōi* movement. Asami is said to have read Chu Hsi's history forty-two times (Earl, *Emperor and Nation,* p. 59).

29. Kate Wildman Nakai, *Shogunal Politics: Arai Hakuseki and the Premises of Tokugawa Rule* (Cambridge, Mass.: Harvard University Press, 1988), p. 346.

30. Maruyama Masao, *Studies in the Intellectual History of Tokugawa Japan,* trans. Mikiso Hane (Princeton, N.J.: Princeton University Press, 1974), p. 142.

31. See Kate Wildman Nakai, "Tokugawa Confucian Historiography: The Hayashi, Early Mito School and Arai Hakuseki," in *Confucianism and Tokugawa Culture,* p. 76. According to Wm. Theodore de Bary, "Patriotism and loyalty to the throne became the paramount themes of Mitsukuni's history, as well as the cardinal doctrines of those who later carried on the tradition of the Mito school. Through them these ideas were to exert a profound influence on the course of Japanese history during the Restoration period" (see de Bary, Chan, and Watson, eds., *Sources of Japanese Tradition,* 1:363).

32. Since the title *shōgun* had itself originated as a term bestowed on generals sent to suppress the "northern barbarians" in Japan—i.e., the Ainu—the Mito scholars, who in the beginning of the nineteenth century were already concerned about how to deal with the new barbarians from overseas, naturally thought in terms of *jōi* in formulating a response.

33. Earl, *Emperor and Nation,* p. 105. Ying-wo Chan has pointed out, in a personal communication, that it was "ghost-written by Fujita Tōkō for Tokugawa Nariaki, the lord of the Mito han. While this piece was written in Chinese by Tōkō, it was based on a draft by Tokugawa Nariaki in *kana.* Tōkō's Chinese draft was shown by Nariaki to Itō Issai, a scholar with deep ties to the Hayashi school, as well as two Mito scholars, Aoyama En'u and Aizawa Seishisai, for comments. Nariaki

then asked Tōkō for his opinion on the comments and, after that, decided the final draft in 1847 (see Seya Yoshihiko's "Kaisetsu" to *Kōdōkanki,* in *Nihon shisō taikei,* vol. 13, *Mitogaku* [Tokyo: Iwanami shoten, 1973], p. 496).

34. Aizawa Seishisai acknowledges his debt to his teacher, and his teacher's influence, in his autobiography, where he notes that "the master's thought is based on the principles of *sonnō* (reverence for the emperor) and *jōi* (expulsion of the barbarian) as they are found in the Spring and Autumn Analects [sic]" (quoted and translated by Harootunian in *Toward Restoration,* p. 59). Harootunian argues that this doctrine of *sonnō jōi* was originally intended not to undermine the Tokugawa feudal system but to strengthen it by anchoring it in timeless moral values. Only later, when it became apparent that the *bakufu* could not respond effectively to the challenge of the West, did it become a revolutionary tool.

35. Maruyama Masao, *Studies in the Intellectual History of Tokugawa Japan,* p. 307.

36. Beasley, *The Meiji Restoration,* p. 208.

37. See the discussion in Harootunian, *Toward Restoration,* pp. xxv–xxxii; and Beasley, *The Meiji Restoration,* pp. 1–12.

38. The characterization is Harootunian's in *Toward Restoration,* p. xxx.

39. I do not understand why the origins of the term *sonnō jōi* in Northern Sung China have not been discussed in the scholarly literature that I have read. I can only guess that, since many of the late Tokugawa thinkers in Japan rejected the principal tenets of the *Shushigaku* school and called for a return to the classics, they were anxious to hide the Sung origins of the term. Why contemporary historians should follow their example is something of a mystery.

40. In fact, the institution of the emperor may have survived in Japan precisely *because* it had no power from very early times. See Morris, *The Shining Prince,* p. 66: "Although later nationalist historians have looked askance at the Fujiwaras for arrogating to themselves powers that were not rightfully theirs, it could quite justifiably be argued that it was they who saved the throne and helped the Japanese imperial dynasty to become (as it is by far) the oldest in the world. For, by removing all real power from the emperor, while at the same time according him the full honours of sovereignty, they set a precedent that was to be maintained during the succeeding centuries by Japan's military rulers, including as recent a leader as General Tojo. If the Heian emperors had been allowed to rule as well as to reign, the imperial family might well have been swept away, or at least supplanted by a new dynasty, when the warrior class took over power from the aristocracy." In a sense, the Japanese accomplished what the neo-

Confucians might also have wished for—separating the power from the authority of the emperor.

41. Herschel Webb has written that "from first to last Japanese theory on the imperial dynasty has asserted a definition of legitimacy which is of the opposite emphasis from the Chinese and European" (*Japanese Imperial Institution*, p. 11).

42. For a more detailed evaluation of the position of the emperor, see Beckmann, *Meiji Constitution*, esp. pp. 29, 84–90. Beckmann concludes his study with these words: "Applying the doctrine that sovereignty rested in the person of a divine emperor, they [the oligarchs] established a government in which they consolidated their control as the emperor's ministers. Thus, in the final analysis, through their dominant position in the cabinet, the supreme command, the Privy Council, and the Imperial Household Ministry, the oligarchs sought to maintain their power in modern political forms sanctioned by a written constitution and buttressed by a renewed emphasis upon Shinto and orthodox Confucianism" (p. 95).

43. John Whitney Hall strongly emphasizes the importance of the emperor in Japan's modernization: "Central to Japan's history of political modernization has been the role of the monarch—the *tenno*—and the institutions and ideas adhering to the imperial institution" ("Monarch for Modern Japan," p. 11). Hall has further speculated on what might have happened had the Japanese abandoned their emperor (the tragedy is that what might have happened in Japan did in fact happen in China, although of course for other reasons as well): "And though the Japanese may look back upon the last hundred years of their history to deny the burden of state authoritarianism which weighed upon them, one wonders whether they are prepared to exchange those conditions for the prospect of national disintegration which could have resulted from a society warring upon itself or under a headless political anarchy" (p. 13). To be sure, by laying the groundwork for the rise of modern Japanese nationalism, the doctrine of *tsun-wang jang-i* also contributed to the rise of singularly antidemocratic (and imperialist) forces. Perhaps that only underlines the essential flexibility of term and demonstrates in graphic terms how the past can be made to serve the present in diverse ways.

44. *ECCP*, p. 207. See Benjamin Elman's thorough study of the rise of the New Text school, *Classicism, Politics, and Kinship*. For further background on the intellectual context of the period, in which the Ch'eng-Chu orthodoxy was displaced among active scholars by the School of Empirical Research (illustrating how philology can affect politics), see Elman, *From Philosophy to Philology*.

45. Liang Ch'i-ch'ao, *Intellectual Trends*, p. 88. Fung, *Chinese Philosophy*, 2:673.

46. Liang Ch'i-ch'ao, *Intellectual Trends*, p. 88.

47. According to Elman, "The renascence of New Text Confucianism, then, was part of a larger transformation of literati perceptions regarding their personal and dynastic responsibilities—a transformation that began during the Ho-shen era. New Text Confucianism was offered as a solution to the ensuing crisis of confidence" (*Classicism, Politics, and Kinship*, p. 114).

48. Quoted in ibid., p. 115.

49. Elman, "Scholarship and Politics," pp. 74–75. Elman notes that Chuang's motives were conservative. Chuang did not intend his views to support "more radical statecraft agendas" that came to be associated with New Text interpretation in the late nineteenth century; rather, they were meant to preserve the existing Sung learning orthodoxy (p. 77). In so doing, then, it appears that, in China as well as Japan, ideas that were originally intended to preserve the existing arrangement ended up being used to attack it. For a discussion of Chuang's role in opposing Ho-shen, see Elman, *Classicism, Politics, and Kinship*, pp. 108–114.

50. Liang Ch'i-ch'ao, *Intellectual Trends*, p. 88. For a detailed discussion of Liu Feng-lu, see Elman, *Classicism, Politics, and Kinship*, pp. 214–256.

51. *ECCP*, p. 520.

52. Elman, *Classicism, Politics, and Kinship*, p. 222.

53. Immanuel C. Y. Hsü, *The Rise of Modern China* (New York: Oxford University Press, 1983), p. 276. See also Teng Ssu-yü and John K. Fairbank, *China's Response to the West: A Documentary Survey, 1839–1923* (Cambridge, Mass.: Harvard University Press, 1965), p. 34.

54. Liang Ch'i-ch'ao, *Intellectual Trends*, p. 89.

55. Treadgold, *The West in Russia and China*, 2:168.

56. Liang Ch'i-ch'ao, *Intellectual Trends*, p. 94.

57. Hsiao, *Modern China*, pp. 94–95.

58. *Biographical Dictionary of Republican China* (New York: Columbia University Press, 1967–1979) s.v. *Liang Ch'i-ch'ao*. For more on Liang's life and thought, see Joseph Levenson, *Liang Ch'i-ch'ao and the Mind of Modern China* (Cambridge, Mass.: Harvard University Press, 1959); Chang, *Liang Ch'i-ch'ao;* and Huang, *Liang Ch'i-ch'ao*.

59. In Donald Treadgold's words, "He strove to reconcile the claims of the individual and the community, emphasizing cooperation as a means of doing so; he endeavored to defend the value of the family, the nation, and private property (which K'ang's Great Community sacrificed). . . . He tried to practice the ideal of a free man, rejecting the outworn, admitting the possibility that evidence might throw in doubt the validity of tenets the Chinese had cherished for millennia or his own current pet idea, whether based on foreign or indigenous

models, constantly seeking to reevaluate his positions, engaging in self-criticism" (*The West in Russia and China,* 2:119–120).

60. See Hellmut Wilhelm, "The Problem of Within and Without: A Confucian Attempt in Syncretism," *JHI* 12 (1951): 48–60.

61. Hsiao, *Modern China,* p. 96.

62. In this respect, modern Korea's experience is not dissimilar to that of China and Japan. In Korea, the ruling class *(yangban)* acted together to protect their own interests and in the process also used Confucian ideology to their own advantage. According to James Palais, "The yangban bureaucrats even turned the normative standards of Confucian thought against the throne. By insisting that the king conform to moral and ethical standards that transcended his right to the arbitrary exercise of power, by setting themselves up as arbiters of those standards by virtue of their knowledge of Confucian texts, and by insisting on their right to remonstrate and the king's obligation to tolerate remonstrance, yangban bureaucrats and literati sought to reduce kings to puppets of their own desires and interests" (*Traditional Korea,* p. 11). Their experience also calls to mind the old motto of the Prussian Junkers, whose relations with the kaiser were often equally ambivalent: "Hoch der König absolut, Wenn er unser Willen tut" (Long live the king, as long as he does our bidding). As quoted in Treadgold, *The West in Russia and China,* 1:155.

63. *The Old Regime and the French Revolution,* trans. Stuart Gilbert (Garden City, N.Y.: Doubleday, 1955), p. xi.

64. Such a venture is also being increasingly advocated by some in the West. One interesting call for that revival is Alasdair MacIntyre's *After Virtue.*

65. See esp. Huang, *Liang Ch'i-ch'ao,* pp. 141–159.

66. Architecture is another form of artistic expression offering a tangible and visible expression of this synthesizing impulse. I look forward to a new generation of Chinese architects, in Taiwan, Hong Kong, Singapore, and even, one hopes, in China, who will design buildings that are fully Chinese and fully modern.

67. Note T'an Ssu-t'ung's comment in a letter to a friend, quoted in Jonathan Spence's *To Change China* (New York: Penguin, 1980): "What you mean by foreign matters are things you have seen, such as steamships, telegraph lines, trains, guns, cannon, torpedoes, and machines for weaving and metallurgy; that's all. You have never dreamed of or seen the beauty and perfection of Western legal systems and political institutions. . . . All that you speak of are the branches and foliage of foreign matters, not the root. . . . Now there is not a single one of the Chinese people's sentiments, customs, or political and legal institutions which can be favorably compared with those of the barbarians" (p. 156). That is an astonishing statement, both for

its insight into the real sources of Western strength and for its complete dismissal of the Chinese tradition.

68. See the epilogue to K. C. Chang, *The Archaeology of Ancient China,* 4th ed. (New Haven, Conn.: Yale University Press, 1986), pp. 414–422. There Chang suggests that the emphasis on cosmological harmony, and the close relation between the political and religious dimensions in ancient China, discouraged the rise of economic or religious institutions that were outside the scope of centralized political power, such that "the modernization of the developing world of today may be seen as an effort—belated and possibly not yet thought through—on the part of the rest of the world to catch up with the West, in a fundamental realignment of cosmology and technology, after a bifurcation more than five thousand years old. . . . It is time that more studies be made of the so-called Asiatic mode of production—not in terms of an established doctrine but as a study of cross-cultural history" (p. 422).

69. That task has already been taken up by scholars far more qualified than I am. They include Hu Shih and Hsiao Kung-ch'üan and, more recently, Frederick Mote, Wm. Theodore de Bary, Benjamin Schwartz, Andrew Nathan, Thomas Metzger, Chang Hao, Yü Ying-shih, and Tu Wei-ming. See also Edwards, Henkin, and Nathan, eds., *Human Rights in Contemporary China;* and several of the essays in Cohen and Goldman, eds., *Ideas across Cultures.*

70. According to John Finnis, "There are, in the final analysis, only two ways of making a choice between alternative ways of coordinating action to the common purpose or common good of any group. There must be either unanimity, or authority. There are no other possibilities" (*Natural Law and Natural Rights,* [New York: Oxford University Press, 1980] p. 232).

71. This optimism in the West was based on an exaggerated hope that reason, set free from the chains of traditional (i.e., Aristotelian or Christian) habits of thinking by the Scientific Revolution and applied to the human world as scientists had applied it to the natural world, would solve most, if not all, human problems. The Romantic movement rose in part as a reaction to those expectations and focused on the forces of darkness in the human personality that lie outside the province of reason. Needless to say, the more balanced view of the Greeks, of a human personality capable of reason but also marred by a tragic propensity to pride, and the Christians, of man created in the image of God but also marred by original sin, represented the mainstream of Western civilization for most of its existence and repudiated any notion of a golden age either in the past or in the future.

72. Of course, it was not all that appealing to Alexander Hamilton either, and many other people in colonial America (and later), who

distrusted the instincts of the hoi polloi. Hamilton regarded the common man as "a great beast" and favored government by the rich and the well born.

73. The literature on the compatibility of the Chinese heritage and Western liberalism and democracy is growing fast. Among the most interesting contributions (aside from those already mentioned, including especially the work of Andrew Nathan, such as *Dilemmas of Reform and Prospects for Democracy*) are de Bary, *The Liberal Tradition in China,* and "Human Rites—an Essay on Confucianism and Human Rights"; and Tu Wei-ming, "Toward a Third Epoch of Confucian Humanism," and "Intellectual Effervescence in China."

74. It was once assumed in the West that one of the important needs of the individual was to surrender some wants in order to promote the public good. Increasingly, many now argue, individual needs are defined primarily as the satisfaction of individual wants that have very little to do with the welfare of family and society.

75. For a stimulating treatment of the contribution of Confucianism to the modernization of East Asia, see Rozman, ed., *The East Asian Region.* See also Roy Hofheinz Jr. and Kent E. Calder, *The Eastasia Edge* (New York: Basic Books, 1982).

Selected Bibliography

Ahern, Emily M. *Chinese Ritual and Politics.* New York: Cambridge University Press, 1981.

Alitto, Guy S. *The Last Confucian: Liang Shu-ming and the Chinese Dilemma of Modernity.* Berkeley and Los Angeles: University of California Press, 1981.

Ames, Roger T. *The Art of Rulership: A Study in Ancient Chinese Political Thought.* Honolulu: University of Hawai'i Press, 1983.

Arendt, Hannah. "What Is Authority?" In *Between Past and Future,* pp. 91–141. New York: Penguin, 1977.

Aristotle. *The Nicomachean Ethics.* Translated by J. A. K. Thomson. New York: Penguin, 1976.

Barfield, Thomas. *The Perilous Frontier: Nomadic Empires and China.* Cambridge, Mass.: Basil Blackwell, 1989.

Barmé, Geremie, and John Minford, eds. *Seeds of Fire: Chinese Voices of Conscience.* New York: Farrar Straus Giroux, 1989.

Beasley, W. G. *The Meiji Restoration.* Stanford, Calif.: Stanford University Press, 1972.

Beattie, Hilary. *Land and Lineage in China: A Study of T'ung-ch'eng County, Anhwei in the Ming and Ch'ing Dynasties.* Cambridge: Cambridge University Press, 1979.

Beckmann, George M. *The Making of the Meiji Constitution.* Lawrence: University of Kansas Press, 1957.

Birdwhistell, Anne D. *Transition to Neo-Confucianism: Shao Yung on Knowledge and Symbols of Reality.* Stanford, Calif.: Stanford University Press, 1989.

Black, Alison Harley. *Man and Nature in the Philosophical Thought of Wang Fu-chih.* Seattle: University of Washington Press, 1989.

Bodde, Derk. "Authority and Law in Ancient China." *JAOS,* suppl. no. 17 (1954): 46–55.

———. "Chinese 'Laws of Nature': A Reconsideration." *HJAS* 39 (1979): 139–155.

Bodde, Derk, and Clarence Morris. *Law in Imperial China.* Cambridge, Mass.: Harvard University Press, 1967.

Bol, Peter Kees. "Culture and the Way in Eleventh Century China." Ph.D. diss., Princeton University, 1982.

———. *Research Tools for the Study of Sung History.* Binghamton, N.Y.: *Journal of Sung-Yuan Studies,* 1990.

———. "The Sung Examination System and the *Shih.*" *Asia Major* 3, no. 2 (1990): 149–171.

———. *"This Culture of Ours": Intellectual Transitions in T'ang and Sung China.* Stanford, Calif.: Stanford University Press, 1992.

Brook, Timothy, ed. *The Asiatic Mode of Production in China.* Armonk, N.Y.: M. E. Sharpe, 1989.

Buck, David. "Forum on Universalism and Relativism in Asian Studies: Editor's Introduction." *JAS* 50 (February 1991): 29–34.

Bush, Susan. *The Chinese Literati on Painting: Su Shih (1037–1101) to Tung Ch'i-ch'ang (1555–1636).* Harvard-Yenching Institute Studies, no. 27. Cambridge, Mass.: Harvard University Press, 1971.

Cahill, James F. "Confucian Elements in the Theory of Painting." In *The Confucian Persuasion,* ed. Arthur F. Wright, pp. 115–140. Stanford, Calif.: Stanford University Press, 1960.

Carter, Thomas F. *The Invention of Printing in China and Its Spread Westward.* Revised by L. C. Goodrich. New York: Ronald Press, 1955.

Chaffee, John W. "Chu Hsi and the Revival of the White Deer Grotto Academy, 1179–1181." *T'oung Pao* 71 (1985): 40–62.

———. *The Thorny Gates of Learning: A Social History of Examinations in Sung China (960–1279 AD).* New York: Cambridge University Press, 1985.

———. "Chu Hsi in Nan-k'ang: *Tao-hsüeh* and the Politics of Education." In *Neo-Confucian Education: The Formative Stage,* ed. Wm. Theodore de Bary and John W. Chaffee, pp. 414–431. Berkeley and Los Angeles: University of California Press, 1989.

Chambers, R. W. *Thomas More.* Ann Arbor: University of Michigan Press, 1958.

Chan, Hok-lam. "Liu Chi (1311–1375): The Dual Image of a Chinese Imperial Advisor." Ph.D. diss., Princeton University, 1967.

———. *Legitimation in Imperial China: Discussions under the Jürchen-Chin Dynasty (1115–1234).* Seattle: University of Washington Press, 1984.

Chan, Hok-lam, and Wm. Theodore de Bary, eds. *Yüan Thought: Chi-*

nese Thought and Religion under the Mongols. New York: Columbia University Press, 1983.

Chan, Wing-tsit. "The Evolution of the Confucian Concept *Jen*." *PEW* 4 (1954–1955): 295–319.

————. *Sourcebook in Chinese Philosophy.* Princeton, N.J.: Princeton University Press, 1963.

————. "The Evolution of the Neo-Confucian Concept *Li* as Principle." *Tsing-hua hsüeh-pao,* n.s., no. 2 (1964): 123–148.

————. "Neo-Confucianism: New Ideas in Old Terminology." *PEW* 17 (1967): 15–35.

————. "Chu Hsi's Completion of Neo-Confucianism." In *Études Song in memoriam Étienne Balazs,* ed. Francoise Aubin. Ser. 2, no. 1. Paris: Mouton, 1973.

————. "Neo-Confucianism as an Integrative Force in Chinese Life and Thought." In *Studia asiatica,* ed. Laurence G. Thompson. San Francisco: Chinese Materials Center, 1975.

————, ed. *Chu Hsi and Neo-Confucianism.* Honolulu: University of Hawai'i Press, 1986.

————. *Chu Hsi: Life and Thought.* Hong Kong: Chinese University Press, 1987.

————. "Chu Hsi and the Academies." In *Neo-Confucian Education: The Formative Stage,* ed. Wm. Theodore de Bary and John W. Chaffee, pp. 389–413. Berkeley and Los Angeles: University of California Press, 1989.

————. *Chu Hsi: New Studies.* Honolulu: University of Hawai'i Press, 1989.

Chang, Carsun. *The Development of Neo-Confucian Thought.* 2 vols. New York: Bookman Associates, 1957–1962.

Chang, Hao. *Liang Ch'i-ch'ao and Intellectual Transition in China, 1890–1907.* Cambridge, Mass.: Harvard University Press, 1971.

————. *Chinese Intellectuals in Crisis: The Search for Order and Meaning, 1890–1911.* Berkeley and Los Angeles: University of California Press, 1987.

Chang, K. C. *Art, Myth, and Ritual: The Path to Political Authority in Ancient China.* Cambridge, Mass.: Harvard University Press, 1983.

Chang, Kang-i Sun. *The Evolution of Chinese Tz'u Poetry: From Late T'ang to Northern Sung.* Princeton, N.J.: Princeton University Press, 1980.

Chao, Kang. *Man and Land in Chinese History: An Economic Analysis.* Stanford, Calif.: Stanford University Press, 1986.

Chaves, Jonathan. *Mei Yao-ch'en and the Development of Early Sung Poetry.* New York: Columbia University Press, 1976.

Ch'en Ch'ing-hsin. "Sung-ju Ch'un-ch'iu yao-yi ti fa-wei yü ch'i cheng-chih ssu-hsiang." *Hsin-ya hsüeh-pao* 10 (1971): 270–368.

Ch'en Ch'un. *Neo-Confucian Terms Explained (The "Pei-hsi tzu-i")*. Translated and edited by Wing-tsit Chan. New York: Columbia University Press, 1986.

Ch'en Fang-ming. "Sung-tai cheng-t'ung-lun ti hsing-ch'eng pei-ching chi nei-jung." *Shih-huo yüeh-k'an* 1 (1971): 418–430.

Ch'en, Kenneth. *Buddhism in China: A Historical Survey*. Princeton, N.J.: Princeton University Press, 1964.

Ch'en Shou-yi. *Chinese Literature: An Historical Introduction*. New York: Ronald Press, 1961.

Ch'eng I. *Ch'un-ch'iu chuan*. In *Ch'eng-shih ching-shuo, Ssu-k'u ch'üan-shu chen-pen ssu-chi* ed., vol. 86. Taipei: Commercial Press, 1973.

Ch'i Ssu-ho. "Professor Hung on the Ch'un-ch'iu." *Yenching Journal of Social Science* 1 (1938): 49–71.

Ch'ien, Edward T. "The Neo-Confucian Confrontation with Buddhism: A Structural and Historical Analysis." *Journal of Chinese Philosophy* 15, no. 2 (December 1988): 347–370.

Ch'ien Mu. "Wang Pi Kuo Hsiang chu I Lao Chuang yung li-tzu t'iao-lu." *Hsin-ya hsüeh-pao* 1 (1955): 135–156.

———. *Sung-Ming li-hsüeh kai-shu*. Taipei: Hsüeh-sheng shu-chu, 1967.

———. *Chung-kuo li-tai cheng-chih te-shih*. Taipei: San-min shu-chu, 1969.

———. *Kuo-shih ta-kang*. Rev. ed. Taipei: Commercial Press, 1977.

———. *Traditional Government in Imperial China*. Translated by George Totten and Chun-tu Hsüeh. New York: St. Martin's Press, 1982.

Chin Chung-shu. "Sung-tai ku-wen yün-tung chih fa-chan yen-chiu." *Hsin-ya hsüeh-pao* 5 (1963): 79–146.

Ching, Julia. "Neo-Confucian Utopian Theories and Political Ethics." *Monumenta serica* 30 (1972–1973): 1–56.

———. "Truth and Ideology: The Confucian Way (Tao) and Its Transmission (Tao-t'ung)." *JHI* 36 (1974): 371–388.

———. *To Acquire Wisdom: The Way of Wang Yang-ming*. New York: Columbia University Press, 1976.

Chou Yü-t'ung. *Ching Chin-Ku-wen hsüeh*. Shanghai: Commercial Press, 1926.

Chow, Tse-tsung. "The Anti-Confucian Movement in Early Republican China." In *The Confucian Persuasion*, ed. Arthur Wright, pp. 288–312. Stanford, Calif.: Stanford University Press, 1960.

———. *The May Fourth Movement: Intellectual Revolution in Modern China*. Stanford, Calif.: Stanford University Press, 1960.

Chu I-tsun. *Ching-i k'ao. Ssu-pu pei-yao* ed. Shanghai: Chung-hua shu-chu, 1936.

Chu Ron-Guey. "Chu Hsi and Public Instruction." In *Neo-Confucian Education: The Formative Stage*, ed. Wm. Theodore de Bary and John W. Chaffee, pp. 252–273. Berkeley and Los Angeles: University of California Press, 1989.

Cohen, Paul. "The Quest for Liberalism in the Chinese Past: Stepping Stone to a Cosmopolitan World or the Last Stand of Western Parochialism? A Review of Wm. Theodore de Bary, *The Liberal Tradition in China.*" *PEW* 35 (1985): 305–310.

Cohen, Paul A., and Merle Goldman, eds. *Ideas across Cultures: Essays on Chinese Thought in Honor of Benjamin I. Schwartz.* Cambridge, Mass.: Harvard University Press, 1990.

Confucius. *The Analects.* Translated by D. C. Lau. New York: Penguin, 1979.

Copleston, Frederick. *Religion and the One: Philosophies East and West.* New York: Crossroads Publishing Co., 1981.

Craig, Albert M. "Restoration Movement in Choshu." *JAS* 18 (February 1959): 187–197.

———. *Choshu in the Meiji Restoration.* Cambridge, Mass.: Harvard University Press, 1961.

Creel, H. G. *Confucius: The Man and the Myth.* New York: Day, 1949.

———. *The Origins of Statecraft in China.* Vol. 1, *The Western Chou Empire.* Chicago: University of Chicago Press, 1970.

Cua, Antonio. "The Concept of *Li* in Confucian Moral Theory." In *Understanding the Chinese Mind,* ed. Robert Allinson, pp. 209–235. Hong Kong: Oxford University Press, 1989.

Daly, James. *Cosmic Harmony and Political Thinking in Early Stuart England.* Transactions of the American Philosophical Society. Philadelphia, 1979.

Dardess, John W. *Confucianism and Autocracy: Professional Elites in the Founding of the Ming Dynasty.* Berkeley and Los Angeles: University of California Press, 1983.

Davis, Richard L. *Court and Family in Sung China, 960–1279: Bureaucratic Success and Kinship Fortunes for the Shih of Ming-chou.* Durham, N.C.: Duke University Press, 1986.

de Bary, Wm. Theodore. "A Reappraisal of Neo-Confucianism." In *Studies in Chinese Thought,* ed. Arthur F. Wright, pp. 81–111. Chicago: University of Chicago Press, 1953.

———. "Chinese Despotism and the Confucian Ideal." In *Chinese Thought and Institutions,* ed. John King Fairbank, pp. 163–203. Chicago: University of Chicago Press, 1957.

———. "Some Common Tendencies in Neo-Confucianism." In *Confucianism in Action,* ed. David S. Nivison and Arthur F. Wright. Stanford, Calif.: Stanford University Press, 1959.

———. "Neo-Confucian Cultivation and the Seventeenth-Century 'Enlightenment.' " In *The Unfolding of Neo-Confucianism,* ed. Wm. Theodore de Bary, pp. 141–216. New York: Columbia University Press, 1975.

———. *Neo-Confucian Orthodoxy and the Learning of the Mind-and-Heart.* New York: Columbia University Press, 1981.

————. *The Liberal Tradition in China.* New York: Columbia University Press, 1983.

————. "Confucian Liberalism and Western Parochialism: A Response to Paul A. Cohen." *PEW* 35 (1985): 339–412.

————. "Human Rites—an Essay on Confucianism and Human Rights." In *Confucianism: The Dynamics of Tradition,* ed. Irene Eber, pp. 109–132. New York: Macmillan, 1986.

————. "Reply to Frederick Mote's 'The Limits of Intellectual History.'" *Ming Studies* 21 (Spring 1986): 77–92.

————. "Chu Hsi's Aims as an Educator." In *Neo-Confucian Education: The Formative Stage,* ed. Wm. Theodore de Bary and John W. Chaffee, pp. 186–218. Berkeley and Los Angeles: University of California Press, 1989.

————. *The Message of the Mind in Neo-Confucianism.* New York: Columbia University Press, 1989.

————. *Learning for One's Self: Essays on the Individual in Neo-Confucian Thought.* New York: Columbia University Press, 1991.

————. *The Trouble with Confucianism.* Cambridge, Mass.: Harvard University Press, 1992.

————. *Waiting for the Dawn: A Plan for the Prince: Huang Tsung-hsi's "Ming-i tai-fang lu."* New York: Columbia University Press, 1993.

de Bary, Wm. Theodore, et al. *A Guide to Oriental Classics.* 3d ed. New York: Columbia University Press, 1989.

de Bary, Wm. Theodore, and Irene Bloom, eds. *Principle and Practicality: Essays in Neo-Confucianism and Practical Learning.* New York: Columbia University Press, 1979.

de Bary, Wm. Theodore, and John Chaffee, eds. *Neo-Confucian Education: The Formative Stage.* Berkeley and Los Angeles: University of California Press, 1989.

de Bary, Wm. Theodore, Wing-tsit Chan, and Burton Watson, eds. *Sources of Chinese Tradition.* New York: Columbia University Press, 1960.

de Bary, Wm. Theodore, and JaHyun Kim Haboush, eds. *The Rise of Neo-Confucianism in Korea.* New York: Columbia University Press, 1985.

de Bary, Wm. Theodore, Ryusaku Tsunoda, and Donald Keene. *Sources of Japanese Tradition.* 2 vols. New York: Columbia University Press, 1964.

d'Entrèves, A. P. *Natural Law: An Introduction to Legal Philosophy.* London: Hutchinson University Library, 1970.

Des Forges, Roger V., Luo Ning, and Wu Yen-bo, eds. *Chinese Democracy and the Crisis of 1989: Chinese and American Reflections.* Albany: State University of New York Press, 1993.

Dull, Jack L. "A Historical Introduction to the Apocryphal (Ch'an-wei) Texts of the Han Dynasty." Ph.D. diss., University of Washington, 1966.

———. "The Evolution of Government in China." In *Heritage of China: Contemporary Perspectives on Chinese Civilization,* ed. Paul S. Ropp, pp. 55–85. Berkeley and Los Angeles: University of California Press, 1990.

Earl, David Margarey. *Emperor and Nation in Japan: Political Thinkers of the Tokugawa Period.* Seattle: University of Washington Press, 1964.

Eber, Irene, ed. *Confucianism: The Dynamics of Tradition.* New York: Macmillan, 1986.

Ebrey, Patricia Buckley. *Family and Property in Sung China: Yüan Ts'ai's Precepts for Social Life.* Princeton, N.J.: Princeton University Press, 1984.

———. "Neo-Confucianism and the Chinese *Shih-ta-fu.*" *American Asian Review* 4 (Spring 1986): 34–43.

———. "The Dynamics of Elite Domination in Sung China." *HJAS* 48 (December 1988): 493–519.

———. *Chu Hsi's "Family Rituals": A Twelfth-Century Chinese Manual for the Performance of Cappings, Weddings, Funerals, and Ancestral Rites.* Princeton, N.J.: Princeton University Press, 1991.

———. *Confucianism and Family Rituals in Imperial China: A Social History of Writing about Rites.* Princeton, N.J.: Princeton University Press, 1991.

Ebrey, Patricia Buckley, and James L. Watson, eds. *Kinship Organization in Late Imperial China, 1000–1940.* Berkeley and Los Angeles: University of California Press, 1986.

Edwards, R. Randle, Louis Henkin, and Andrew J. Nathan. *Human Rights in Contemporary China.* New York: Columbia University Press, 1986.

Egan, Ronald Christopher. *The Literary Works of Ou-yang Hsiu (1007–1072).* Cambridge: Cambridge University Press, 1984.

Elman, Benjamin A. *From Philosophy to Philology: Intellectual and Social Aspects of Change in Late Imperial China.* Cambridge, Mass.: Harvard University Press, 1984.

———. "Scholarship and Politics: Chuang Tsun-yü and the Rise of the Ch'ang-chou New Text School in Late Imperial China." *Late Imperial China* 7 (June 1986): 63–86.

———. *Classicism, Politics, and Kinship: The Ch'ang-chou School of New Text Confucianism in Late Imperial China.* Berkeley and Los Angeles: University of California Press, 1990.

———. "Education in Sung China." *JAOS* 111 (January–March 1991): 83–93.

————. "Political, Social, and Cultural Reproduction via Civil Service Examinations in Late Imperial China." *JAS* 50 (February 1991): 7–28.

Elman, Benjamin A., and Alexander Woodside, eds. *Education and Society in Late Imperial China, 1600–1900.* Berkeley and Los Angeles: University of California Press, 1994.

Elvin, Mark. *The Pattern of the Chinese Past: A Social and Economic Interpretation.* Stanford, Calif.: Stanford University Press, 1973.

Etzioni, Amitai. *A Comparative Analysis of Complex Organizations.* New York: Free Press, 1961.

Finkel, Donald, trans. *A Splintered Mirror: Chinese Poetry from the Democracy Movement.* San Francisco: North Point Press, 1991.

Fisher, Carney T. "The Ritual Dispute of Sung Ying-tsung." *Papers on Far Eastern History* 36 (September 1987): 109–138.

Freeman, Michael Dennis. "Lo-yang and the Opposition to Wang An-shih: The Rise of Confucian Conservatism, 1068–1086." Ph.D. diss., Yale University, 1973.

Friedrich, Carl J. *Tradition and Authority.* New York: Praeger, 1972.

Fu Zhengyuan. *Autocratic Tradition and Chinese Politics.* Cambridge: Cambridge University Press, 1993.

Fumoto, Yasutaka. *Hoku-sō ni okeru jugaku no tenkai.* Tokyo: Shoseki bumbutsu ryūtsūkai, 1968.

Fung Yu-lan. *A History of Chinese Philosophy.* Translated by Derk Bodde. 2 vols. Princeton, N.J.: Princeton University Press, 1952–1953.

Gardner, Daniel K., trans. *Learning to Be a Sage.* By Chu Hsi. Berkeley and Los Angeles: University of California Press, 1990.

————. "Modes of Thinking and Modes of Discourse in the Sung: Some Thoughts on the *Yü-lu* ('Recorded Conversations') Texts." *JAS* 50 (August 1991): 574–603.

Ginzburg, Carlo. *The Cheese and the Worms: The Cosmos of a Sixteenth-Century Miller.* Translated by John Tedeschi and Anne Tedeschi. New York: Penguin, 1982.

Golas, Peter. "Rural China in the Song." *JAS* 39 (February 1980): 291–325.

————. "The Sung Economy: How Big?" *Bulletin of Sung Yuan Studies* 20 (1988): 90–94.

Goldman, Merle. *Sowing the Seeds of Democracy in China: Political Reform in the Deng Xiaoping Era.* Cambridge, Mass.: Harvard University Press, 1994.

Goodrich, L. C. "The Development of Printing in China and Its Effects on the Renaissance under the Sung Dynasty (960–1279)." *Journal of the Hong Kong Branch of the Royal Asiatic Society* 3 (1963): 36–43.

Graham, A. C. *Two Chinese Philosophers, Ch'eng Ming-tao and Ch'eng Yi-ch'uan.* London: Lund Humphries, 1958.

————. *Disputers of the Tao: Philosophical Argument in Ancient China.* La Salle, Ill.: Open Court Press, 1989.

Guy, Kent. *The Emperor's Four Treasures.* Cambridge, Mass.: Harvard University Press, 1987.

Haboush, Jahyun Kim. *A Heritage of Kings: One Man's Monarchy in the Confucian World.* New York: Columbia University Press, 1988.

Haeger, John. "The Intellectual Context of Neo-Confucian Syncretism." *JAS* 31 (1972): 499–513.

Haley, John Owen. *Authority without Power: Law and the Japanese Paradox.* New York: Oxford University Press, 1991.

Hall, John Whitney. "A Monarch for Modern Japan." In *Political Development in Modern Japan,* ed. Robert E. Ward, pp. 11–64. Princeton, N.J.: Princeton University Press, 1968.

Han Minzhu, ed. *Cries for Democracy: Writings and Speeches from the 1989 Chinese Democracy Movement.* Princeton, N.J.: Princeton University Press, 1990.

Handlin, Joanna F. *Action in Late Ming Thought: The Reorientation of Lu K'un and Other Scholar-Officials.* Berkeley and Los Angeles: University of California Press, 1983.

Hansen, Chad. "Individualism in Chinese Thought." In *Individualism and Holism: Studies in Confucian and Taoist Values,* ed. Donald Munro, pp. 35–56. Ann Arbor: University of Michigan Center for Chinese Studies, 1985.

Hansen, Valerie. *Changing Gods in Medieval China, 1127–1276.* Princeton, N.J.: Princeton University Press, 1990.

Harbsmeier, Christoph. "Marginalia Sino-logica." In *Understanding the Chinese Mind: The Philosophical Roots,* ed. Robert E. Allinson, pp. 125–166. Hong Kong: Oxford University Press, 1989.

Harootunian, H. D. "Confucianism: Two Reviews." Journal of Japanese Studies 7 (1981): 111–131.

————. *Things Seen and Unseen: Discourse and Ideology in Tokugawa Nativism.* Chicago: University of Chicago Press, 1988.

Hartman, Charles. *Han Yü and the T'ang Search for Unity.* Princeton, N.J.: Princeton University Press, 1986.

Hartwell, Robert M. "A Revolution in the Chinese Iron and Coal Industries during the Northern Sung, 960–1126." *JAS* 21 (1962): 153–162.

————. "A Cycle of Economic Change in Imperial China: Coal and Iron in Northeast China, 750–1350." *Journal of the Economic and Social History of the Orient* 10 (1967): 102–159.

————. "The Evolution of the Early Northern Sung Monetary System." *JAOS* 87 (1967): 280–289.

————. "Classical Chinese Monetary Analysis and Economic Policy in T'ang–Northern Sung China." *Transactions of the International Conference of Orientalists in Japan* 13 (1968): 70–81.

———. "Financial Expertise, Examinations and the Formulation of Economic Policy in Northern Sung China." *JAS* 30 (1971): 281–314.

———. "Historical Analogism, Public Policy, and Social Science in Eleventh- and Twelfth-Century China." *AHR* 76 (1971): 690–727.

———. "International Commerce and Monetary Policy in Sung China." Paper prepared for the Seminar on Traditional China, Columbia University, November 1971.

———. "Demographic, Political, and Social Transformations of China, 750–1550." *HJAS* 42 (1982): 365–442.

———. "New Approaches to the Study of Bureaucratic Factionalism in Sung China: A Hypothesis." *Bulletin of Sung-Yüan Studies* 18 (1986): 33–40.

Hatch, George. "The Thought of Su Hsün (1009–1066): An Essay in the Social Meaning of Intellectual Pluralism in Northern Sung." Ph.D. diss., University of Washington, 1972.

Henderson, John B. *The Development and Decline of Chinese Cosmology.* New York: Columbia University Press, 1984.

———. *Scripture, Canon, and Commentary: A Comparison of Confucian and Western Exegesis.* Princeton, N.J.: Princeton University Press, 1991.

Ho, Ping-ti. "Early-Ripening Rice in Chinese History." *Economic History Review* 9 (1956–1957): 200–218.

———. *The Ladder of Success in Imperial China: Aspects of Social Mobility.* New York: Columbia University Press, 1962.

———. "An Estimate of the Total Population of Sung-Chin China." In *Études Song in memoriam Étienne Balazs,* ed. Francoise Aubin, ser. 1, *Histoire et Institutions,* pp. 33–53. Paris: Mouton, 1970.

Hooker, Richard. *Of the Laws of Ecclesiastical Polity.* 2 vols. New York: Dutton, Everyman's Library, 1954.

Hsiao Kung-chuan. "Legalism and Autocracy in Traditional China." *Tsing-hua hsüeh-pao,* n.s., no. 2 (1964): 108–121.

———. *A Modern China and a New World: K'ang Yu-wei, Reformer and Utopian, 1858–1927.* Seattle: University of Washington Press, 1975.

———. *A History of Chinese Political Thought.* Vol. 1. Translated by Frederick W. Mote. Shanghai: Commercial Press, 1945–1946; Princeton, N.J.: Princeton University Press, 1979.

———. *Chung-kuo cheng-chih ssu-hsiang shih.* Taipei: Lien-ching ch'u-pan shih-yeh kung-ssu, 1982.

Hsieh Shan-yüan. *The Life and Thought of Li Kou, 1009–1059.* San Francisco: Chinese Materials Center, 1979.

Hsü, Cho-yün. *Ancient China in Transition: An Analysis of Social Mobility, 722–222 B.C.* Stanford, Calif.: Stanford University Press, 1965.

Hsün Tzu. *The Works of Hsüntze.* Translated by Homer Dubs. London: Probsthain, 1928.

Hu An-kuo. *Ch'un-ch'iu Hu-shih chuan. Ssu-pu ts'ung-k'an hsü-pien* ed. Shanghai: Commercial Press, 1933.

Hu Shih. "The Natural Law in the Chinese Tradition." In *University of Notre Dame Natural Law Institute Proceedings,* vol. 5, ed. Edward F. Barrett, pp. 119–153. Notre Dame, Ind.: University of Notre Dame Press, 1953.

Huang, Pei. *Autocracy at Work: A Study of the Yung-cheng Period, 1723–1735.* Bloomington: Indiana University Press, 1974.

Huang, Philip C. *Liang Ch'i-ch'ao and Modern Chinese Liberalism.* Seattle: University of Washington Press, 1972.

Huang, Ray. *1587, Year of No Significance: The Ming Dynasty in Decline.* New Haven, Conn.: Yale University Press, 1981.

Huang Tsung-hsi. *The Records of Ming Scholars.* Edited by Julia Ching with the collaboration of Chaoying Fang. Honolulu: University of Hawai'i Press, 1987.

Hucker, Charles. *Dictionary of Official Titles in Imperial China.* Stanford, Calif.: Stanford University Press, 1985.

Hummel, Arthur. "The Case against Force in Chinese Philosophy." *Chinese Social and Political Science Review* 9 (1925): 334–350.

Hymes, Robert P. *Statesmen and Gentlemen: The Elite of Fu-chou, Chianghsi, in Northern and Southern Sung.* New York: Cambridge University Press, 1986.

————. "Lu Chiu-yüan, Academies, and the Problem of the Local Community." In *Neo-Confucian Education: The Formative Stage,* ed. Wm. Theodore de Bary and John W. Chaffee, pp. 432–456. Berkeley and Los Angeles: University of California Press, 1989.

Hymes, Robert P., and Conrad Schirokauer, eds. *Ordering the World: Approaches to State and Society in Sung Dynasty China.* Berkeley and Los Angeles: University of California Press, 1993.

International Encyclopedia of the Social Sciences. New York: Macmillan, 1968.

Jansen, Marius B., and Gilbert Rozman. *Japan in Transition: From Tokugawa to Meiji.* Princeton, N.J.: Princeton University Press, 1986.

Johnson, David. *The Medieval Chinese Oligarchy.* Boulder, Colo.: Westview, 1977.

Juan Chih-sheng. "Ts'ung Kung-yang-hsüeh lun Ch'un-ch'iu ti hsingchih." Ph.D. diss., National Taiwan University, 1969.

Kalgren, Bernhard. "On the Authenticity and Nature of the Tso Chuan." *Göteborgs Högskolas Årsskrift* 32 (1926): 1–65.

Kao Ming. *Li-hsüeh hsin-t'an.* Hong Kong: Chinese University of Hong Kong, 1963.

Kasoff, Ira E. *The Thought of Chang Tsai (1020–1077)*. New York: Cambridge University Press, 1984.

Kato Shigeshi. "On the Hang or the Associations of Merchants in China." *Memoirs of the Research Department of the Toyo Bunko* 8 (1938): 45–83.

Kennedy, George. "Interpretation of the Ch'un-ch'iu." *JAOS* 62 (1942): 40–48.

Kern, Fritz. *Kingship and Law in the Middle Ages*. Oxford: Blackwell, 1939.

Kinugawa, Tsuyoshi, ed. *Collected Studies on Sung History Dedicated to Professor James T. C. Liu in Celebration of His Seventieth Birthday*. Tokyo: Dohosha, 1989.

Knechtges, David Richard. "Yang Shyong, the Fuh, and Hann Rhetoric." Ph.D. diss., University of Washington, 1968.

Knoblock, John. *Xunzi: A Translation and Study of the Complete Works*. Vols. 1 and 2. Stanford, Calif.: Stanford University Press, 1988–.

Koschmann, J. Victor. *The Mito Ideology: Discourse, Reform, and Insurrection in Late Tokugawa Japan, 1790–1864*. Berkeley and Los Angeles: University of California Press, 1987.

Kracke, E. A., Jr. "Family vs. Merit in Chinese Civil Service Examinations under the Empire." *HJAS* 10 (1947): 103–123.

———. *Civil Service in Sung China, 960–1067*. Cambridge, Mass.: Harvard University Press, 1953.

———. "Sung Society: Change within Tradition." *FEQ* 14 (1955): 479–488.

———. "Sung K'ai-feng: Pragmatic Metropolis and Formalistic Capital." In *Crisis and Prosperity in Sung China*, ed. John Winthrop Haeger, pp. 49–77. Tucson: University of Arizona Press, 1975.

———. *Translations of Sung Civil Service Titles*. 2d ed. San Francisco: Chinese Materials Center, 1978.

Kwon, Yon-Ung. "The Imperial Lecture of Sung China." *Journal of Social Sciences and Humanities* 48 (December 1978): 103–113.

Labadie, John Richard. "Rulers and Soldiers: Perception and Management of the Military in Northern Sung China (960–ca.1060)." Ph.D. diss., University of Washington, 1981.

Langlois, John D., Jr., ed. *China under Mongol Rule*. Princeton, N.J.: Princeton University Press, 1981.

———. "Law, Statecraft, and *The Spring and Autumn Annals* in Yüan Political Thought." In *Yüan Thought: Chinese Thought and Religion under the Mongols*, ed. Hok-lam Chan and Wm. Theodore de Bary, pp. 89–152. New York: Columbia University Press, 1982.

Latourette, Kenneth Scott. *The Chinese: Their History and Culture*. 3d ed. New York: Macmillan, 1960.

Lau, D. C., trans. *Mencius*. New York: Penguin, 1970.

Lee, Thomas H. C. "Education in Northern Sung China." Ph.D. diss., Yale University, 1974.

———. "Life in the Schools of Sung China." *JAS* 37 (1977): 45–60.

———. "The Social Significance of the Quota System in Sung Civil Service Examinations." *Journal of the Institute of Chinese Studies* 13 (1982): 287–317.

———. *Government Education and the Examinations in Sung China*. Hong Kong: Chinese University Press, 1985.

———. "Sung Schools and Education before Chu Hsi." In *Neo-Confucian Education: The Formative Stage*, ed. Wm. Theodore de Bary and John W. Chaffee, pp. 105–136. Berkeley and Los Angeles: University of California Press, 1989.

Legge, James, trans. *The Chinese Classics*. Vol. 1, *Confucian Analects, the Great Learning, and the Doctrine of the Mean*. Vol. 2, *Mencius*. Vol. 3, *The Shoo King*. Vol. 4, *The She King*. Vol. 5, *The Ch'un Ts'ew with the Tso Chuen*. London: Henry Frowde, 1862–1872. Reprint, Hong Kong: Hong Kong University Press, 1961.

———. *Li Chi: Book of Rites*. Edited by Ch'u Chai and Winberg Chai. 2 vols. New Hyde Park, N.Y.: University Books, 1967.

Lei Tsung-hai. "The Rise of the Emperor System in Ancient China." *Chinese Social and Political Science Review* 20 (1936): 251–265.

Levenson, Joseph R. *Confucian China and Its Modern Fate: A Trilogy*. Berkeley: University of California Press, 1958, 1964, 1965.

Lewis, C. S. *The Discarded Image: An Introduction to Medieval and Renaissance Literature*. Cambridge: Cambridge University Press, 1964.

Li Ming-fu. *Ch'un-ch'iu chi-yi. Ssu-k'u ch'üan-shu ch'u-chi* ed. Shanghai: Commercial Press, 1935.

Liang Ch'i-ch'ao. *Intellectual Trends in the Ch'ing Period*. Translated by Immanuel C. Y. Hsü. Cambridge, Mass.: Harvard University Press, 1959.

Little, Daniel. "Rational-Choice Models and Asian Studies." *JAS* 50 (February 1991): 35–52.

Liu Ch'ang. *Ch'un-ch'iu chuan. T'ung-chih t'ang ching-chieh* ed. Taipei: Ta-t'ung shu-chu, 1969.

———. *Ch'un-ch'iu yi-lin. T'ung-chih t'ang ching-chieh* ed. Taipei: Ta-t'ung shu-chu, 1969.

Liu, James T. C. "An Early Sung Reformer: Fan Chung-yen." In *Chinese Thought and Institutions*, ed. John K. Fairbank. Chicago: University of Chicago Press, 1957.

———. *Reform in Sung China: Wang An-shih (1021–1086) and His New Policies*. Cambridge, Mass.: Harvard University Press, 1959.

———. "An Administrative Cycle in Chinese History: The Case of Northern Sung Emperors." *JAS* 21 (1962): 137–152.

————. "The Neo-Traditional Period (ca. 800–1900) in Chinese History." *JAS* 24 (1964): 105–107.

————. *Ou-yang Hsiu: An Eleventh-Century Neo-Confucianist.* Stanford, Calif.: Stanford University Press, 1967.

————. "Sung Roots of Chinese Political Conservatism: The Administrative Problem." *JAS* 26 (1967): 457–463.

————. "How Did a Neo-Confucian School Become the State Orthodoxy?" *PEW* 23 (1973): 483–505.

————. "The Sung Emperors and the Ming-T'ang or Hall of Enlightenment." In *Études Song in memoriam Étienne Balazs,* ed. Francoise Aubin, series 2, vol. 1, *Civilisation,* pp. 45–58. Paris: Mouton, 1973.

————. *China Turning Inward: Intellectual-Political Changes in the Early Twelfth Century.* Cambridge, Mass.: Harvard University Press, 1988.

————. "A Note on Classifying Sung Confucians." *Bulletin of Sung Yuan Studies* 21 (1989): 1–7.

Liu, James T. C., and Peter J. Golas, eds. *Change in Sung China: Innovation or Renovation?* Boston: D. C. Heath, 1969.

Liu, Kwang-ching, ed. *Orthodoxy in Late Imperial China.* Berkeley and Los Angeles: University of California Press, 1990.

Liu Po-chi. *Sung-tai cheng-chiao shih.* 2 vols. Taipei: Chung-hua shu-chu, 1971.

Liu Te-han. "Ch'un-ch'iu Kung-yang chuan tui Hsi-Han cheng-chih ti ying-hsiang." *Shu-mu chi-k'an* 11 (1977): 31–57.

Liu Wu-chi. *An Introduction to Chinese Literature.* Bloomington: Indiana University Press, 1966.

Lo Jung-pang. "Maritime Commerce and Its Relation to the Sung Navy." *Journal of the Economic and Social History of the Orient* 12 (1969): 57–101.

Lo, Winston W. *The Life and Thought of Yeh Shih.* Hong Kong: Chinese University of Hong Kong Press, 1974.

————. *An Introduction to the Civil Service of Sung China: With Emphasis on Its Personnel Administration.* Honolulu: University of Hawai'i Press, 1987.

Lu Kuang-huan. "The Shu-yüan Institution Developed by Sung-Ming Neo-Confucian Philosophers." *Chinese Culture* 9 (1969): 98–122.

Ma, Laurence J. C. *Commercial Development and Urban Change in Sung China, 960–1279.* Ann Arbor: University of Michigan Press, 1971.

MacIntyre, Alasdair. *After Virtue: A Study in Moral Theory.* Notre Dame, Ind.: University of Notre Dame Press, 1981.

McKnight, Brian E. *Village and Bureaucracy in Southern Sung China.* Chicago: University of Chicago Press, 1971.

————. "Patterns of Law and Patterns of Thought: Notes on the Specifications *(shih)* of Sung China." *JAOS* 102 (April/June 1982): 323–331.

————. *Law and the State in Traditional East Asia: Six Studies on the Sources of East Asian Law.* Honolulu: University of Hawai'i Press, 1987.

McMullen, David. "Han Yü: An Alternative Picture." *HJAS* 49 (December 1989): 603–657.

Mair, Victor H. *T'ang Transformation Texts: A Study of the Buddhist Contribution to the Rise of Vernacular Fiction and Drama in China.* Cambridge, Mass.: Harvard University Press, 1989.

Malmqvist, Göran. "Studies on the Gongyang and Guuliang Commentaries." *Bulletin of the Museum of Far Eastern Antiquities* 43 (1971): 67–222; 47 (1975): 19–69.

Maruyama Masao. *Studies in the Intellectual History of Tokugawa Japan.* Translated by Mikiso Hane. Princeton, N.J.: Princeton University Press, 1974.

Maspero, Henri. "La composition et la date du Tso Tchouan." *Mélanges chinois et bouddhiques* 1 (1931–1932): 137–215.

————. *China in Antiquity.* Translated by Frank A. Kierman Jr. Kent: Wm. Dawson & Son, 1978.

Metzger, Thomas A. *Escape from Predicament: Neo-Confucianism and China's Evolving Political Culture.* New York: Columbia University Press, 1977.

Miyakawa Hisayuki. "An Outline of the Naitō Hypothesis and Its Effects on Japanese Studies of China." *FEQ* 14 (August 1955): 533–552.

Miyazaki Ichisada. *China's Examination Hell.* Translated by Conrad Schirokauer. New Haven, Conn.: Yale University Press, 1981.

Moody, Peter R., Jr. *Political Opposition in Post-Confucian Society.* New York: Praeger, 1988.

Morohashi Tetsuji. "Jūgaku no mokuteki to Sō-ju no katsudō." In *Morohashi Tetsuji chosaku shū,* 1:167–557. Tokyo, 1975.

Morris, Christopher. *Political Thought in England: Tyndale to Hooker.* London and New York: Oxford University Press, 1953.

Morris, Ivan. *The World of the Shining Prince: Court Life in Ancient Japan.* New York: Penguin, 1964.

Mote, Frederick W. "The Growth of Chinese Despotism: A Critique of Wittfogel's Theory of Oriental Despotism as Applied to China." *Oriens extremus* 8 (1961): 1–41.

————. "Chinese Political Thought." In *IESS.* New York: Macmillan, 1968.

————. "The Limits of Intellectual History?" *Ming Studies* 19 (Fall 1984): 17–25.

Mote, Frederick W., and Denis Twitchett. *Cambridge History of China.* Vol. 7, *The Ming Dynasty, 1368–1644.* Pt. 1. New York: Cambridge University Press, 1988.

Mou Jun-sun. "Liang Sung *Ch'un-ch'iu* hsüeh chih chu-liu." In *Sung-shih yen-chiu chi,* 3:103–121. Taipei: Chung-hua shu-chü, 1966.

Mungello, David. *Leibniz and Confucianism: The Search for Accord.* Honolulu: University of Hawai'i Press, 1977.

Munro, Donald J. *Individualism and Holism: Studies in Confucian and Taoist Values.* Ann Arbor: University of Michigan Center for Chinese Studies, 1985.

———. *Images of Human Nature: A Sung Portrait.* Princeton, N.J.: Princeton University Press, 1988.

Myers, Ramon H. "Transformation and Continuity in Chinese Economic and Social History." *JAS* 33 (February 1974): 265–277.

Najita, Tetsuo. *Visions of Virtue in Tokugawa Japan.* Chicago: University of Chicago Press, 1987.

Najita, Tetsuo, and Irwin Scheiner, eds. *Japanese Thought in the Tokugawa Period, 1600–1868: Methods and Metaphors.* Chicago: University of Chicago Press, 1978.

Nathan, Andrew. *Chinese Democracy.* Berkeley and Los Angeles: University of California Press, 1986.

———. *Dilemmas of Reform and Prospects for Democracy.* New York: Columbia University Press, 1990.

Needham, Joseph. *Science and Civilisation in China.* 6 vols. Cambridge: Cambridge University Press, 1954–.

Nosco, Peter, ed. *Confucianism and Tokugawa Culture.* Princeton, N.J.: Princeton University Press, 1984.

Ou-yang Hsiu. *Hsin wu-tai shih.* Peking: Chung-hua shu-chü, 1974.

Painter, Sidney, and Brian Tierney. *Western Europe in the Middle Ages, 300–1475.* 3d ed. New York: Alfred A. Knopf, 1978.

Palais, James B. *Politics and Policy in Traditional Korea.* Cambridge, Mass.: Harvard University Press, 1975.

Pan Ku. *The History of the Former Han Dynasty.* Translated by Homer H. Dubs. 2 vols. Baltimore: Waverly Press, 1944.

Pennock, J. Roland, and John W. Chapman, eds. *Authority Revisited: Nomos XXIX.* New York: New York University Press, 1987.

Peterson, Willard. "Another Look at *Li.*" *Bulletin of Sung-Yüan Studies* 18 (1986): 13–32.

P'i Hsi-jui. *Ching-hsüeh li-shih.* Edited and annotated by Chou Yü-t'ung. Hong Kong: Chung-hua shu-chü, 1961.

Prusek, Jaroslav. "The Narrators of Buddhist Scriptures and Religious Tales in the Sung Period." *Archiv Orientalni* 10 (1938): 375–389.

————. "Researches into the Beginnings of the Chinese Popular Novel." *Archiv Orientalni* 11 (1939): 91–132; 23 (1955): 620–662.

————. *Chinese Statelets and the Northern Barbarians in the Period 1400–300 B.C.* New York: Humanities Press, 1971.

Pulleyblank, Edwin G. "Neo-Confucianism and Neo-Legalism in T'ang Intellectual Life, 755–805." In *The Confucian Persuasion,* ed. Arthur F. Wright, pp. 77–114. Stanford, Calif.: Stanford University Press, 1960.

Pye, Lucian W. *Asian Power and Politics: The Cultural Dimensions of Authority.* Cambridge, Mass.: Belknap Press, 1985.

Reese, M. M. *The Cease of Majesty: A Study of Shakespeare's Plays.* London: Edward Arnold, 1961.

Robinson, Thomas W. *Democracy and Development in East Asia: Taiwan, South Korea, and the Philippines.* Lanham, Md.: American Enterprise Institute Press, 1991.

Ropp, Paul S., ed. *Heritage of China: Contemporary Perspectives on Chinese Civilization.* Berkeley and Los Angeles: University of California Press, 1990.

Rosemont, Henry, Jr., ed. *Explorations in Early Chinese Cosmology.* Chico, Calif.: Scholar's Press, 1984.

Rossabi, Morris, ed. *China among Equals: The Middle Kingdom and Its Neighbors, 10th–14th Centuries.* Berkeley and Los Angeles: University of California Press, 1981.

Rozman, Gilbert, ed. *The East Asian Region: Confucian Heritage and Its Modern Adaptation.* Princeton, N.J.: Princeton University Press, 1991.

Sabine, George H. *A History of Political Theory.* 3d ed. New York: Holt, Rinehart & Winston, 1961.

Sanaka Sō. "Sōgaku ni okeru iwayuru hihan-teki kenkyū no tanchō ni tsuite." *Shigaku Zasshi* 54 (1943): 1124–1141.

Sariti, Anthony William. "Monarchy, Bureaucracy, and Absolutism in the Political Thought of Ssu-ma Kuang." *JAS* 33 (1972): 53–76.

Schirokauer, Conrad. "Chu Hsi's Political Career: A Study in Ambivalence." In *Confucian Personalities,* ed. Arthur Wright and Denis Twitchett. Stanford, Calif.: Stanford University Press, 1962.

————. "Neo-Confucians under Attack: The Condemnation of *Wei-hsüeh.*" In *Crisis and Prosperity in Sung China,* ed. John Winthrop Haeger. Tucson: University of Arizona Press, 1975.

————. "Chu Hsi and Hu Hung." In *Chu Hsi and Neo-Confucianism,* ed. Wing-tsit Chan. Honolulu: University of Hawai'i Press, 1986.

Schneider, Laurence A. *Ku Chieh-kang and China's New History: Nationalism and the Quest for Alternative Traditions.* Berkeley: University of California Press, 1971.

———. *A Madman of Ch'u: The Chinese Myth of Loyalty and Dissent.* Berkeley and Los Angeles: University of California Press, 1983.

Schram, Stuart R., ed. *The Scope of State Power in China.* New York: St. Martin's Press, 1985.

———, ed. *Foundations and Limits of State Power in China.* London: School of Oriental and African Studies, 1987.

Schurmann, H. F. "Traditional Property Concepts in China." *FEQ* 15 (August 1956): 507–516.

Shiba Yoshinobu. *Commerce and Society in Sung China.* Translated by Mark Elvin. Ann Arbor: University of Michigan Press, 1970.

———. "Commercialization of Farm Products in the Sung Period." *Acta asiatica* 19 (1970): 77–96.

———. "Urbanization and the Development of Markets in the Lower Yangtze Valley." In *Crisis and Prosperity in Sung China,* ed. John Winthrop Haeger, pp. 13–48. Tucson: University of Arizona Press, 1975.

———. "Sung Foreign Trade: Its Scope and Organization." In *China among Equals: The Middle Kingdom and Its Neighbors, 10th–14th Centuries,* ed. Morris Rossabi, pp. 89–115. Berkeley and Los Angeles: University of California Press, 1981.

Shih Chieh. *Shih Tzu-lai chi. Ts'ung-shu chi-ch'eng* ed., vols. 2361–2362. Shanghai: Commercial Press, 1936.

Shih, Vincent Y. C. "Metaphysical Tendencies in Mencius." *PEW* 12 (1962–1963): 319–341.

Sibley, Mulford Q. *Political Ideas and Ideologies: A History of Political Thought.* New York: Harper & Row, 1970.

Simon, Yves R. *The Tradition of Natural Law: A Philosopher's Reflections.* Edited by Vukan Kuic. New York: Fordham University Press, 1965.

Skinner, Quentin. *The Foundations of Modern Political Thought.* Vol. 1, *The Renaissance.* Vol. 2, *The Age of Reformation.* Cambridge: Cambridge University Press, 1978.

Smith, Kidder, Jr., Peter K. Bol, Joseph A. Adler, and Don J. Wyatt. *Sung Dynasty Uses of the I Ching.* Princeton, N.J.: Princeton University Press, 1990.

Ssu-k'u ch'üan-shu tsung-mu t'i-yao. Taipei: Commercial Press, 1971.

Ssu-ma Kuang. *Ch'ien-hsü. Ts'ung-shu chi-ch'eng* ed., vol. 697. Shanghai: Commercial Press, 1936.

Sun Chüeh. *Ch'un-ch'iu chuan. T'ung-chih t'ang ching-chieh* ed. Taipei: Ta-t'ung shu-chü, 1969.

Sun Fu. *Ch'un-ch'iu tsun-wang fa-wei.* T'ung-chih t'ang ching-chieh ed. Taipei: Ta-t'ung shu-chü, 1969.

———. *Sun Ming-fu hsiao-chi. Ssu-k'u ch'üan-shu chen-pen* (the 8th collection) ed., vol. 148. Taipei: Commercial Press, 1978.

Sung-shih. Compiled by T'o T'o (1313–1355). Peking: Chung-hua shu-chü, 1977.

Sung Ting-tsung. "Hu An-kuo Ch'un-ch'iu pien Sung shuo." *Ch'eng-kung ta-hsüeh hsüeh-pao* 13 (May 1978): 135–154.

Tain, Tzey-yueh. "Tung Chung-shu's System of Thought: Its Sources and Its Influence on Han Scholars." Ph.D. diss., University of California, Los Angeles, 1974.

Talmon, J. L. *Origins of Totalitarian Democracy.* New York: W. W. Norton, 1970.

Tao Jing-shen. "The Influence of Jürchen Rule on Chinese Political Institutions." *JAS* 30 (November 1970): 121–130.

———. "Barbarians or Northerners: Northern Sung Images of the Khitans." In *China among Equals: The Middle Kingdom and Its Neighbors, 10th–14th Centuries,* ed. Morris Rossabi, pp. 66–86. Berkeley and Los Angeles: University of California Press, 1983.

———. *Two Sons of Heaven: Studies in Sung-Liao Relations.* Tucson: University of Arizona Press, 1988.

Taylor, Rodney L. *The Religious Dimensions of Confucianism.* Albany: State University of New York Press, 1990.

Taylor, Romeyn. "Chinese Hierarchy in Comparative Perspective." *JAS* 48 (August 1989): 490–511.

Tillman, Hoyt Cleveland. *Utilitarian Confucianism: Ch'en Liang's Challenge to Chu Hsi.* Cambridge, Mass.: Harvard University Press, 1983.

———. *Confucian Discourse and Chu Hsi's Ascendancy.* Honolulu: University of Hawai'i Press, 1992.

———. "A New Direction in Confucian Scholarship: Approaches to Examining the Differences between Neo-Confucianism and *Tao-hsüeh.*" *PEW* 42 (July 1992): 455–474.

Treadgold, Donald W. *The West in Russia and China: Religious and Secular Thought in Modern Times.* vol. 1, *Russia, 1472–1917.* and vol. 2, *China, 1542–1949.* Cambridge: Cambridge University Press, 1973.

Ts'ai Yung-ch'un. "The Philosophy of Ch'eng I." Ph.D. diss., Columbia University, 1950.

Tu Wei-ming. *Confucian Thought: Selfhood as Creative Transformation.* Ithaca: State University of New York Press, 1985.

———. "Toward a Third Epoch of Confucian Humanism: A Background Understanding." In *Confucianism: The Dynamics of Tradition,* ed. Irene Eber, pp. 3–21. New York: Macmillan, 1986.

———. "Intellectual Effervescence in China." *Daedalus* 121 (Spring 1992): 251–292.

———. *Way, Learning, and Politics: Essays on the Confucian Intellectual.* Albany: State University of New York Press, 1993.

Twitchett, Denis Crispin. *Printing and Publishing in Medieval China.* New York: Frederic C. Beil, 1983.

Übelhör, Monika. "The Community Compact *(Hsiang-yüeh)* of the Sung and Its Educational Significance." In *Neo-Confucian Education: The Formative Stage,* ed. Wm. Theodore de Bary and John W. Chaffee, pp. 371–388. Berkeley and Los Angeles: University of California Press, 1989.

von Glahn, Richard. *The Country of Streams and Grottoes: Expansion, Settlement, and the Civilizing of the Sichuan Frontier in Song Times.* Cambridge, Mass.: Harvard University Press, 1987.

Wakabayashi, Bob Tadashi. *Anti-Foreignism and Western Learning in Early-Modern Japan.* Cambridge, Mass.: Harvard University Press, 1986.

Wakeman, Frederic, Jr. *The Great Enterprise: The Manchu Reconstruction of Imperial Order in Seventeenth-Century China.* 2 vols. Berkeley and Los Angeles: University of California Press, 1983–1985.

Walton, Linda. "Kinship, Marriage, and Status in Song China: A Study of the Lou Lineage of Ningbo, c. 1050–1250." *Journal of Asian History* 18 (1984): 35–77.

———. "The Institutional Context of Neo-Confucianism: Scholars, Schools, and *Shu-yüan* in Sung-Yüan China." In *Neo-Confucian Education: The Formative Stage,* ed. Wm. Theodore de Bary and John W. Chaffee, pp. 457–492. Berkeley and Los Angeles: University of California Press, 1989.

Wang Gungwu. *The Structure of Power in North China during the Five Dynasties.* Kuala Lumpur: University of Malaya Press, 1963.

———. "The Rhetoric of a Lesser Empire: Early Sung Relations with Its Neighbors." In *China among Equals: The Middle Kingdom and Its Neighbors, 10th–14th Centuries,* ed. Morris Rossabi, pp. 47–65. Berkeley and Los Angeles: University of California Press, 1983.

Wang Hsi-yüan. "Liu-shih nien lai chih Ku-liang hsüeh." In *Liu-shih nien lai chih kuo-hsüeh,* ed. Ch'eng Fa-jen, pp. 431–468. Taipei: Cheng-chung shu-chü, 1972.

Wang, John C. Y. "Early Chinese Narrative: The *Tso-chuan* as Example." In *Chinese Narrative: Critical and Theoretical Essays,* ed. Andrew H. Plaks, pp. 3–20. Princeton, N.J.: Princeton University Press, 1977.

Wang Pi. *Commentary on the "Lao Tzu."* Translated by Ariane Rump, in collaboration with Wing-tsit Chan. Honolulu: University of Hawai'i Press, 1979.

Watson, Burton. *Ssu-ma Ch'ien, Grand Historian of China.* New York: Columbia University Press, 1958.

―――. *Early Chinese Literature.* New York: Columbia University Press, 1962.

―――, trans. *Basic Writings of Mo Tzu, Hsün Tzu, and Han Fei Tzu.* New York: Columbia University Press, 1967.

―――, trans. *The Tso Chuan: Selections from China's Oldest Narrative History.* New York: Columbia University Press, 1989.

Watson, Walter. "Chu Hsi, Plato, and Aristotle." *Journal of Chinese Philosophy* 5 (1978): 149–174.

Webb, Herschel. *The Japanese Imperial Institution in the Tokugawa Period.* New York: Columbia University Press, 1968.

Weber, Max. "The Types of Authority." In *Theories of Society,* ed. Talcott Parsons, 1:632–641. New York: Free Press of Glencoe, 1961.

Wechsler, Howard. *Offerings of Jade and Silk: Ritual and Symbol in the Legitimation of the T'ang Dynasty.* New Haven, Conn.: Yale University Press, 1985.

Wilhelm, Hellmut. "Chinese Confucianism on the Eve of the Great Encounter." In *Changing Japanese Attitudes toward Modernization,* ed. Marius Jansen, pp. 283–310. Princeton, N.J.: Princeton University Press, 1965.

Wilhelm, Richard, trans. *The I Ching.* 3d ed. Princeton, N.J.: Princeton University Press, 1967.

Winch, Peter. "Authority." In *Political Philosophy,* ed. Anthony Quinton, pp. 97–111. London: Oxford University Press, 1967.

Wittfogel, Karl A. *Oriental Despotism: A Comparative Study of Total Power.* New Haven, Conn.: Yale University Press, 1957.

Wong Hon-chiu. "Government Expenditures in Northern Sung China (960–1127)." Ph.D. diss., University of Pennsylvania, 1975.

Worthy, Edmund Henry, Jr. "The Founding of Sung China, 950–1000: Integrative Changes in Military and Political Institutions." Ph.D. diss., Princeton University, 1975.

―――. "Regional Control in the Southern Sung Salt Administration." In *Crisis and Prosperity in Sung China,* ed. John Winthrop Haeger, pp. 101–141. Tucson: University of Arizona Press, 1975.

Wu, Pei-yi. "Education of Children in the Sung." In *Neo-Confucian Education: The Formative Stage,* ed. Wm. Theodore de Bary and John W. Chaffee, pp. 307–324. Berkeley and Los Angeles: University of California Press, 1989.

Yang Hsiang-k'uei. "T'ang Sung shih-tai ti ching-hsüeh ssu-hsiang." *Wen shih che* 5 (1958): 7–17.

Yearley, Lee H. *Mencius and Aquinas: Theories of Virtue and Conceptions of Courage.* Albany: State University of New York Press, 1990.

Yoshikawa, Kojiro. *An Introduction to Sung Poetry.* Translated by Burton Watson. Cambridge, Mass.: Harvard University Press, 1967.

Zelin, Madeleine. *The Magistrate's Tael: Rationalizing Fiscal Reform in Eighteenth Century Ch'ing China*. Berkeley and Los Angeles: University of California Press, 1984.

Zurndorfer, Harriet T. *Change and Continuity in Chinese Local History: The Development of Hui-chou Prefecture, 800–1800*. Leiden: E. J. Brill, 1989.

Index